Who Understands Comics?

ALSO AVAILABLE FROM BLOOMSBURY

Who Understands Comics?

Questioning the Universality of Visual Language Comprehension

NEIL COHN

BLOOMSBURY ACADEMIC
LONDON • NEW YORK • OXFORD • NEW DELHI • SYDNEY

BLOOMSBURY ACADEMIC
Bloomsbury Publishing Plc
50 Bedford Square, London, WC1B 3DP, UK
1385 Broadway, New York, NY 10018, USA

BLOOMSBURY, BLOOMSBURY ACADEMIC and the Diana logo are trademarks of
Bloomsbury Publishing Plc

First published in Great Britain 2021

Cover design by Rebecca Heselton
Comic image : Asterix Comic Book © Art Directors & TRIP/Alamy Stock Photo

A catalogue record for this book is available from the British Library.

Library of Congress Cataloging-in-Publication Data
Names: Cohn, Neil, author.
Title: Who understands comics? : questioning the universality of visual language
comprehension / Neil Cohn.
Description: London, UK ; New York, NY : Bloomsbury Academic, 2020. |
Includes bibliographical references and index.
Identifiers: LCCN 2020027573 (print) | LCCN 2020027574 (ebook) |
ISBN 9781350156043 (hardback) | ISBN 9781350156067 (ebook) |
ISBN 9781350156050 (epub)
Subjects: LCSH: Comic books, strips, etc.—Semiotics. | Sequence (Linguistics) |
Visual literacy. | Semiotics—Psychological aspects.
Classification: LCC PN6714 .C6326 2020 (print) | LCC PN6714 (ebook) |
DDC 741.501/9—dc23
LC record available at https://lccn.loc.gov/2020027573
LC ebook record available at https://lccn.loc.gov/2020027574

ISBN: HB: 978-1-3501-5603-6
        PB: 978-1-3501-5604-3
        ePDF: 978-1-3501-5606-7
        eBook: 978-1-3501-5605-0

Typeset by RefineCatch Limited, Bungay, Suffolk
Printed and bound in Great Britain

To find out more about our authors and books visit www.bloomsbury.com
and sign up for our newsletters.

This book is dedicated to my uncle, Ben Hall.

CONTENTS

FIGURES

TABLES

PREFACE

I first began theorizing about the structure of visual narratives like comics when I was in college. I was then concerned mostly with how sequences of images might be structured: what are the organizing principles that make up a drawing and a sequence of pictures? However, at that time I hadn't much considered what it took for a person to actually comprehend these image sequences. Following my graduation, a few experiences began changing this . . .

First, I began drawing the non-fiction graphic novel *We the People*, where I translated political writings into graphic form. During this process, I found that my editors had difficulty recognizing or construing certain aspects of the "comic medium" that seemed familiar to me. I wondered, why might this be? Weren't these elements of comics obvious and transparent?

At the same time, I was auditing classes with Dan Slobin at UC Berkeley on language acquisition, which made me wonder: How might kids come to be able to understand sequential images? Weren't kids supposed to understand image sequences easily and effortlessly?

The final moment of curiosity came from a meeting I had a few years later with Marie Coppola while at the University of Chicago. She showed me video of fieldwork she had done with an individual who had never learned a full language, where she was surprised to find that this individual also had difficulty construing the meaning of sequences of images. Was it possible that sequences of images weren't understandable by some people, and if so, why?

As I later set out to explore these questions, I found many papers describing both cross-cultural research and studies of children's development of sequential image understanding. However, this work was scattered across many academic fields, from psychology and anthropology to linguistics and art education. Two observations were apparent: First, there was a pervasive belief held by experimenters, often also maintained by scholars of comics, that sequences of images were universally understandable and transparent. This then led to surprise by researchers when this assumption was not upheld when participants did *not* seem to construe the sequence. Second, despite these findings repeating consistently across a fairly extensive body of literature, there was no cohesive field or theoretical framework that tied this work together, and researchers often had little knowledge of each other's work.

This book aims to address these observations by questioning this abiding belief in the universal comprehension of sequences of images and thereby to integrate it into a theoretical framework. It is a substantially expanded and supplemented account of ideas that first appeared in Cohn (2020a), "Visual narrative comprehension: universal or not?" Each chapter describes a different aspect of diversity or variance in sequential image understanding or development, from cross-cultural variation in structure and comprehension to children's developmental trajectories and neurodiverse conditions like Autism Spectrum Disorder, Schizophrenia Spectrum Disorder, Developmental Language Disorder, and in cases of brain damage like aphasia.

My hope is that this work provides a coherent picture of the state of our understanding about visual narrative comprehension, given the disparate body of literature on the topic. Integrating this material can hopefully lay the groundwork for subsequent research that can go beyond these foundations.

I am grateful to several colleagues and mentors for their insights and influence contributing to this book. My consideration of these topics would not have taken hold without encouraging discussions and interactions with Marie Coppola, Jun Nakazawa, Dan Slobin, David Wilkins, and Brent Wilson. My knowledge of clinical aspects of visual narrative in Chapter Eight, particularly Autism Spectrum Disorder, owes greatly to my collaborator Emily Coderre.

The overall framework of this work is informed by my mentor Ray Jackendoff, while my other mentors Phil Holcomb, Gina Kuperberg, and Marta Kutas greatly influenced my model of the neurocognition of visual narrative processing, presented in Chapter Two. This model also benefited from discussions with my collaborators Tom Foulsham, Joe Magliano, Mirella Manfredi, Les Loschky, Martin Paczynski, Kaitlin Pederson, and Joost Schilperoord. Early drafts of papers forming these ideas benefited from feedback by Katalin Bálint, Jan Engelen, Renske van Enschot, Kara Federmeier, Fons Maes, and Joost Schilperoord. Readers hopefully appreciate the work of my editor Kelly J. Cooper as much as I do for helping to aid further clarity to my writing.

The Visual Language Research Corpus, discussed in Chapter Three, was coded by enthusiastic student assistants at UC San Diego and Tilburg University, which includes work by Jessika Axnér, Michaela Diercks, Mark Dierick, Ryan Huffman, Lincy van Middelaar, Kaitlin Pederson, Ryan Taylor, Rebecca Yeh, and Vivian Wong.

I am always thankful for the encouragement of my family and friends who have supported me throughout this pursuit, particularly Leigh, Lindsey, and Charlie Cohn, as well as Maaike Verest.

Finally, I am ever appreciative of the growing engagement of both scholars and laypeople with my research. Hopefully this work can further fuel the spirit of inspiration and discovery that motivates us all.

Neil Cohn
Tilburg, Netherlands
December 2019

CHAPTER ONE

An Assumption of Universality

Sequential images are so pervasive in contemporary society that we may take their understanding for granted. Here, I broadly refer to sequences of images bound by meaningful connections, including the ubiquitous instruction manuals and signage. *Visual narratives* are a particular type of sequential image, often drawn, which typically convey meaning through a continuous event sequence, particularly to tell a story. Visual narratives often appear in contexts combined with writing, as in comics or picture stories, among other contexts. These latter types of visual narratives are among the first literature that children engage with, while reading storybooks with caregivers. All this makes sequences of images appear simple to understand, and this feeling of transparency has underlined a broad assumption that sequential images are universally comprehended.

Theorists of comics have followed these notions. In his treatise *Understanding Comics*, Scott McCloud stated that "Pictures are received information. We need no formal education to 'get the message'" which contrasts with his statement that "writing is perceived information. It takes time and specialized knowledge to decode the abstract symbols of language" (McCloud 1993: 49). Echoes of these sentiments have carried over statements by scholars studying comics, who widely presume the transparency of their sequential images in contrast to language (e.g., Miodrag 2013; Szawerna 2017). Others have also stated without evidence that learning to understand or produce visual narratives is akin to other deliberately learned skills like playing an instrument, unlike the naturalistic acquisition of language (e.g., Kowalewski 2018).

Similar thinking motivates the growing advocacy for using comics in a range of communicative contexts. The past decades have seen a surge of advocates promoting the use of comics in educational settings (Cary 2004; Sousanis 2015). Recent work has also pushed for using comics for health (Green and Myers 2010) and science communication (Bach et al. 2017; Farinella 2018). Similar notions have underscored efforts to use visual narratives in humanitarian settings for decades (Cooper et al. 2016; Fussell and Haaland 1978; Stenchly et al. 2019). Indeed, recent partnerships by the United Nations, UNICEF, and NGOs aim to teach sustainable development using "the universal visual language and transformative power of comics to educate people in every corner of the globe" (comicsunitingnations.com).

These studies have advocated for the use of visual narratives like comics in education and communication, and indeed various empirical studies have suggested such benefits in these contexts (Mayer 2009; Nalu 2011; Wong et al. 2017). Nevertheless, many of the motivations behind such activism indicate tacit assumptions that sequences of images combined with text will be universally understood and thus confer an advantage to comprehension by sidestepping the need to decode the visual information while allowing it to supplement or aid the verbal.

Similar assumptions of universality pervade psychology studies. Researchers have used visual narratives in intelligence (IQ) testing and clinical assessments for decades (Kaufman and Lichtenberger 2006; Wechsler 1981), and sequential images are widely used as stimuli in experimental and anthropological research. These studies assume that visual narratives will be universally understood, including for children and/or illiterate populations, thus narrative sequential images have been used in tasks to explore a range of cognitive capacities. These include social intelligence (Campbell and McCord 1996), Theory of Mind (Baron-Cohen, Leslie, and Frith 1986; Sivaratnam et al. 2012), action planning and event sequencing (Tinaz et al. 2006; Tinaz, Schendan, and Stern 2008), sequential reasoning (Zampini et al. 2017), temporal cognition (Boroditsky, Gaby, and Levinson 2008), and discourse comprehension (Gernsbacher, Varner, and Faust 1990), among others.

1.1 Why Might They Be Universal?

There are several reasons sequential images might be presumed to be understood universally. We can start at the level of *single pictures*. Images are iconic—they look like what they represent (e.g., Peirce 1931)—and naïve beliefs about drawing hold that they represent what is seen either by vision or a mental image, not culturally constrained and learned schematic patterns (like language). If drawings represent what people see, they should be universal, since all people ostensibly have the same perceptual capacities. Differences in producing drawings thus reduce to a matter of "talent," despite the assumed universality in understanding images (for review, see e.g., Arnheim 1978; Cohn 2014b; Willats 2005; Wilson 1988).

Similar assumptions extend to *sequential* image understanding: if comprehending events and actions in general should be universal, and images simply depict perception, images depicting events should also be transparent. This renders sequential image understanding as a matter of visual perception and event cognition (Loschky et al. 2020), which otherwise requires no learning, decoding, or specialized knowledge. Under this view, simply seeing and knowing events provides enough basis to understand sequences of drawn images.

Beliefs about the simplicity and universality of sequential images are no doubt reinforced by their ubiquity across cultures and history. Like most drawings, sequential images appear in diverse historical and cultural contexts recorded as far back as cave paintings (McCloud 1993; Petersen 2011). In contemporary industrialized societies, sophisticated visual narratives appear in comics, picture books, and storyboarding, in addition to sequential images in instruction manuals and signage. This ubiquity appears to span across human cultures and history without relying on appropriation from a particular origin—i.e., visual narratives do not seem to have a place they were "invented" and then spread across the world. Rather, the production of graphic images, including in sequence, appears to be a "universal" potential of human communication and cognition.

Thus, the idea that sequences of images are transparent and universally understood is widespread and pervasive. Though the cross-cultural ubiquity of sequential images supports them as a "universal" aspect of human communication, it does not mean that they are understood *universally*. Indeed, these ideas are merely an *assumption*, guided largely by the intuitions of adults with longstanding familiarity with visual narratives. As such, I will call this belief the *Sequential Image Transparency Assumption* (SITA).

How would we know whether sequences of images are universally understood? To show that sequential images are *not* universally transparent, we would need evidence where people could *not* construe their meaning, or have difficulty comprehending visual narratives. As it turns out, there are several examples where sequences of images cannot be construed. One example comes from cross-cultural cases where individuals had not been exposed to Western-style visual narratives. Another case is from children, who have difficulty understanding visual sequences while they are below certain ages (typically under the age of 4). In fact, comprehension of visual sequences varies even among people with different frequencies of reading comics and visual narratives. Also, individuals with various neurodiversities sometimes have challenges processing image sequences, including people with Autism Spectrum Disorder, Schizophrenia Spectrum Disorder, and Developmental Language Disorder.

All of these cases provide evidence that the SITA is not supported. This research has been dispersed across many different fields, including comics studies, anthropology, linguistics, art education, and including the subfields of developmental, cognitive, and clinical psychology. This wide dispersion implies two things. First, the diverse and multifaceted perspectives across these fields all recognize that visual narratives are an important aspect of human expression and communication. Yet, second, because they are so distributed, no clear field studying the comprehension of these materials has been consolidated. As a result, most of this research has remained unknown across disciplines, rendering the perception that such scholarship has not been undertaken.

This book seeks to rectify this widespread dispersion by synthesizing this literature on the understanding of *sequential* images, particularly visual narratives. Indeed, this wealth of research suggests that sequential images are not simplistic or universally transparent. Rather, the understanding of image sequences seems to require a *fluency*—i.e., a proficiency acquired through exposure to and practice with a system of visual narrative. Such fluency is comparable to the natural, extensive, and often passive exposure and practice required to comprehend language.[1]

Although language is a cognitively "universal" and "innate" system in the sense that all typically developing human brains have the cognitive structures necessary to speak languages (Jackendoff 2002), language *fluency* is not developmentally inevitable and requires exposure to and practice with an external system. For spoken or signed languages, only in unfortunate circumstances do individuals fail to receive the requisite exposure and practice necessary to learn a language (Goldin-Meadow 2003). For visual narratives, a lack of drawing skill may be more widespread and viewed as culturally permissible, particularly since they are less integrated into everyday interactive communication (although, for a cross-cultural counterpoint, see Wilkins 1997/2016). However, this does not excuse visual narrative fluency from the same interaction between nature and nurture as fluency in language, despite different cultural assumptions and practices.

1.2 Visual Language Theory

This notion of fluency applied to sequential image understanding is in line with *Visual Language Theory* (VLT), a framework arguing that creating and understanding graphic images, particularly those in sequence, taps into analogous and/or overlapping structures and cognition as language (Cohn 2013b). A language is made up of a set of patterns in a person's mind/brain. The patterns for an individual constitute their own *idiolect*, which is developed from the patterns they are exposed to and practice with across their lifespan. To the extent that a person's idiolect aligns with those of other people, they share a common "language."

Although we treat such "languages" as monolithic cultural artifacts, they are aggregates of the many cognitive idiolects of their producers. This aggregation is what constitutes their manifestation as cultural systems (which in turn create a feedback loop as such a system provides exposure to future learners of that system). As a result, patterns may be diverse across groups of people, given the divisions that occur across regional, economic, cultural, occupational, or other societal factors. As a result, there is no universal language, and diverse languages occur across the world. This conception of language holds for spoken and signed languages, and is argued by VLT to also be true of *visual languages*—the systems guiding people's abilities to produce and comprehend graphic expressions (i.e., drawings), particularly those in sequences.

This argument places visual languages of drawn information as equal to spoken and signed languages as human expressive capacities. It is worth emphasizing that this is not an analogy saying that "visual language *is like* verbal language." Rather, there are abstract principles that the mind/brain uses to structure information, and these mechanisms apply to both the spoken and graphic modalities, with no "ranking" of either form as a baseline. This position is articulated in the Principle of Equivalence, which posits that *the mind/brain treats expressive modalities in similar ways, given modality specific constraints* (Cohn 2013b). Thus, it is not a comparison of one modality "being like" another, but rather that their structure and cognition draw from similar resources. Indeed, a growing body of literature supports that neural mechanisms involved in processing visual narratives overlap with those involved in verbal languages (Cohn 2020b), as will be discussed in Chapter Two.

Because graphic expression occurs in a myriad of manifestations, visual languages appear in many contexts of society. One such context of fairly complex visual languages is in comics of the world. Just as novels may be *written in* a written language, comics are a cultural artifact *drawn in* a visual language and/or *written in* a written language. It is important to emphasize this separation between the notion of a visual language and "comics." **Comics themselves are not a (visual) language.** It would be odd to say that "novels are written language," and this is equally odd of the misnomer that "comics are a visual language."

Rather, comics are a context in which certain fairly sophisticated visual languages are used, and the particular visual language may depend on the country and/or genre of the comic. For example, Japanese Visual Language (JVL) characterizes the visual style and storytelling used in manga, while "Kirbyan" American Visual Language is most associated with the graphic system used in superhero comics from the United States (Cohn 2013b). These designations characterize the "drawing and storytelling styles" most associated with these particular contexts. Yet, manga and superhero comics are not defined only by their stereotypical visual languages, nor are those visual languages constrained to the contexts of comics. Manga is not a synonym for JVL (Kacsuk 2018), and indeed JVL could be used to draw superhero comics in the United States or a myriad of other contexts that would not necessarily garner the label of "manga." The "visual languages" are defined by the patterns used by their authors (elaborated on in Chapter Three), while "comics" are defined by a web of sociocultural ideas including their cultural context, genres, and possibly the specific visual language(s) that they use.

For drawings to constitute a full visual language though, certain criteria need to be met about their structural makeup. Here I follow linguistic research where a language manifests from the interaction between three primary structural components (Jackendoff 2002; Jackendoff and Audring 2018). First, languages express a *meaning* through a mapping to a *modality*. In spoken languages, the auditory-vocal modality uses sounds guided by a phonological structure, while in visual languages the visual-graphic modality of drawn marks is organized by a graphic structure. Units created out of the systematic mapping between a modality and a meaning create its lexicon. Thus, patterns of sounds that map to meanings constitute conventionalized morphemes, words, phrases, and idioms. Similarly, patterned graphics—i.e., configurations of lines and shapes with regular and repeatable forms— create the "visual vocabularies" of visual languages, both for patterned parts of images, whole images, and image sequences (Cohn 2013b). However, to become a full language, in any modality, meaningful expressions alone are not enough. Such expressions must be ordered using a *grammar*, a combinatorial system that organizes meaningful expressions into a coherent expression. Thus, while expressions can be made that do not use all of these components (Cohn 2016b), full languages require all three: *meaning*, which becomes expressed by a *modality*, and is organized by a *grammar*.

These component parts of a language mutually interface in a *parallel architecture* (Jackendoff 2002; Jackendoff and Audring 2018), meaning that they are independent structures that unite to create the whole of expression. As depicted in Figure 1.1, these structures operate across both units (here, individual images) and sequences of those units (here, sequential images). This parallel structuring means that, in the case of the visual languages used in comics, structure does not descend hierarchically from a

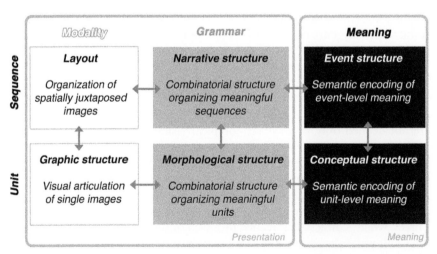

FIGURE 1.1 *A model of the architecture of visual narratives incorporating the primary components of a modality, grammar, and meaning for both the unit and sequence levels. Creative Commons License.*

page to a panel to image content in a singularly divisible structure. Rather, despite being independent components, the structures within the parallel architecture mutually coalesce to give us the perception of a holistic experience.

Let's analyze each of these components in more detail with an example. Consider the wordless comic in Figure 1.2, from *JA!* by Ángela Cuéllar and Jonás Aguilar. The sequence starts in panel one with a man entering a pet shop with his pets, a dog and a cat. Next, the cat looks at a fish in a bowl (panel two), and then gazes into it with a menacing smile (panel three). The man then wonders where his dog is (panel four), only for the final panel to reveal the dog crammed into the fish bowl. The punchline appears to be that the cat stuffed the dog into the bowl, confounding the expectation that he was gazing into the fishbowl with the intent to eat the fish.

Below, I will describe each component of the parallel architecture of visual language in reference to this sequence. I begin with aspects of the

FIGURE 1.2 *An example visual narrative from* JA! *by Ángela Cuéllar and Jonás Aguilar (© 2016; https://revista-exegesis.com/2016/01/ja/). Creative Commons License.*

modality (graphic and layout structures), then move on to grammar (morphology and narrative structures), and then finish with the conceptual and event structures.

1.2.1 *Graphic Structures*

Visual languages are created in the *graphic modality*. This means that drawn expressions are composed of lines and shapes in configurations, and the system that organizes these elements is a **graphic structure**. Such a structure is analogous to the phonological structures which govern the modality of articulated sound in spoken languages. Like the phonemes that make up speech, *graphemes* are the cognitive building blocks that correspond to the graphic marks that make up visual depictions, like lines (straight, curved) and dots. These elements in turn are organized using principles of combination that may optimize their understanding, such as the line junctions that arise when joining lines together (Willats 1997). For example, lines forming a junction shaped like a "T" signal that one object might be behind another (occlusion), while a Y-shaped junction will cue the interpretation of an angular corner.

If configurations of lines are patterned as "graphic schemas," they can constitute parts of a **visual lexicon** (Cohn 2013b) stored in the long-term memory of the drawer and recognized as such by a comprehender. These patterns can range in size from the small subparts of images (hands, eyes, head-shapes, etc.), to larger composites like whole figures in particular postures, and even to full scenes. For example, in Figure 1.2 the man's hair is consistently drawn in the same way, as are the shapes of the cat's and dog's heads, both of the pets' bodies, and the fishbowl. The consistency of these visual features allows for recognition that they index the same characters and objects across panels (discussed further later). A visual lexicon would also have to include non-iconic graphic patterns as well, such as speech balloons, thought bubbles, motion lines, and other conventionalized aspects of visual "morphology" (Cohn 2013b).

Visual lexicons, whether of an individual or across a group of people, are what characterize the "visual style" of drawings. All of these patterns must be stored in the minds of people who draw them. This means that becoming proficient in drawing is a matter of building up a visual lexicon of graphic schemas (Cohn 2012a; Wilson and Wilson 1977), facilitated by exposure to and imitation of the drawings in a learner's environment (Cox 1998; Huntsinger et al. 2011; Okada and Ishibashi 2017; Wilson and Wilson 1977; Wilson 1988). This drive for learners to imitate a visual lexicon of patterns would explain why many people appear to stagnate in their process of learning to draw around puberty, as it is the apex of a learning period for easy acquisition of a visual vocabulary (Cohn 2012a; Wilson 1988). Thus, the sentiment of "I can't draw" reflects the insufficient learning of a visual vocabulary.

The ability for people to recognize that visual styles index different cultures (America, Japan, Maya, etc.) and different functional purposes (superhero comics, instruction manuals) are a testament to the recognition of the systematic nature of patterned visual lexicons. If there was no such structure to drawings, we would not have such codified associations between drawing "styles" and their contexts. For comprehenders, the iconic nature of images (i.e., they resemble what they look like) may facilitate easier comprehension—and the feeling of transparency—but cross-cultural findings imply that drawings are not always comprehended in ways that conform to Western expectations (for review, see Arbuckle 2004; de Lange 2000; Goldsmith 1984).

1.2.2 *External Compositional Structure*

Another feature of the modality of graphic expression extends beyond the composition of individual image units—i.e., *panels*—and to the organization of images relative to each other. The *external compositional structure*, or layout, is the juxtaposition of images in a physical arrangement, be it temporal or spatial. *Temporally sequential* juxtapositions present images one after the other successively in *time*, be it unfurling in a slide-show, sketched on a chalkboard, or drawn in sand (Cohn 2013b). For example, Aboriginals from Central Australia create narratives by drawing a highly codified visual vocabulary in the sand, unfurling in time (Green 2014; Munn 1986; Wilkins 1997/2016). Figure 1.3a imagines the panels of Figure 1.2 as if they were unfurled one a time in the same space in succession, as might occur in a slideshow or on a computer screen. This sequence would progress in time, but not across a physically juxtaposed space.

Spatially sequential juxtapositions arrange images next to each other. To start, spatially sequential juxtapositions involve recognizing that the spatial array is decomposable into smaller parts, each of which are their own units. For example, Figure 1.2 is not just one big image, but also contains five individual panels. We can describe this "big image" as the *canvas* on which a layout is made—whether it's a page, a wall, or a webpage. It is the panels within this canvas that are then spatially juxtaposed to create a sequence (though canvases might be juxtaposed as well, such as sequential pages). This creates a tension between the holistic space of a canvas and the segmented panel units (Bateman and Wildfeuer 2014; Fresnault-Deruelle 1976; Groensteen 2007; Molotiu 2012).

Spatially sequential juxtapositions might be fairly simple in book form with one image per page (as in picture books), or multiple panels in a complex spatial arrangement (as in comics). Basic spatial juxtapositions may use linear horizontal (Figure 1.3b) or vertical sequences (Figure 1.3c), as found in historical sequential images on tapestries or stained-glass, or in today's comic strips. More complicated page layouts appear in contemporary comic pages, grounded in the basic grid pattern, as in the original layout of the comic in Figure 1.3d. However, complex arrangements of panels vary from the grid, involving staggering of panels, embedded vertical columns, inset panels placed inside of other panels, separation or overlap between panels, and various other features (Bateman et al. 2016; Cohn 2013b; Gavaler 2017).

As long as the order of images in a sequence is retained, the same meaningful content can have several different arrangements (horizontally, vertically, grids, etc.). As a practical example, comic strips sometimes use

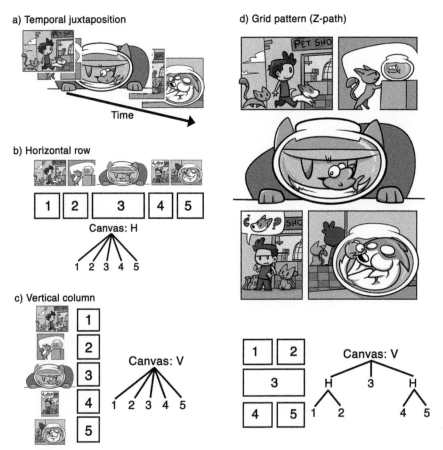

FIGURE 1.3 *Variations in layout for the comic in Figure 1.2. A sequence could be conveyed one image at a time in a temporal sequence. Spatially, so long as the order of reading the panels does not change, construal of the content does not change if depicted as (b) a single vertical (V) column or (c) a single horizontal (H) row, or in (d) its original grid layout of three horizontal (H) rows each with two panels, embedded in a vertical (V) column.*

four square panels in case editors decide to alter their layouts to fit a space in a newspaper page or a website. Some scholars emphasize that variation in page layout can serve functional, meaningful roles (Bach et al. 2018; Bateman and Wildfeuer 2014; Caldwell 2012; Groensteen 2007; Peeters 1998 [1991]). However, layout is separate from—yet interfaces with— structures governing meaning (Cohn 2014a). In addition to the flexibility of layouts shown in Figure 1.3, this separation in structure also arises in empirical observations. Readers have explicit preferences for panel arrangements even without content (Cohn 2013a; Cohn and Campbell 2015), and layouts have distinctive properties independent of meaning (Bateman et al. 2016; Cohn 2013b; Gavaler 2017).

Nevertheless, some authors may intentionally play with the relationship between these structures, using the physical layout to convey meaning. This might arise from using panel shape in an expressive way (such as panels in the shape of the scope of a gun or binoculars), or by aligning the depiction within panels with the layout between panels (such as a person falling downward across panels stacked vertically in a column). Even more overt coupling of layout and meaning occurs when the content of a sequence interacts with the layout itself. This happens when characters physically rip panels in half to create two separate panels, or when a character passes something from a panel in the middle of an upper row to the middle panel in a lower row. All of these cases exploit the *interface* between the structures of meaning and layout, but they do not imply that those structures are inseparable. The fact that these layouts are noticeable deviations is evidence for such a normative separation in the first place.

The external compositional structure reflects the physical makeup of panels on a canvas but does not account for how readers then engage with those layouts. An additional ***navigational*** or ***assemblage structure*** governs how a comprehender moves through a layout and constructs its structure in their mind. Navigation of complex layouts within comics appears to draw on constraints that do not rely on the contents of the panels, as suggested by studies where readers' eyes were tracked as they moved through layouts (Bateman, Beckmann, and Varela 2018; Omori, Ishii, and Kurata 2004), and where comprehenders stated their navigational preferences in layouts without content (Cohn 2013a; Cohn and Campbell 2015). While most readers adopt the ordering principles from writing systems, such as the left-to-right-and-down "Z-path" of the Latin alphabet, or its reverse in Asian scripts (Cohn 2013a; Spinillo and Dyson 2001), complex layouts may require alternate routes constrained by conventionalized ordering that deviates from the Z-path, and/or by basic "Gestalt" perceptual principles like the proximity or contiguity of panels to each other (Cohn 2013a). Variation in the distance or alignment between panels provides cues to flout the Z-path and choose alternative routes throughout the layout (Cohn 2013a; Cohn and Campbell 2015).

1.2.3 Morphological Structures

While the graphic marks might connect to meaning (discussed later), this information is organized by a *morphological structure*, which encodes the ways in which elements combine to form expressible units. Here, we focus on two basic types of morphological elements: units that can stand alone and units that need to be attached to other units. Panels as image-units can be composed of sub-units that stand alone (like a single character) or combinations of them (like a scene). In Figure 1.2, all of the panels depict interacting characters, a morphological type that I have termed a "macro" panel because it contains multiple morphological elements that could stand alone. However, these panels could also be framed to have single characters (a "mono" panel), to select only portions of characters (a "micro" panel), or to depict only the background aspects of the environment (an "amorphic" panel), as in Figure 1.4a. Nevertheless, in Figure 1.2, the macro panels each enclose different characters, thereby cutting up the overall conceptualized environment in various ways. These different framings are depicted in Figure 1.4b. This capacity for panels to cut up a scene lets them serve as *attention units*, framing certain portions of a scene while leaving out others.

Units that cannot exist in isolation are *bound morphemes*, similar to the affixes in spoken or signed languages that need to attach to stems that can stand alone (Cohn 2013b, 2018). For example, in English, the affix *un-* can combine with the stem *happy* to create a new word *unhappy*. But *un-* cannot stand alone. Similarly, visual affixes like speech balloons attach to a stem of a speaker, like in the fourth panel of Figure 1.2, as labeled in Figure 1.4. The stem (the speaker) could stand alone without the balloon, but the affix (the balloon) could not float in the air on its own without the stem. Other visual affixes include hearts or stars floating above characters' heads or substituted for eyes, motion lines attached to moving objects, or dotted lines replacing solid lines to signal invisibility (Cohn 2013b; Forceville 2011). This combinatorial quality of units can also be hierarchic: lightbulbs might float above a head to show inspiration, but the lightbulb might also have affixes of radiating lines to show it is lit up. Thus, an affix (radial lines) attaches to an affix (lightbulb) which attaches to a stem (a face) in a hierarchic way.

Visual affixes use combinatorial principles that are highly conventionalized and constrained, and their understanding is modulated by familiarity and experience reading comics (Cohn, Murthy, and Foulsham 2016; Forceville 2011; Newton 1985). While speech balloons and hearts for eyes have become fairly ubiquitous across cultures' comics (and emoji), other morphology might be harder to understand without knowing their culture-specific origins. For example, in Japanese manga, nosebleeds depict lust or a bubble out of the nose indicates sleep (Cohn 2013b; Cohn and Ehly 2016), which have now been appropriated by emoji in messaging applications. The symbolic meaning of these representation is fairly opaque without knowing their conventionalized meanings. Visual morphemes use a variety of

FIGURE 1.4 *Morphological structure highlighted from Figure 1.2, depicting a) affix-stem relationships and various types of framing of panel content, and b) how panels serve as attention units to cut up the overall conceptual space related to these characters. Creative Commons License.*

meaning-making strategies, including the use of purely symbolic signs (hearts), the visual manifestations of basic conceptual categories (like motion lines depicting paths), or the evocation of conceptual metaphors (Cohn 2013b, 2018; Forceville 2011; Szawerna 2017). For example, steam blowing out of the ears uses a metaphor that evokes the head as an overflowing pressurized container (Forceville 2005), while gears spinning above a head imply that the mind is a machine (Cohn 2018).

Because of their conventional nature, these types of visual affixes require exposure and practice to be understood. The meanings of morphemes like speech balloons and motion lines are reported as not understood by people of cultures unfamiliar with these representations (Duncan, Gourlay, and Hudson 1973; Kennedy and Ross 1975; San Roque et al. 2012; Winter 1963). Some morphemes can be recognized when comprehenders are fairly young, like speech balloons and thought bubbles, which appear to be understood by around 4 years old (Wellman, Hollander, and Schult 1996).

Others, like motion lines, obtain only a moderate understanding around age 6 but progress to a full understanding by age 12 (Carello, Rosenblum, and Grosofsky 1986; Friedman and Stevenson 1975; Gross et al. 1991; Mori 1995; Nakazawa 2016). In general, understanding of visual morphology appears to get better with both age and experience with comics (Nakazawa 2016), and possibly with the frequency that they appear in comics (Newton 1985).

1.2.4 *Narrative Structures*

Beyond physical juxtaposition in layout, sequential meaning can be organized and ordered through a *grammar*. There are several levels of complexity for a grammatical system, depending on the type of sequencing involved in creating a mapping between a modality and meaning (Jackendoff and Wittenberg 2014, 2017). At the lowest levels of complexity, the grammar itself contributes little to the overall expression, while at higher levels the grammar provides more structures of its own.

At a basic level, visual sequences might use a *linear grammar*—a simple concatenation of units in a linear sequence where meaning alone guides the relations between images (Jackendoff and Wittenberg 2014, 2017). Note that here "linear" is understood in the sense of "construing the meaning of one unit after another," regardless of its physical layout. Because grammars govern the links between the content of images, their layout remains an independent, parallel structure concerned with arranging that content *physically*. Based on the characteristics of the semantics of the images, we can characterize two types of simple sequencing involved in linear grammars.

Unordered sequences appear as visual lists, as found pervasively in a culture's instruction manuals and signage. This unordered nature can be tested by rearranging the elements of the sequence: If reordering the images does *not* disrupt the message, then it is likely unordered. Consider the unordered linear grammars in Figure 1.5a, taken from various signage, which each provide lists telling the viewer what to do or not to do in various situations. Rearranging these images would have no real impact on how the sequence is understood. These types of visual lists can also provide an inventory of items, such as the various tools one will need to build something in the assembly instructions for furniture. Unordered linear grammars often are used in emoji sequencing, like a sequence of various emoji related to celebrations and birthdays (Cohn, Engelen, and Schilperoord 2019; Gawne and McCulloch 2019).

Ordered linear sequences appear as basic step-by-step instructions (i.e., step one, step two, step three), which also appear in instruction manuals and signage. As in Figure 1.5b, linear grammars are often instructions on how to do things. This might include how to perform different tasks, like how to do CPR, how to put on an oxygen mask, or how to build furniture. It could

a) Unordered linear grammars

b) Ordered linear grammars

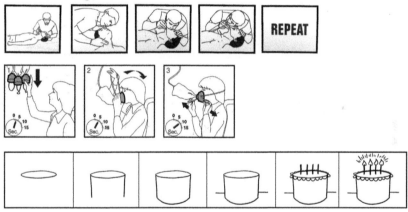

FIGURE 1.5 *Sequences of images that use a) unordered and b) ordered linear grammars.*

also be the step-by-step instructions for how to draw something. These sequences unfold in an ordered manner, and thus could not be rearranged in their sequence. In both unordered and ordered sequences, each unit carries roughly the same importance and role, with omission of any unit just as impactful as any other.

More complicated sequencing differs from linear grammars with a variety of characteristics, particularly in differentiating the role that units play and segmenting a sequence into hierarchic constituents, which organize panels into groupings, and embed those clusters inside of each other. These traits allow units to connect panels across distances or negotiate ambiguous structures with multiple possible semantic interpretations. Such characteristics require a *narrative structure* (Cohn 2010b, 2013b). For example, there are several ways that the situations in Figure 1.2 could have been conveyed. The final sequence is guided by choices for how to convey these situations, including what information to show and when, and what to omit and when. The resulting sequence conveys a narrative where the opening panel establishes the characters and setting, while the next two panels initiate the assumed primary relationship between the cat and fish(bowl). The final panels have a climactic reveal of the dog stuffed into the bowl. Note, however, that the true climactic event is never shown: We never see the act of the cat cramming the dog into the bowl, and instead are left to infer this event. The narrative roles played by panels also apply at higher levels to form hierarchic constituents (Cohn 2013b; Cohn et al. 2014). Modification of visual sequences can introduce further complexity, such as repetition of narrative categories that show different characters in frames, zooms of information, and other constructional patterns (Cohn 2013b, 2015, 2019b). These structures will be elaborated on in the next chapter.

1.2.5 *Conceptual and Event Structures*

Finally, visual narratives convey meanings both in their individual image-units and across sequences. In understanding the units, a comprehender would need to recognize the referential information about entities and locations, such as that in Figure 1.2 there are characters of a man, a dog, a cat, and a fish. It is also recognized that these entities belong in the place of a pet store and some of them in a fishbowl. A comprehender would also need to recognize the events that these entities undertake, such as their actions and experiences. In Figure 1.2, the first panel shows the man, dog, and cat all in the action of walking, as cued by their postures (specifically, outstretched legs). In panel four, the man is quizzically speaking, cued both by his posture (one hand on hip, one on chin) and by the symbolic speech balloon.

To construe these units as a *sequence*, a comprehender must track elements across images and observe their changes. First, a comprehender must recognize that the characters and objects in one image are the same referential entities repeated in subsequent images (Bornens 1990; Lefèvre 2000b; Saraceni 2001; Stainbrook 2016; Stoermer 2009). Thus, a *continuity constraint* guides a comprehender to recognize that each image does not depict different characters, but contains the *same characters* repeated across different images. In Figure 1.2, this means that same man, cat, dog, and fish are interpreted as depicted in all the panels, rather than five unconnected images, each with a different man, cat, dog, and/or fish, which would be the interpretation if the continuity constraint was not followed.

FIGURE 1.6 *The referential continuity of entities across panels. Creative Commons License.*

This continuity is schematized in Figure 1.6a for the primary characters across panels.

Continuity relies on visual features of the images to map to a common referential entity. In Figure 1.6a, the man has the same hair and clothing across multiple images, while the same basic linework is used for the cat and dog. If the visual features changed between images, it would challenge the assumption of continuity that these are the same characters repeated across frames. A comprehender must distinguish between which cues may be relevant for maintaining continuity, while filtering out changes or alterations that may impede it (i.e., changes in viewpoint, size, occlusion, etc.).

Nevertheless, some differences in depiction may signal shifts in time, viewpoint, causal relationships, and construal of other alterations in states. Thus, an *activity constraint* characterizes the recognition that, insofar as elements repeat across images, differences in their depiction might cue an understanding of a change in state (temporal, causal, viewpoint, etc.). Thus, in Figure 1.2, the difference in the cat's mouth between panel two and panel three motivates the understanding that it smiled. Because not all repetitions of elements, nor differences between visual elements, are proxies for recognizing successive states, a comprehender must differentiate these instances.

Failing to follow these constraints would result in the inability to recognize a sequence of images *as a sequence*. Without referential continuity, each entity in a panel would be its own unique character, not the same character repeated (i.e., each panel in Figure 1.2 shows a different man, cat, dog, etc.). Maintaining continuity without activity would lead to an interpretation of the same character in unrelated separate scenes (i.e., each panel in Figure 1.2 shows the same man, cat, fish, etc., but in unconnected scenes). Finally, a lack of both continuity and activity constraints would lead to the interpretation that each image depicts totally separate characters in unconnected scenes.

It is important to note that these constraints are primarily a byproduct of layouts with spatially sequential juxtapositions, because the spatial arrangements require that the entities that are repeated in each frame be continuous. No such constraints would operate on a temporally sequential juxtaposition, because elements drawn in a single space might persist across time without repetition (Cohn 2013b). However, interpretations that belie activity or continuity might be possible if removing the temporal context (Green 2014). Thus, the type of layout can have consequences for the semantic interpretation.

With continuity established, comprehenders must incorporate differences in the representations across images into a growing mental model characterizing the understanding of the scene (Cohn and Kutas 2015; Loschky et al. 2018). Between images, changes occur to characters, spatial locations, time, and/or events (McCloud 1993; Magliano and Zacks 2011; Saraceni 2001; Zwaan and Radvansky 1998). Small semantic changes between images may only require mappings into a mental model, but larger discontinuity may prompt the generation of inferences to resolve the missing information, thereby requiring a larger updating process (Cohn and Kutas 2015; Loschky et al. 2018).

Consider the changes that take place across panels in Figure 1.2. Between the first three panels, fairly minimal changes occur between panels, which would require only updating of which characters are being focused on. The man and pets are shown in panel one, which shifts to the cat and fish only in panels two and three. Panel two introduces the fish. However, other panels require further inference. At the final panel, inferences are needed about event structures (the cat crammed the dog into the bowl) and the intentions and goals of the characters (the dog is in the bowl because the cat crammed it there, which is why it was smiling in panel three). Many of these inferences can be made only retroactively, after the subsequent event has already been viewed.

1.3 Multimodality

Finally, visual languages often appear in *multimodal* interactions with other modalities, particularly written or spoken language. In contexts like comics, picture books, and many instruction manuals, sequences of images combine with writing to form cohesive multimodal units. Indeed, various researchers have been examining multimodal combinations between text and drawn narratives both theoretically (Cohn 2016b; Forceville and Urios-Aparisi 2009; McCloud 1993; Saraceni 2003; Stainbrook 2016; Tseng and Bateman

2018) and with experimentation (Kirtley et al. 2018; Laubrock, Hohenstein, and Kümmerer 2018; Manfredi, Cohn, and Kutas 2017; Manfredi et al. 2018).

Here, I've argued that both verbal and visual languages appear as singular experiences, but actually comprise numerous interacting subparts. In this same vein, the combination of these modalities is not merely the interaction between two holistic expressions; perceiving them as such limits the analysis of such multimodal messages. Rather, since both of those systems involve various substructures, multimodality must be understood as an interaction between those parts, which in turn yields the whole of the multimodal experience (Cohn 2016b).

As both the verbal and visual languages involve units and sequencing comprised of a modality, meaning, and grammar, interactions between these components creates various types of multimodal expressions. Combinations of text and image require the integration of meaning across two different types of input, although neurocognitive research suggests that they ultimately activate a shared system of comprehension (Baggio 2018; Cohn 2020b; Kutas and Federmeier 2011). Indeed, empirical work has shown that visual sequences can modulate the semantic processing of written and spoken language (Manfredi, Cohn, and Kutas 2017; Manfredi et al. 2018), just as sentence contexts can modulate the meaning of images (Ganis, Kutas, and Sereno 1996; Weissman and Tanner 2018).

Consider the comic strips from *Journal Comics* by Drew Weing in Figure 1.7. These sequences balance messages in both text and images. However, in both cases the semantics are a bit more "weighted" towards the written language (Cohn 2016b)—i.e., the gist is conveyed more by the verbal modality rather than the visual modality. This is evident when deleting the text (Figure 1.7c and 1.7d), which results in both sequences losing key information about the overall message. Note that omitting the images would alter the overall gist slightly less, suggesting that the written language is indeed carrying more "semantic weight" of the multimodal message than the visual modality.

The omission of text reveals another difference between these strips though: the nature of their sequencing (i.e., their grammars). Figure 1.7a/c, conveys a successive temporal order with a narrative progression across the images. If rearranged, the overall meaning of the sequence would change. However, Figure 1.7b/d does not use such a dedicated sequence, and instead uses a linear grammar—it is essentially a "visual list" of images related to the binding idea of smells. Rearrangement of these panels would make little difference to the overall gist of the sequence. Because meaning is more weighted to the verbal expression, this difference in visual sequencing may be harder to discern, although it yields a different type of multimodal interaction. Thus, multimodal expressions require the comprehender to balance meaning not only across visual and verbal modalities, but also their grammars.

FIGURE 1.7 *Comic strips (a & b) that combine text and image from* Journal Comic *(© Drew Weing). Both use more written than graphic information but differ in their sequencing: a/c) uses a dedicated narrative order to the image sequence while b/d) uses an unordered linear grammar, linked together through a semantic field about smells.*

1.4 Outline of the Book

Each of the structures in the parallel architecture of visual language (Figure 1.1) contribute to the holistic experience of a visual narrative sequence. This book then seeks to examine how these structures are comprehended in the minds of readers, and how might that comprehension be varied across cultural, developmental, and/or neurodiverse conditions. Several prior works have investigated the way that proficiency factors into the understanding of individual pictures and their parts. Here, our focus is less on the proficiency related to the units of visual narratives, but more with their sequencing. To what degree are sequences of images transparent and universally understood, and to what degree do they require a fluency?

The structures outlined in the parallel architecture for visual narratives contribute to the organization of narrative sequences of images, which can also combine with the structures of verbal language to create multimodal interactions (Cohn 2016b). Clearly, to account for the full architecture and comprehension of most visual narratives (like picture books or comics), we must address these multimodal interactions in full. However, without comprehensive understanding of the visual modality on its own, addressing their multimodal interaction with text will always remain limited. Thus, we here focus primarily on the comprehension of the visual modality.

So far, we have discussed the structures comprising visual narratives that may be stored in the mind of a comprehender, but we also need to account for *how* comprehension unfolds while a person engages visual narrative sequences. That is, what are the (neuro)cognitive processes that guide a comprehender to understand a sequence of images? A growing body of literature within the psychological sciences has begun to provide an explanation of these mechanisms (Cohn 2020b; Loschky et al. 2020), and Chapter Two thus reviews the current state of these cognitive models. This basis for the processes of comprehension lay the groundwork for our further discussion of how such comprehension might be disrupted when people fail to construe a sequence of images.

In addition, the structures involved in visual languages described so far treat these building blocks in the abstract. In actuality, these structures may appear in diverse manifestations across the world. Indeed, just as languages vary around the world, so too do visual languages. Chapter Three thus examines how comics differ from around the world from a corpus of 290 annotated comics, specifically targeting their sequencing structures. As will be discussed, this cross-cultural diversity results in two levels of potential fluency: proficiency with visual sequences in general and proficiency for culture-specific visual narrative patterns. This would be analogous to the distinction between language competency in general and fluency in specific languages around the world.

Another possibility with languages is a lack of fluency altogether. Here, we begin to fully challenge the Sequential Image Transparency Assumption by investigating reports where people could not construe a sequence of images *as a sequence*. Chapter Four thus reviews cross-cultural findings where individuals appear to not understand spatially sequential visual narratives, largely due to a lack of exposure and practice with their properties. Related to this issue of exposure is that of development. Specifically, how do children come to comprehend a sequence of images?

Although visual narratives are stereotyped as associated with children's literature, Chapter Five will show that children learn to understand and produce sequences of images with age and experience.

These chapters primarily explore situations where individuals may lack a fluency in a spatially sequential visual language or may be developing such fluency. We can also ask, does fluency differ among adults who have already had exposure to visual narratives, and have already developed an understanding of them? In Chapter Six, we review two approaches to assessments of proficiency in visual languages and show that comprehension of sequential images varies based on people's frequency of reading visual narratives like comics.

Another place to examine variation in comprehension ability is to study individuals with atypical cognitive abilities. The study of clinical populations is informative both for better understanding neurodiversity and for comparing their capacities to those of neurotypical individuals to better understand how systems like visual narratives work. This is especially important for the comparison between visual language and verbal languages, as there is a widespread belief that many neurodiverse populations have impaired language processing, but intact abilities to comprehend visual materials. This "Visual Ease Assumption" (Coderre 2020) presumes that verbal and visual processing rely on fairly different cognitive resources, in contrast to hypotheses made by Visual Language Theory. Chapter Seven thus reviews the research on three neurodiverse populations of individuals with Autism Spectrum Disorder, Schizophrenia Spectrum Disorder, and Developmental Language Disorder (previously called Specific Language Impairment), as well as findings related to individuals with aphasia—i.e., with brain damage associated with deficits in language.

Finally, visual narratives do not appear only in drawn form, but also in film. Film does not necessarily use a visual language (unless it uses drawings, like animation), but it still conveys units of meaning in temporally sequential sequences. Chapter Eight thus first compares the affordances of the static, spatial drawn visual narratives and the dynamic, moving filmic visual narratives and the consequences that these differences in modality have on their structure and comprehension. It then surveys the cross-cultural and developmental literature on film comprehension to explore how these findings align with those reviewed in prior chapters. Finally, the central question of Chapter Eight is whether comprehension in film might be transferable to that of drawn visual narratives: Does watching TV or movies help a person read or draw comics?

As will be demonstrated across these chapters, this extensive empirical literature implies that the understanding of sequences of images involves a fluency, acquired across a developmental trajectory, given exposure and practice with visual narratives that manifest across diverse variations across the world. Chapter Nine will thus tie together this work and discuss its implications on the understanding of comics and visual narratives, and their study and use in education, communication, psychology, and beyond.

CHAPTER TWO

Comprehending
Visual Narratives

If we are to examine whether people comprehend narrative visual sequences in a transparent way, we first need to address the nature of those comprehension processes. One motivation for the Sequential Image Transparency Assumption might come from the belief that visual narratives imitate the perception of real-life situations, only clothed in the graphic structures of drawn lines. Since we understand how events and actions take place, why should a drawn sequence of events be difficult to construe?[1]

Research on event cognition itself has rapidly grown in the past two decades (Radvansky and Zacks 2014), and this knowledge does indeed seem to transcend our understanding of both perceived events and their manifestation in expressive forms like language or films (Loschky et al. 2018; Loschky et al. 2020; Radvansky and Zacks 2014). However, even if understanding of a sequence of images taps into this knowledge, which it seems to do, it does not mean that event cognition and visual perception are the only requirements to understand an image sequence. Indeed, emerging research on visual narrative comprehension suggests that this perception of an effortless understanding masks more complex processes.

As discussed in Chapter One, visual narratives like comics involve several levels of structure. Let's consider such complexity in Figure 2.1, from Ben Costa's *Pang: The Wandering Shaolin Monk, Volume 2*. First, we can consider its physical make-up. In its layout, this sequence spans two actual pages. The first panel is taken from a prior page, originally in the bottom right corner, but altered here for simplicity. The second page uses three rows, vertically stacked, with two, three, and then two panels in each row, where panels themselves are horizontally staggered. Thus, this layout uses an overall grid structure using only a left-to-right and down Z-path for navigation.

Next, let's shift to what the images themselves convey. The content within the panels show an encounter between a monk held in bondage (Pang, the titular wandering Shaolin monk) and a tiger. It begins with Pang and the tiger facing each other (panel one), and then Pang offers himself to be eaten by the tiger instead of a character not depicted here (panel two) while the tiger looks prepared to attack (panel three). Pang closes his eyes (panel four) expecting to be eaten (panel five) only to open his eyes (panel six) and realize the tiger was leaving (panel seven). It ends with Pang gasping in relief (panel eight).

A reader must decode several levels of complexity to comprehend this sequence. First, we need to understand that this is not one image (or even two physical pages), but a holistic structure with several sub-units (panels) which have an arrangement that is intended to be read in a particular order. The lines and shapes within each panel depict basic meaningful information, like a person (Pang), a tiger, and a forest. We also need to recognize the continuity of this information across panels: that each depicted person is the same person (Pang) and not a unique character or scene in each panel. Not all of the characters are shown in every panel, which means we also need to infer the things that occur "off-panel" and that the narrative world does not stop with the frame of the panel.

Based on the depictions within the panels (poses, expressions, etc.) we also understand that the depicted characters (Pang, tiger) are involved in actions and events, and we might also make expectations about what might happen next. For example, we might fear that Pang could be eaten by the tiger at the start of the sequence, and thus feel relief when the tiger leaves and he remains unscathed. This also involves knowing that characters have intentions and goals that might motivate these events, such as the tiger's goal to have dinner and Pang's desire not to be that meal (despite his selfless intent).

The content of this sequence is also presented in a particular way, with information depicted or withheld to evoke a response in the reader. This presentation extends beyond the linear relationships between the panels, since panels three and seven of the tiger are separated by three panels depicting only Pang. These panels of Pang could also be deleted, reinforcing this distant connection between the panels of the tiger. In a nice confluence of content and layout, these panels of Pang also comprise their own row in the layout, so exiting this chunk of content involves exiting the physical row as well.

Although comprehending this sequence might seem simple, it involves all of this complexity and more. This chapter thus asks: What are the cognitive mechanisms involved in this comprehension process?

Below, we discuss the stages and mechanisms involved with navigating and understanding a sequence of images. The research informing this work has primarily used experiments with participants who are neurotypical college-aged adults or older from industrialized societies, with exposure and practice with visual narratives, particularly comics. As we will see in later chapters, it is important to know the participants involved in these studies as both age and experience may modulate how sequences of images might

FIGURE 2.1 *Example sequence from* Pang: The Wandering Shaolin Monk, Volume 2, *by Ben Costa, where a captured monk, Pang, is confronted by a tiger. The first panel comes from a separate page, for which the layout has been altered for clarity. Sequence © 2013 Ben Costa.*

be understood. Thus, although the findings presented here are likely generalizable—with modulation for various populations—they must be taken with the caveat that they reflect the processing of a specific population.

Here we will explore the processes related to visual narrative *sequences*: their layout, semantics, and narrative structure. I will argue that processing each of these components involves a similar progression. In each case, a comprehender works to build a *cognitive structure* that characterizes that domain, reflecting an organizational architecture aggregating information of a given cognitive process. For example, a cognitive structure associated with the meaning of a sequence of images (or words and sentences) is a *situation model,* which is a mental model combining the meaningful information of a discourse as it unfurls (Kintsch and van Dijk 1978; Zwaan and Radvansky 1998). Since a situation model is the aggregated understanding of a (visual or multimodal) discourse as it progresses, its construction is the aim of the comprehension process.

The building of a cognitive structure might be characterized simplistically by a three-part process. First, an incoming stimulus (like a picture or word) allows a comprehender to *access* some type of knowledge which can be used to construct a cognitive structure suited to the given domain of processing. This can facilitate *predictions* about subsequent information, both through activation of bottom-up features (i.e., what is available in the stimulus), and through top-down stored knowledge (i.e., information already encoded in the mind). Confirmation of these predictions allows the cycle to begin again. However, when incoming information may be discontinuous with those prior expectancies, it triggers an *updating* process whereby the structure is revised and/or a new structure is generated. These stages characterize an ongoing process that is cyclic and iterative throughout the reading and comprehension process. Below, I will argue that these stages can characterize each of the structures involved with processing of visual narrative sequences, thereby running in parallel.

2.1 Navigating Visual Narratives

We start our discussion by examining the most surface aspect of a visual narrative sequence: its layout. As discussed in Chapter One, spatially sequential layouts are a visual display that contain sub-units that are spatially arranged on a physical canvas, such as a comic page. This spatial arrangement requires a way to navigate through these panels in an ordered way. This task could be complex, given that there are numerous ways panels can be manipulated relative to each other, altering their alignment, proximity, and positions (Bateman et al. 2016; Cohn 2013b). While content no doubt interacts with the ways that readers navigate a page layout, the processing of layout and content are ultimately separate (discussed below). Here we shortly review the basic processes of navigating a spatial layout, particularly of comic pages, while the remainder of this chapter investigates the processes involved with comprehension of the content. While some exploratory work has begun to look at how layout and content interact (Bateman, Beckmann, and Varela 2018; Mikkonen and Lautenbacher 2019; Omori, Ishii, and Kurata 2004), careful experimentation remains needed to understand this relationship further.

Overall, I will hypothesize that the three stages discussed above—access, prediction, and updating—are involved in how a reader navigates through a page layout. First, a reader accesses a unit of the layout—i.e., a panel. The panel is part of a larger *assemblage structure* which reflects the cognitive structure of how a given page is organized and how it is navigated. Then, on the basis of the panel's location and its surrounding cues, readers make predictions about where to go next drawing on knowledge encoded in their long-term memory or being constructed in their working memory. Upon acting on these predictions (i.e., going to the next panel), confirmation of a prediction will allow the cycle to start again, but a perceived discontinuity with those expectations will trigger an updating process. This process then begins again with each subsequent panel. We will explore each of these stages below.

The first task confronted by a reader when engaging a page is to *access* the units of navigation—the panels. There are two potential options for how such a process begins. First, it has been hypothesized that readers engage in *global visual search* processes whereby their eyes explore a page prior to committing to any panels (e.g., Groensteen 2007). Some evidence of such search processes has been shown in an uncontrolled experiment tracking subjects' eyes during free reading of comic pages (Mikkonen and Lautenbacher 2019). However, in this experiment, pages from different comics were shown one at a time, decoupled from their context in a sequential story. This meant that each page could not carry expectations from prior pages in a work and readers may have needed more orientation given that each presented page changed in authors, stories, etc.

A second possibility is that readers have targeted expectations of where a page begins. Indeed, readers appear consistent for their preferences to start a page in the upper corner (leftward for readers of left-to-right dominant layouts) even without content (Cohn 2013a). Also, readers have been observed to make dedicated saccades—i.e., rapid eye movements between locations where the eye fixates—to this upper-left position in experiments where the layout of a comic strip was a predictable grid (Foulsham, Wybrow, and Cohn 2016). Indeed, some fixations prior to landing on the upper-corner panel may involve intermediate positions within the saccades moving to this position (Mikkonen and Lautenbacher 2019). Thus, expectations of an upper-corner panel may motivate readers to forego global search processes for more direct looking.

Once a reader has accessed a particular panel position, they then need to choose where to go next. One hypothesis might be that content motivates where a reader navigates from panel-to-panel. This would require that a participant explores all possible adjacent panels (at least) before committing to the next panel. When measured with eye tracking, this would imply that their eyes would look back and forth between the current panel and all other options. Experimental data mostly does not support this, as eye-movements generally remain smooth between panels (Foulsham, Wybrow, and Cohn 2016; Mikkonen and Lautenbacher 2019; Omori, Ishii, and Kurata 2004), especially for experienced comic readers (Bateman, Beckmann, and Varela 2018; Nakazawa 2002a; Zhao and Mahrt 2018). Such findings of smooth eye-movements across comic panels go against claims that "the eye's movements on the surface of the page are relatively erratic and do not respect any precise protocol" (Groensteen 2007: 47).

If readers are not relying on content, then what motivates where they go next? The relatively smooth eye-movements in combination with a modulation by expertise implies that readers draw upon various sources of information to guide their decisions about navigational order. Thus, when at a particular panel, readers make ***structural predictions*** for where to go next based on the constraints they have encoded. There are four basic types of information that readers likely negotiate when deciding where to go next (Cohn 2013a):

1 *Rule-based ordering* – Some constraints are motivated by a conventionalized order which is stored in long-term memory. These would be the type of orders inherited from writing systems involving the basic reading directions, such as the left-to-right and down "Z-path" consistent with alphabetic scripts. Although Japanese and Chinese scripts use a top-to-bottom and rightward "N-path," their overall pages (as in manga) appear to use a right-to-left and down "S-path" (Cohn et al. 2019). The encoding of such rules would thus guide predictions for how to navigate panels.

2 *Perceptual constraints* – Some navigational preferences are guided by aspects of Gestalt groupings, such as cues related to the alignment and proximity of panels. In general, greater misalignment and separation of panels leads to preferences for an alternative reading order from the conventionalized Z-path (Cohn 2013a; Cohn and Campbell 2015). Such cues may follow general perceptual preferences, but their application to the navigation of layouts may be stored as constraints in long-term memory.

3 *Layout schemas* – In addition to general constraints, comprehenders encode patterns of layout structures in their long-term memory. These layout schemas may consist of conventionalized panel arrangements and their preferred navigation (like blockage—a vertical column of panels adjacent to a panel spanning that column), or additional navigational conventions (such as arrows or trails between panels). As will be shown in the next chapter, layouts vary in systematic ways across cultures, genres, and time periods (Bateman, Veloso, and Lau 2019; Cohn et al. 2019; Laubrock and Dubray 2019; Pederson and Cohn 2016). This implies that authors of comics store preferences in long-term memory for certain configurations of panels. Such knowledge thereby becomes encoded for readers of comics who use those preferences, which in turn influences readers' navigational choices through layouts.

4 *Assemblage structure* – The navigation of a page layout creates a hierarchic organization hypothesized to be constructed in the course of navigating a page layout. Such an organizational structure groups panels into hierarchic clusters on the basis of their arrangements (Cohn 2013a; Tanaka et al. 2007), as depicted in Figure 2.2. This structure would thus be held in working memory during the navigation of a page but would then be released from working memory once the next page is reached.

These sources of information are hypothesized as belonging in a constraint-based system, where they can be balanced in relation to each other, and may carry different probabilistic weights of influence. As stated earlier, the smooth saccades demonstrated in eye tracking studies provide support for the concept that stored structures guide the comprehender's navigation of layouts. Additional evidence comes from experiments where participants consciously choose the order of panels in layouts with empty panels (Cohn 2013a; Cohn and Campbell 2015). In these experiments, participants were fairly consistent about their choices for panel orderings, which were modulated incrementally by both rule-based and Gestalt constraints. For example, as panel borders became less aligned and more separated, the Z-path became less preferred. Such constraints are also influenced by the assemblage structure. The aim of navigation is not just to progress through an ordered route throughout a page, but rather to construct an assemblage structure of the page (Figure 2.2).

These knowledge structures would provide the basis for the predictions that readers make for how to progress from panel to panel. Thus, because Figure 2.1 maintains a fairly standard grid structure, when a reader reaches any of the panels inside of a row, it would be predicted that they would move laterally to the next panel. This would be guided by the alignment of the horizontal gutters between panels (n, m), as depicted in the assemblage structure in Figure 2.2a. When reaching the end of the row, the page border should serve as a cue to read diagonally left to start a new row, rather than, for example, downward to the vertically adjacent panel. Such predictions may be aided by subtle parafoveal peripheral vision—i.e., the visual field outside the central, focal aspects of vision—which picks up on surrounding visual cues to satisfy viewing choices prior to full saccades (Laubrock, Hohenstein, and Kümmerer 2018).

Thus, navigation of where to read next would involve the interaction of two sources of information. Bottom-up information comes from the physical cues of panel relationships, such as alignment or proximity of panel borders to each other, or the edge of a page. Among these might be misalignment of horizontal panel borders, which can motivate a reader to move downward in a vertical column, rather than horizontally (Cohn 2013a; Cohn and Campbell 2015). These bottom-up cues then interact with top-down expectations, constrained from the stored knowledge listed above, as well as the hierarchic groupings constructed online throughout the navigation of layout (Figure 2.2). Thus, if a reader is at a panel within a row or column, they may predict that they will remain in that grouping, barring bottom-up cues to the contrary.

When readers' expectations are disconfirmed about which panel should be viewed next, or when the layout presents multiple conceivable options, readers may *update* their structure to create a new navigational path. This revision process manifests physically in regressive eye movements, which is where the eyes rebound to prior locations after exploring new places. In

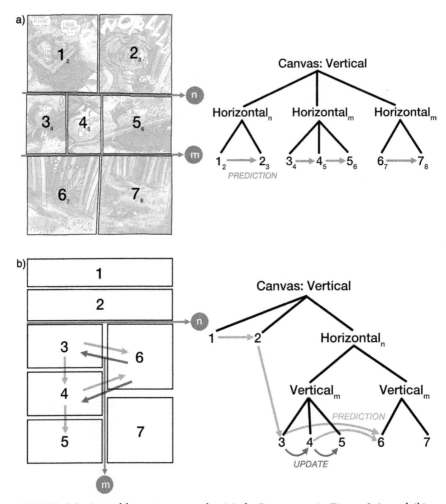

FIGURE 2.2 *Assemblage structures for (a) the* Pang *page in Figure 2.1, and (b) a mock-up page. In (a) large numbers represent panel numbers on this page and subscripts align with the panel numbers in Figures 2.4 and 2.6. Lighter arrows represent predictions, with darker arrows representing updating.*

simple grid layouts, regressions have been observed most frequently between physically adjacent panels, but less frequently moving diagonally across rows (Foulsham, Wybrow, and Cohn 2016). Regressive eye movements are also more common in layouts that deviate from the standard Z-path, again with variation in the alignment or proximity of panels (Bateman, Beckmann, and Varela 2018; Chiba et al. 2007; Omori, Ishii, and Kurata 2004). Thus, we would expect that regressive eye movements would be more likely to come from greater variance in the probabilistic likelihood that a given panel should be ordered next within a given layout. In other words, a comprehender is more likely to look backwards once they reach a panel if there was less certainty of which panel came next, given all the constraints described earlier.

As the layout of the page in Figure 2.1 maintains a fairly simple grid structure, we would expect relatively few updating processes, given the high likelihood of maintaining the Z-path throughout this arrangement. As a contrast, consider Figure 2.2b, a layout which has been shown to create variable preferences for navigation (Cohn and Campbell 2015). Let us assume that the numbering of the panels is the intended reading order, though similar processes described later might occur with an alternate reading order (such as 1-2-3-6-4-5-7).

Consider the processes that might occur upon reaching panel three. Here, a reader may predict that they should follow the Z-path and move laterally to panel six, given the alignment of the top borders. However, alignment of the panels' vertical borders and the misalignment of the lower borders (a vertical stagger) might motivate a downward order to panel four. Note also that the bottom border of panel six also does not line up with panel four, which would create a "blockage" arrangement with more confident recognition of a column (Cohn and Campbell 2015). Thus, after a disconfirmation that panel six is the next panel, a reader would be expected to regress to panel three before moving downward to panel four. Given the misalignment between borders of panels four, five, and six, a similar process may repeat here. However, it is possible panel four could be recognized as within the middle of a vertical segment cued by the alignment of vertical borders (m), leading to a higher probability to "stay in this segment" and move downward.

Ambiguities in layout thus create further costs for the process of how a layout might be navigated. Consider then how more experimental "artistic" layouts might challenge a reader's navigation, where the layout further deviates from top-down expectations. Similar experiences might hold from layouts with less dedicated reading orders, such as infographics or other spatial arrays. These layouts may thus demand more updating guided by bottom-up cues, because they would be less able to rely on expectations motivated from top-down knowledge.

Thus, to summarize, the extant work on the structure and navigation of page layouts related to comic pages indicates three overall stages. A reader *accesses* a particular unit of the layout (a panel), then makes *predictions* for a subsequent spatial position informed by their internalized structures related to layouts, and they then *update* their ordering when those expectations might be disconfirmed. As we will see in the rest of this chapter, similar stages can characterize the processing of the semantic and narrative content. How these processing stages in layout align with those in semantics and narrative remains an open question for future research.

2.2 Comprehending Visual Narratives

The processing of the content of visual narrative involves interactions between numerous cognitive systems and two frameworks have emerged to describe the stages of this processing. First, the *Scene Perception and Event Comprehension Theory (SPECT)* (Loschky et al. 2018; Loschky et al. 2020) emphasizes how perceptual processing combines with mental model construction throughout visual narrative comprehension, drawing from the research traditions of scene perception, event cognition, and discourse comprehension. Second, the *Parallel Interfacing Narrative-Semantics (PINS) Model* (Cohn 2020b) stresses neurocognition, and how comprehension combines semantic representations that provide the meaning, with a narrative structure which organizes that meaning into a sequence. The PINS Model, depicted in the right side of Figure 2.3, draws more from psycholinguistics and cognitive neuroscience. In particular, it is informed by studies of the brain using event-related potentials (ERPs), a direct measurement of the electrical activity of the brain over time, which results in brainwaves. Many of the neural responses that appear in brainwaves create repeatable patterns that have become recognized as indexes for specific cognitive functions. Below, I describe the flow of processing a sequence of images while integrating insights from SPECT and the PINS Model.

As in the discussion of page layouts above, I will argue that comprehension processes involve three broad stages of *accessing* information to build a structure, using this information to make *predictions*, and then *updating* that structure on the basis of incoming information. This overall procedure is cyclic and operates across both the semantic and narrative levels of representation, as in Figure 2.3. These stages will be elaborated on below.

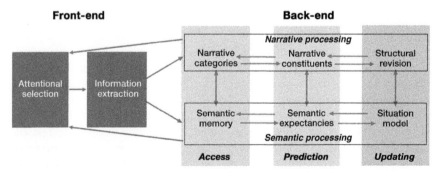

FIGURE 2.3 *Schematization of the step-by-step processing stages for comprehending a visual narrative sequence, integrating insights from SPECT and the PINS Model.*

2.3 Semantic Processing

As "comprehension" often revolves around how a reader consumes and retains the meaning of an expression, let us here first address the *semantic processing* associated with such meaning-making. The SPECT model makes a useful distinction between two interacting domains of processing that broadly relate to mechanisms of perception and comprehension (Loschky et al. 2018; Loschky et al. 2020). *Front-end processes* describe the aspects of perception and attention involved in extracting information from visual images, primarily within a single eye fixation. These are the processes involved with exploring the sensory experience of the visual modality itself. In other words, front-end processes characterize how the eye and mind interact to negotiate the content of the image. In contrast, *back-end processes* relate to the stages involved in constructing a *situation model*, i.e., the mental model incorporating the understanding of the entities and events of an unfolding (visual) discourse (Zwaan and Radvansky 1998). That is, back-end processes are how the mind/brain construct meaning, given what was experienced by the eye. Front-end processes typically precede back-end processes, as perceptual experiences provide the materials for subsequent understanding of that information. However, back-end processes can also feed back into the front-end perceptual processes, such as when the expectations or demands of a mental model influence how and where an eye will move through an image.

2.3.1 Front-end Processing: Information Extraction

The comprehension of the content of a sequence of images begins with the front-end perceptual processes, as readers must find the specific cues within images that will be relevant for the sequential context. This includes *attentional selection*, which involves the eyes searching throughout an image to find which information to process, and the subsequent *information extraction* to pull out the relevant meaning. Research tracking readers' eyes has suggested that focus within the picture content of a panel is primarily given to characters and their parts (especially faces) compared to backgrounds (Kirtley et al. 2018; Laubrock, Hohenstein, and Kümmerer 2018), along with the specific cues within images that motivate the sequential meaning (Foulsham, Wybrow, and Cohn 2016; Hutson, Magliano, and Loschky 2018; Jain, Sheikh, and Hodgins 2016). This search, selection, and extraction process happens rapidly, with general fixation durations to content of panels occurring under 250 milliseconds (Laubrock, Hohenstein, and Kümmerer 2018). Decent comprehension even maintains when images in a sequence are presented with rapid exposure, such as 150 milliseconds per panel (Hagmann and Cohn 2016; Inui and Miyamoto 1981).

Readers also appear to be fairly directed in finding the important content of panels (Foulsham, Wybrow, and Cohn 2016; Laubrock, Hohenstein, and Kümmerer 2018), with the narrative sequence informing readers where to direct their attention. Certain areas of panels contain the cues that are relevant for their meaning within the sequence (Foulsham and Cohn forthcoming; Hutson, Magliano, and Loschky 2018), as evident in findings that attention is more focal to these areas when panels are placed in a coherent order than in a scrambled order (Foulsham, Wybrow, and Cohn 2016). Indeed, framing of a panel with only the focal cues—such as panels using a zoomed-in viewpoint—provides enough information as framing of the whole scene for comprehending a visual narrative sequence (Foulsham and Cohn forthcoming).

A schematization of semantic processing for Figure 2.1 is depicted in Figure 2.4. The front-end information extraction is represented by the second tier, whereby the most pertinent information of a panel is pulled out. These would be the areas that would receive the most fixations. In panel two, the primary information might include the text (here excluded), Pang's worried face and his bound hands, but not the whole image and its background. Sometimes a panel will only depict this primary information by using the panel frame as an "attentional unit" for a more constrained view of the scene. Panel five essentially does this, by framing Pang's grimacing face alone,

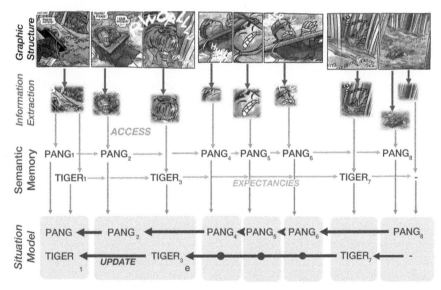

FIGURE 2.4 *A schematization of semantic processing for a visual narrative sequence. Forward-looking expectancies are noted with rightward arrows in semantic memory, while backward-looking updating is notated with leftward arrows within the situation model.*

leaving out all surrounding details and context that appear in other panels. This zoom functions both to bring focus (i.e., attention) to Pang's emotion, but also to exclude information about the rest of the scene (i.e., the location of the tiger), thereby raising the tension of the scene at that unit.

2.3.2 Back-end Processing: Semantic Access and Expectancies

With the information extracted through the front-end processes of visual search and attentional selection, this information can be fed into back-end processes to construct an understanding of the sequence. Information extracted from the visual surface of a panel will activate information in semantic memory. In studies of neurocognition measured by event-related brain potentials (ERPs), this process of *semantic access* is indexed by the "N400" brainwave response. The N400 gets its name because it is a *negative* polarity response occurring roughly 300 to 500 milliseconds after a stimulus is presented (i.e., a word or image), which reaches its peak around 400 milliseconds (Kutas and Federmeier 2011). In other words, the N400 is a brain response associated with the processing of meaning that occurs less than half a second after a comprehender experiences that information.

The N400 was first discovered in studies of sentence processing (Kutas and Hillyard 1980), but it has been observed occurring in response to the manipulation of meaning across many domains (Kutas and Federmeier 2011), including to single images and to panels in visual narratives (Cohn et al. 2012; West and Holcomb 2002).[2] For example, Figure 2.5a depicts the N400s evoked by panels from sequences that balance their semantic associations with a narrative structure (dotted and dashed lines) compared to panels from normal sequences (solid line). In this case, the fewer semantic associations that exist between panels, the greater the N400 effect. The N400 is thought to reflect a default neural response that occurs to all meaningful information, given the relationship of an incoming stimulus (like a word or picture) to its prior context (Kutas and Federmeier 2011). This means that unexpected or incongruous information thus evokes larger N400s than more expected information.

Let's consider again our example sequence, schematized in Figure 2.4, where vertical lines depict how the extracted information feeds into semantic memory. For simplicity, this example focuses only on the referential information about characters, but a reader's full comprehension would also include the knowledge about the events that take place, characters' goals and intents, the spatial location, and various other meaningful information (Zwaan and Radvansky 1998). The information fed into semantic memory thus activates features related to the specific characters in the sequence (Pang, tiger), but also concepts associated with those characters (Chinese monks, big cats, daily meals, etc.).

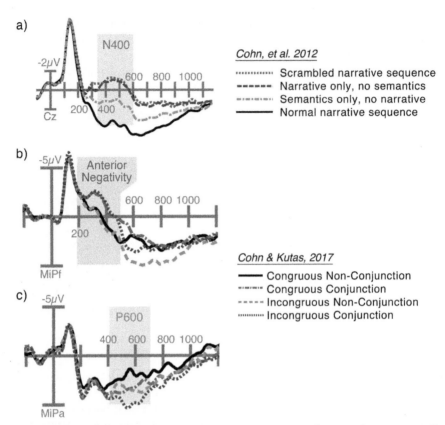

FIGURE 2.5 *The primary brainwaves occurring to manipulations of narrative and/ or semantic structures in visual narratives: a) the N400 elicited by semantic incongruity, which is insensitive narrative structure (Cohn et al. 2012). b) An anterior negativity elicited by narrative patterning is insensitive to semantic incongruity. The c) P600 is modulated by both narrative and semantics (Cohn and Kutas 2017). Each graph depicts one electrode site, along the midline of the scalp, either center (Cz), prefrontal (MiPf), or parietal (MiPa). The x-axis depicts the time-course in milliseconds, while the y-axis depicts amplitude, with negative up. Separation of waves indicates a difference in processing, with relevant time-windows highlighted.*

Once activated, these features become predisposed to be (re)activated by information in subsequent panels. Thus, characters (Pang, tiger) or spatial locations (a bamboo forest) that appear in a panel should be easier to reactivate if they appeared in a previous panel. Likewise, information that is associated with the activated features should be easier to access than unrelated information. For example, because a tiger is depicted in the scene, an incongruous, non-sequitur panel of a lion inserted into this sequence will be easier to process than one of an iguana or a dinosaur—because tigers are semantically associated to lions as both being predatory cats. Closely related information thus leads to a reduced amplitude of the N400—i.e., less cost for accessing the meaning in semantic memory—while incongruous or unexpected information leads to a greater N400.

Indeed, as readers progress through a visual narrative they make various probabilistically based *expectations* about incoming information relative to its prior sequential context. There are several types of information that may allow for forward-looking semantic expectancies in visual narrative sequencing:

1 *Continuity constraint* – In spatially sequential visual narrative sequences like Figure 2.1, readers may expect a high likelihood that the characters and objects in one panel will persist in subsequent panels (i.e., the continuity constraint). Such expectations also lead readers to make more directed eye-movements to where those elements are assumed to appear, implying that the front-end process of information extraction is facilitated by these back-end expectancies (Foulsham, Wybrow, and Cohn 2016). This information extraction for continuity is not perceptually trivial, since characters and objects may change in how they are depicted across images, be it different postures, viewpoints, sizes, framing, or visual style. All of these differences involve linking varied configurations of graphic lines to a common conceptual identity. As we will see in later chapters, recognition of such continuity is not always maintained by individuals with less exposure to visual narratives.

2 *Predictive inferences* – Readers may also make more active predictions about "what might happen next" in a sequence, similar to "predictive inferences" discussed in the discourse literature (McKoon and Ratcliff 1986). Subtle cues throughout a narrative can motivate broad foreshadowing (Magliano, Dijkstra, and Zwaan 1996), such as objects introduced into a story which are then used in later parts of the narrative. For example, a weapon introduced in the first part of a story might be expected to be used in a later part (a.k.a. the principle of "Chekhov's gun"). Such expectancies would be information incorporated into a situation model and then marked as relevant for subsequent events.

3 *Event schemas and scripts* – Other predictions may connect the content of images to a broader event schema or script, which is the stored knowledge about how events are organized (Jackendoff 2007; Radvansky and Zacks 2014; Schank and Abelson 1977). This includes information about the postures and motions that actions require, and how events progress from their start to finish. For example, characters in preparatory postures (like reaching back an arm to punch) create expectations that their actions (a punch) will be completed (Cohn and Paczynski 2013), and indeed removing these postural cues leads to costs for interpreting the events (Cohn, Paczynski, and Kutas 2017).

4   *Idiosyncratic themes or tropes* – More specific event schemas may be
    contextual to certain stories. If you are reading a *Peanuts* comic and
    know their tropes, you might expect that if Charlie Brown is running
    toward a football, Lucy will pull it away so he embarrassingly falls
    on his back. This prediction would be stored in memory because of
    the familiarity with this particular comic strip, and indeed other
    stories may carry their own idiosyncratic contextual expectancies.

Because the N400 is sensitive to the expectancy of incoming information
given its prior context, affirmation of a prediction will lead to a smaller
N400 (Kutas and Federmeier 2011). Thus, in studies of language, words
that have a higher probability of being expected in a sentence lead to easier
processing, as evident in smaller N400 amplitudes and faster reading times
(Delong, Urbach, and Kutas 2005; van Berkum et al. 2005). We found
comparable results in our studies of visual narratives. In fact, the N400 is
modulated in a graded way based on how much an event is expected as
"what happens next": the more predictable an event, the smaller the N400
(Coderre et al. forthcoming). Because both words and images in sequence
are modulated by such expectancies, it implies that sensitivity to predictability
is a feature of processing meaning in general, not tied to any one modality.

Thus, when expectations are continually reinforced across a sequence,
the N400 becomes smaller at each subsequent panel of the visual narrative
(Cohn et al. 2012), just like the N400 reduces across positions of words in
a sentence (Van Petten and Kutas 1991). Indeed, the N400 is often greatest
at the first panel of a visual narrative sequence, where this process of
semantic access is just starting and a comprehender must first access the
meanings necessary to comprehend a discourse (Cohn et al. 2012). This
process serves to "lay a foundation" for the subsequent comprehension of
the narrative (Gernsbacher 1990), and it is also reflected in the way that
readers also spend a longer time viewing the first panel of a sequence than
subsequent panels (Cohn and Wittenberg 2015; Foulsham, Wybrow, and
Cohn 2016). Thus, information at the start takes more effort to process, but
comprehension of subsequent information becomes easier, depending on its
congruity with the sequential context.

2.3.3 *Back-end Processing:*
Situation Model Construction

Information that becomes activated in semantic memory then becomes
incorporated into a situation model, which is an aggregation of the meaning
of the constructed visual discourse (Cohn 2020b; Loschky et al. 2018;
Loschky et al. 2020). Comprehension of a (visual) narrative is reflected in
the process of building a situation model. As it is constructed throughout the
reading of a visual narrative, a situation model is held in working memory,

but it then gets stored in episodic long-term memory where it is retained into the future (Magliano et al. 2012). In other words, your understanding of a narrative while engaging a discourse arises in the building of a situation model, after which aspects of that model maintain for what you remember about that story.

Construction of a situation model is sensitive to the shifts that occur throughout a sequence. While a reader progresses through a visual discourse, they monitor for changes in characters, postures, events, spatial locations, and other meaningful dimensions that may shift across panels. Discontinuity in the information extracted from panels relative to the prior context triggers an *updating* process where the situation model needs to be revised to account for this new information (McNamara and Magliano 2009; Zwaan and Radvansky 1998). That is, as new information comes in, a backwards-looking process checks it against the current situation model, which is revised accordingly. This updating process is posited as continuous and ongoing at each unit of the visual discourse, not just in response to incongruous information.

Updating processes can vary in their magnitude for how much alters within the situation model depending on the amount of information being revised. SPECT makes a distinction between *mapping* and *shifting* (Loschky et al. 2018; Loschky et al. 2020). Backward-looking "mapping" occurs when discontinuity is detected between incoming information and the situation model, when prior expectations may be disconfirmed, and/or when too much information changes between images. Such mapping can thus be incremental in nature (Huff, Meitz, and Papenmeier 2014; Kurby and Zacks 2012), and similar notions have been posited by theoretical approaches to meaningful relations between panels in visual narrative sequencing (Bateman and Wildfeuer 2014; Saraceni 2016; Stainbrook 2016). When changes between panels become untenable for mapping, the sequence may be segmented by a "shift" to a new situation model (Gernsbacher 1990; Loschky et al. 2020; McNamara and Magliano 2009; Zwaan and Radvansky 1998).

Figure 2.4 represents the situation model with rounded boxes, each incorporating the characters in the sequence (Pang, tiger). Leftward arrows depict the backward-looking updating processes that occur relative to the preceding model. Note, for example, the changes between panel two, which shows only Pang, and panel three, which shows only the tiger. This type of shift between characters incurs a cost (Cohn and Kutas 2017), but because these panels depict only a portion of the scene, the broader spatial location would need to be inferred, as notated by "e" (for "environment"). Further updating may be required where the tiger remains unseen from panel three until appearing again in panel seven. The tiger would thus need to be held in memory across panels four to six, which focus on Pang. Updating costs thus may occur at panel seven both for the reactivation of the tiger, and because it is shown leaving, an action that might confound the foreshadowed expectation that it may be attacking Pang off-panel in panels four to six.

In some cases, discontinuity between the content of a situation model and the depictions in panels may warrant the need to derive an inference. For example, imagine if in Figure 2.1 we omitted the penultimate panel showing the tiger walking away, so that the sequence would begin showing Pang in danger from the tiger, and upon opening his eyes the tiger would be gone. A reader would then need to reconcile this depiction (Pang alone in the woods) with the earlier information (he was threatened by the tiger) by inferring what event occurred to result in that difference (the tiger left). Inferencing of this type would incur costs to working memory in order to update the situation model with the relevant information (Cohn and Kutas 2015; Cohn and Wittenberg 2015; Hutson, Magliano, and Loschky 2018; Magliano et al. 2015).

Inference generation has long been a focus of how visual narratives are understood, with many theories emphasizing how readers "fill in" information between two panels (Gavaler and Beavers 2018; McCloud 1993). With this view of situation model updating in mind, we can thus summarize the above by distinguishing between changes in the flow of information between panels. Incremental changes between images do not rise to the full level of inferences, but instead characterize simple *mappings* between situation models—such as changes between characters or differences in the posture of a character to imply an action. *Shifting* characterizes large revisions of a situation's understanding, such as changing between two scenes. Full *inferences* only arise when information is missing that, if not reconciled, would render a scene difficult to otherwise understand—such as a primary event of the sequence going undepicted. Thus, not all updates of a situation model between panels might require "filling in" information. This is further apparent in that authors use several conventionalized techniques to cue a reader to generate inferences, rather than such "filling in" just occurring by happenstance of a sequence (Cohn 2019a).

In research measuring ERPs, updating processes have been posited to be indexed by a "P600", a *positive* polarity neural response appearing over the posterior part of the scalp, which typically begins around 400 milliseconds after experiencing a stimulus (like seeing an image or word) and peaks around 600 milliseconds. In language research, P600s were first recognized in contexts of syntactic processing (Hagoort, Brown, and Groothusen 1993; Osterhout and Holcomb 1992), but they have come to be associated with the update, revision, and/or integration of incoming information given the expectancies of a prior context (Baggio 2018; Brouwer et al. 2016; Kuperberg 2013, 2016). This interpretation is consistent with work arguing that the P600 is part of a broader family of brain responses associated with mental model updating (Donchin and Coles 1988; Leckey and Federmeier 2019; Van Petten and Luka 2012).

In visual narratives, P600s have been observed in both congruous and incongruous circumstances, supporting the idea that updating is a continuous and ongoing process throughout a visual sequence (Cohn and Kutas 2015;

Magliano and Zacks 2011). For example, P600s are evoked by changes in characters or events, both when they might be congruous (Cohn and Kutas 2015) or incongruous in the context of the sequence (Cohn and Kutas 2017; Cohn and Maher 2015). Such an example appears in the experiment that generated the brainwaves in Figure 2.5c. In this study, greater P600s were shown in response to panels that changed between characters than panels that repeated characters, while even greater positivity (i.e., more "downward") occurred to panels that had discontinuous changes between characters (Cohn and Kutas 2017). As P600s most often appear in response to changes or alterations of information in a sequence, they appear to reflect the updating processes most associated with mapping.

A different brain response appears more associated with inferential processing. This seems to arise in ERPs with "sustained negativities" starting around 400ms that appear with a central or frontal distribution across the scalp (Baggio 2018). Research on language has attributed these negativities to the demands for holding onto information in working memory and/or searching through a situation model to resolve ambiguities related to characters (Hoeks and Brouwer 2014; van Berkum 2009) or events (Baggio, van Lambalgen, and Hagoort 2008; Bott 2010; Paczynski, Jackendoff, and Kuperberg 2014; Wittenberg et al. 2014). Sustained negativities have also been observed in visual narrative processing, particularly at the panel following the omission of an event—i.e., where an inference would be expected to be generated (Cohn forthcoming; Cohn and Kutas 2015).

Evidence of inferential processing also occurs outside of measurements of the brain. Readers spend a longer time viewing panels following the position of an omitted event (Cohn and Wittenberg 2015; Magliano et al. 2015; Magliano et al. 2017), and this timing can be modulated by intervening working memory demands (Magliano et al. 2015). In addition, readers search through these post-omission panels more than when previous information is provided overtly, reflecting their attempts to reconcile the missing information (Hutson, Magliano, and Loschky 2018). All told, evidence of building a situation model arises in both neural (ERPs) and behavioral measurements (reading times, eye movements). Yet, the differences between brain responses for updating processes like mapping and shifting (P600s) and full inferences (sustained negativities) imply varied mechanisms related to interpretive processing in visual narrative comprehension.

To summarize, comprehending the meaning of a visual narrative sequence—its *semantic processing*—involves both front-end processes and back-end processes. Front-end processes use attentional selection and information extraction to negotiate which information in the visual depiction might be relevant to be understood. In back-end processes, this information activates semantic memory and gets incorporated into a growing situation model which is updated based on how the visual discourse progresses. Comprehension thus involves both forward-looking expectancies related to activated information and backward-looking updating which reconcile those expectations with incoming information. Overall, these processes are consistent with the types of comprehension processes posited by theories of discourse processing in language (Graesser, Millis, and Zwaan 1997; McNamara and Magliano 2009; van Dijk and Kintsch 1983), although they become adapted to the unique affordances of the visual-graphic modality (Magliano et al. 2013; Magliano, Higgs, and Clinton 2019).

2.4 Narrative Processing

Understanding of a visual narrative sequence involves constructing a situation model, as characterized earlier. However, there are several reasons why this semantic processing alone remains insufficient to explain how readers comprehend visual narrative sequences. First, discourse researchers have stressed that this type of iterative cycle of extraction, activation, and updating persist both for discourse and for understanding events as we perceive them in daily life (Radvansky and Zacks 2014). Yet, we recognize that *narratives* differ from everyday events, meaning that some non-trivial cognitive understanding must distinguish narratives from our lived experiences.

Second, parts of a visual narrative sequence play discernable roles that transcend just a flowing sequence of ever-shifting meanings. In Figure 2.1, the first panel's function is to set-up the situation, while the penultimate panel shows its climax before an aftermath in the final panel. Description of such roles go back at least as far as Aristotle's "Beginning-Middle-End" pattern (Butcher 1902) and narrative theories generally converge on the nature of such roles (Brewer 1985; Cohn 2013c; Cutting 2016). Third, and relatedly, visual narrative sequencing uses recognizable patterns (Bateman 2007; Branigan 1992; Cohn 2015, 2019b). Such patterns vary systematically across cultures and time periods (Cohn 2013b, 2019b; Cohn, Taylor, and Pederson 2017), and readers appear to process these patterns differently based on their frequency of exposure (Cohn and Kutas 2017). Neither narrative roles nor sequencing patterns occur in our everyday experiences of events, again implying that such information is encoded in a cognitive system beyond our active processing of meaning.

Fourth, various relationships between panels extend beyond image-to-image juxtapositions (Magliano and Zacks 2011; McCloud 1993; Saraceni 2016; Stainbrook 2016). Consider panels four to six in Figure 2.1, which only show Pang worried about being eaten, while the tiger remains off-panel. By not showing the tiger from panel three to seven, we need to make a distance connection between the set-up of the situation (Pang and the tiger) and its non-juxtaposed climax (where the tiger leaves). The Pang panels (four to six) can also be deleted with little recourse on the understanding of the sequence, suggesting that they create a center-embedded clause—a grouping of units placed within that of another sequence. This embedding is framed by the distance dependency of the tiger panels (three and seven). In addition, sequences may be ambiguous, with multiple interpretations and/or parsings (Cohn 2010b, 2015), may use metaphorical sequential relationships not motivated by an event structure (Cohn 2010a; Tasić and Stamenković 2015), or may depict the same general meaning in multiple different ways (Brewer and Lichtenstein 1981; Cohn 2013c, 2015; McCloud 1993). These phenomena all require a system beyond monitoring the meaningful changes between images.

Finally, all of these traits of sequencing reflect the choices that authors make in presenting which information a reader sees and when. In the center-embedded clause of panels four to six in Figure 2.1, the author chose to show only Pang, while keeping the tiger and its actions (or lack thereof) out of the view of the panels' frames. This has an impact on how the sequence is understood: withholding the tiger from view thus increases the tension for the comprehender because they do not know what the tiger is doing. These aspects of the sequence all reflect choices made by the author (here Ben Costa), and constitute the *narrative structure* of the sequence, as argued within the parallel architecture presented in Figure 1.1 of Chapter One.

Thus, within the PINS Model (Cohn 2020b) in Figure 2.3, an additional level of narrative processing runs parallel to semantic processing. As with layout and semantics, this level of representation constructs a cognitive structure. The theory of Visual Narrative Grammar (VNG), argues that this cognitive structure is a *narrative grammar*, which is diagrammed for Figure 2.1 in Figure 2.6, and is discussed below. This narrative grammar functions to organize the semantic information of a visual sequence analogous to how syntactic structure organizes the meaning of a sentence (Cohn 2013c). Like syntax, this narrative structure uses architectural principles that assign units to categorical roles and arrange them into hierarchic structures. Nevertheless, this narrative grammar operates at a higher level of information structure than sentences, closer to the level of a discourse, since most individual images contain more information than individual words (Cohn 2013c, 2015).

In the analogy between narrative and syntax, VNG has surface resemblance to previous grammars posited for stories (Mandler and Johnson 1977; Rumelhart 1975) or the sequencing of film (Carroll 1980; Colin 1995). However, VNG attempts to address several features of structure previously critiqued in these prior theories (Black and Wilensky 1979; de Beaugrande 1982; Garnham 1983). In particular, older models used procedural phrase structure rules based on Chomskyan generative grammars (Chomsky 1965), thereby resulting in ambiguous distinctions between grammar and semantics. In contrast, VNG is modeled after construction grammars (Culicover and Jackendoff 2005; Goldberg 1995), which posit sequencing patterns encoded as schema in long-term memory, along with correspondence rules to an explicitly separate semantics (see Cohn 2013c,

2015). Unlike with phrase structure rules, "unification" serves as a combinatorial mechanism, which is posited as a process that assembles stored schema into larger structures, given the prior context (Hagoort 2016, 2005; Jackendoff 2002). Finally, unlike other generative accounts of narrative, VNG also posits schema that elaborate or modify the canonical order (Cohn 2013c, 2015), along with idiosyncratic patterns comparable to syntactic constructions and idioms (Cohn 2013b, 2019a).

Within VNG, panels are assigned to categorical roles which differentiate the parts of a sequence, organized in the *canonical narrative schema* (see Table 2.1a). This basic pattern specifies that narrative sequences often begin with an Establisher, which sets up the basic characters and situations of the sequence. In Figure 2.1, the first panel is indeed an Establisher, where Pang first meets the tiger (diagrammed in Figure 2.6). An Initial then anticipates subsequent events, such as panels two and three of Pang and the tiger, where they engage each other but no event yet manifests (like the tiger attacking or leaving). An occurrence may be delayed from the Initial in a Prolongation, as in Figure 2.1/2.6 across panels four to six, where we wait to discover whether Pang will be attacked. These panels prolong the narrative tension. A sequence will then climax in the Peak. In this sequence, the Peak is relatively anticlimactic, as Pang is indeed *not* attacked and the tiger is shown walking away. The aftermath or resolution then occurs in the Release, which dissolves the narrative tension. This occurs with Pang finding relief in the final panel at not having been eaten.

Although the canonical schema specifies that these categories must go in this order, not all categories are mandatory in every sequence. In addition, the surface sequence may not always follow the canonical schematic order, since categories can apply both to panels and to groupings of panels. In Figure 2.6, the top level of the narrative structure does follow the canonical narrative sequence, progressing *Establisher-Initial-Prolongation-Peak-Release*. This is what gives the overall sequence the feeling of a narrative arc. Within this, panels four to six also form their own narrative constituent, with an Establisher of Pang being worried, an Initial of his anticipation of being attacked, and then a Peak of him opening his eyes wondering what is happening. As mentioned before, this is a *center-embedded clause* which

TABLE 2.1 Basic sequencing patterns used in Visual Narrative Grammar

a) Canonical narrative schema:	$[_{\text{Phase X}}$ (Establisher) – (Initial) – (Prolongation) – Peak – (Release)$]$
b) Conjunction schema	$[_{\text{Phase X}} X_1 - X_2 - \ldots X_n]$

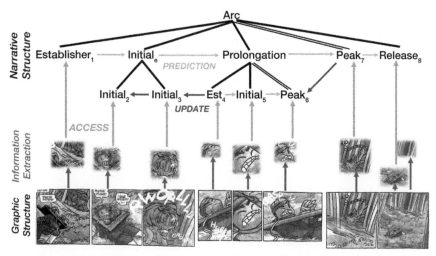

FIGURE 2.6 *The narrative structure of Figure 2.1 illustrated by a hierarchic tree structure. Vertical lines represent the access of narrative categories via the extracted visual cues. Rightward lines represent forward-looking structural predictions, while leftward lines represent backward-looking structural revision.*

could exist as its own sequence or could be omitted without disrupting the well-formedness of the full sequence. Nevertheless, these panels together function as a Prolongation, which serves to delay the main climax of the sequence in the Peak (panel seven) from the anticipation of the tiger's attack in the earlier Initial (panel three).

It is worth noting that the overall surface structure of this sequence does not follow the canonical narrative sequence (*E-I-I-E-I-P-P-R*), but the grouping structure allows for the canonical structure to be followed within each of its parts. Both the upper, matrix clause and the embedded Prolongation clause are motivated internally by their Peaks (panels six and seven), which function as the "heads" of their groupings. These panels thus carry the key message of their respective constituents, as would be relevant for a higher-level sequence. The topmost node is assigned as an Arc, which is a grouping that plays no other role in a sequence (and this sequence would indeed lose its Arc status if we returned it to its context in the original story). Thus, overall, the canonical schema allows for the embedding of narrative constituents inside each other. This recursion can feasibly lead to ever higher levels of embedding, including whole plotlines, which then consist of similar patterns across multiple sub-narrative constituents.

Further elaboration of a sequence can be introduced with modifiers, which are patterns that alter or elaborate on the sequencing of the canonical narrative schema. Specific constructions may be between different characters within a constant narrative state or zoom-in on information in surrounding panels (Cohn 2015, 2019b). The sequence in Figure 2.1 uses one of these modifiers in panels two and three, which each show only Pang and the tiger, but do not show them together in the same frame. Both of these panels function as Initials in the narrative structure, and thereby combine using the conjunction schema (Table 2.1b) which specifies that multiple units playing the same categorical role (i.e., "X") can combine in a constituent of that same category (a grouping of "X"). This is comparable to conjunction in syntax, which also combines words that share a common grammatical category into a common phrase (e.g., *dogs and cats* is a noun phrase with two nouns). Thus, I will here use the term "conjunction" in narrative grammar to describe an organizational principle analogous to that in syntax.

In panels two and three of Figure 2.1, the conjunction involves two Initials that depict different characters, meaning that their semantics demand the inference of a common environment. This inference in the situation model is annotated with the subscript "e" (for "environment") in Figure 2.4 and is then co-indexed to the Initial constituent of these panels, as in Figure 2.6. Conjunctions can also extend beyond this type of construction of scenes and they can also depict parts of a character or object to imply the whole; sub-events or iterations of actions; or various elements within a broader semantic field (Cohn 2015).

Narrative categories, constituents, and conjunctions illustrate why a narrative structure is necessary as a separate level of representation from semantics. For example, panels two and three could be depicted either with the two panels in the original (i.e., mono panels), or with a single panel depicting both Pang and the tiger in the same spatial location, like in the preceding panel (i.e., a macro panel). In addition, panels four to six show only Pang while omitting the tiger, which could also show both of them in each frame. These narrative patterns are structural choices for which information is shown and when it is shown, thereby requiring a level of representation separate from the encoding of that information itself.

2.4.1 Narrative Categories

One way that narrative structure packages information is to distinguish units from each other, thereby specifying the way that they function relative to the global sequence. Some panels may be more important, containing crucial climactic information, while others are more expendable, such as ones that function to just set up subsequent situations. These roles are the *narrative categories*. Such roles would not be played, for example, in a sequence that relies only on semantic relationships between panels, such as the linear grammars discussed in Chapter One (Figure 1.5), where all units carry the same relative value in the sequence.

Several studies have provided evidence that panels are differentiated in their narrative categories, because consistent behaviors distinguish them from each other. For example, when participants are asked to choose panels to delete from a sequence, they consistently choose to delete Establishers and Releases more often than Peaks and Initials (Cohn 2014c). Complementary results occur when participants are asked to recognize which panels may have been omitted from a sequence. Here, Establishers were recognized as missing less often than Peaks, and then Initials and Releases (Cohn 2014c; Magliano et al. 2017). Thus, the sequence in Figure 2.1 would remain fairly congruous if the Establishers of panel one or four were deleted, but not if the Peaks of panels five or six were deleted. In addition, brain responses distinguish between panels that violate or maintain the narrative categories expected by the sequence context (Cohn 2012b; Cohn and Kutas 2015). Such findings support that panels do not function in uniform ways within a sequence, and consistent tendencies are characterized by different narrative categories.

Narrative categories are *accessed* from the bottom-up semantic cues that may be extracted from a panel that would be relevant for a sequence (Figure 2.3). In Figure 2.6, this process is depicted with the vertical arrows extending up from the extracted information to the narrative categories. For an Establisher, the most prototypical cues would be passive actions that introduce entities, as in the first panel of Figure 2.1 (and Figure 2.6). Preparatory actions often cue Initials, such as the tiger approaching Pang in panel three. Peaks often depict completed actions or interruptions of actions. Figure 2.1 varies in this regard. In the subordinate Peak of panel six, there is a completed action of Pang opening his eyes. However, the main Peak shows the tiger leaving, a relatively passive climax compared to the expectation of Pang being attacked. Releases then often show the coda of an action, as in the tiger leaving in the final panel.

While these types of bottom-up cues can inform the assignment of a narrative category by linking them to semantics of the depicted content, their context in the sequence can also influence their categorical roles. Narrative categories do not exist in isolation, they are embedded within the canonical narrative schema. This means that, as will be discussed later, a panel following an Establisher may be probabilistically expected to be followed by an Initial because of the order of categories in the canonical schema. This top-down information can also influence the way that image content is assigned to narrative categories. For example, in studies where participants are given unordered panels and instructed to arrange them into a meaningful sequence, panels functioning as Establishers or Releases are often reversed in their positions (Cohn 2014c). Similarly, when these same panels are reversed in a sequence, readers view them at the same pace, which is different from reversals involving Initials or Peaks, where readers slow down for the mixed-up information (Cohn 2014c). This implies that the same content might function in different contexts of a sequence, again supporting a separation between the narrative structure and semantics.

2.4.2 *Narrative Constituents and Prediction*

Top-down context can influence category assignment because the canonical narrative schema (Table 2.1) has a particular order that allows for *structural predictions*. This type of prediction is not about what events may happen next, like in the semantic expectancies discussed previously in the section on semantic processing (such as predictive inferences). Rather, these are predictions about what narrative structure may probabilistically occur based on the ordering of the sequencing schemas. There are several types of information that might inform predictions of subsequent narrative information:

1 *General narrative schemas* – Because narrative categories belong to a canonical schema entrenched in memory, as in Table 2.1, accessing one category will generate predictions for subsequent categories in the schema. Thus, if a reader is at an Initial, there is a relatively high likelihood that a Peak will come next, since Peaks follow Initials in the canonical schema. If the incoming semantic cues satisfy the contextual constraints of the schema, then a category should be easier to assign. Similarly, if a comprehender is at a Release, they should predict a high likelihood of the subsequent panel beginning a new constituent, since Releases are the final category of the canonical schema (Cohn and Bender 2017).

2 *Narrative constructions* – Beyond predictions about categories from the canonical schema, other probabilistic expectancies may be generated about narrative patterns (Cohn 2015, 2019b), which may involve the basic schemas in Table 2.1. Such patterns may be culturally variable (Cohn 2019b), meaning that such probabilities may be modulated by a reader's familiarity with those patterns given the visual narratives they read (Cohn and Kutas 2017).

Structural predictions are thus forward-looking probabilistic expectations generated on the basis of prior context and stored knowledge. Violations of such predictions in ERPs result in "anterior negativities," often with a left or bi-lateralized distribution on the scalp (i.e., they appear in the frontal part of the head, either on the left side or both sides). These anterior negativities have been thought to index disconfirmation of structural predictions (Kluender and Kutas 1993; Yano 2018), or increased cost due to the "unification" processes involved in structure building (Hagoort 2017). Similar negativities have also been observed in response to violations of syntactic structure in sentence processing (Hagoort 2017; Kaan 2007). Anterior negativities have been observed in response to: disruptions of narrative constituents in visual narratives (Cohn et al. 2014), to the difference between semantically incongruous sequences that varied in their narrative structure (Cohn et al. 2012), and to sequencing patterns using narrative conjunction compared to those without conjunction (Cohn and Kutas 2017), as depicted in Figure 2.5b.

It is worth emphasizing that narrative constituents are not necessarily contingent on semantic discontinuity between panels. Discourse theories have stressed that narrative segments are triggered by the update of a situation model caused by semantic discontinuity like changes in characters, locations, or events (Gernsbacher 1990; Loschky et al. 2020; Magliano and Zacks 2011). This interpretation has typically come from tasks observing that situational changes often characterize where participants choose to divide visual narratives into segments (Gernsbacher 1990; Magliano and Zacks 2011), and thus a causal relationship has been assumed. This would imply that narrative constituents would occur only from backward-looking updating, meaning that the boundary between groupings would be recognized only after it had already been passed. While semantic discontinuities may interface with narrative constituent structures (Cohn and Bender 2017), as reflected in the vertical arrow linking them in the PINS Model in Figure 2.3, narrative and semantic predictions rely on different representations.

While backward-looking updating does factor into narrative processing (as discussed later), several findings suggest semantic discontinuity alone does not motivate narrative structure. First, semantic discontinuity is actually less predictive of narrative segmentation than "illegal narrative bigrams" (Cohn and Bender 2017), which are pairs of narrative categories that are out of order from the canonical narrative schema. In Figure 2.6, there is a *Peak-Peak* bigram in panels five and six, which does not follow the order of the canonical narrative schema, and therefore is "illegal." This order should thus trigger either a constituent break (as is the diagrammed parsing) or should incorporate these panels into a conjunction schema with both Peaks inside a larger Peak constituent (Cohn and Kutas 2017). Both outcomes would violate the primary structural prediction of a subsequent Release following a Peak from the canonical schema.

Second, we have observed different brain responses for discontinuity of semantics and narrative structure. N400s, which are indicative of semantic processing, do not seem sensitive to narrative structure. This was evident in comparisons between sequences that did or did not have a well-formed narrative structure and/or coherent semantic associations between panels (Cohn et al. 2012). The crucial comparison was between fully scrambled sequences and those with only a narrative structure but no meaningful relationships between panels. Both of these sequences lacked semantic relationships and correspondingly evoked comparable N400s, which were both larger than those evoked by coherent narrative sequencing. Yet, despite not differing in their N400 effects, the presence of narrative structure modulated an anterior negativity between these otherwise incongruous visual sequences (Cohn et al. 2012). Conversely, anterior negativities, which are evoked by grammatical processing, are sensitive to differences in narrative patterning, but are not modulated by semantic discontinuities like incongruous character changes (Cohn and Kutas 2017). This suggests that different brain responses distinguish between the processing of semantic (N400) and narrative (anterior negativities) levels of representation in visual sequences.

Third, anterior negativities are evoked in situations where backward-looking updating would be impossible. These results were obtained in a study where participants viewed sequences one panel at a time, and blank white "disruption" panels were inserted into the sequence either at the natural break between constituents or disrupting the groupings (Cohn et al. 2014). Larger anterior negativities appeared in response to the disruptions within constituents than those that appeared between groupings, no matter whether that disruption fell before or after the constituent boundary. The crucial finding was this: When the disruption appeared inside the first constituent, this negativity was evoked *prior* to the break between constituents. It would have been impossible for any panel to have triggered semantic discontinuity, since the boundary had not yet been crossed. Thus, backward-looking discontinuity could not have motivated this result, and it *must* have been the disconfirmation of a forward-looking prediction.

2.4.3 Structural Revision

When incoming information does not conform to narrative predictions, it may trigger a **structural revision** (Figure 2.3). This backward-looking reanalysis may occur if the cues of an incoming panel conflict with the predictions of what might come next. As this is another type of updating process, here applied to structure instead of semantics, structural revision also manifests in the brainwave response of a P600. Studies of sentence processing actually first observed P600s in contexts requiring syntactic revision (Hagoort, Brown, and Groothusen 1993; Osterhout and Holcomb 1992) before this brain response was argued to index more general integration or updating processes (Baggio 2018; Brouwer et al. 2016; Kuperberg 2013, 2016).

In studies of visual narrative processing, P600s have implicated structural revision when panels cue unexpected changes in narrative categories (Cohn 2012b), even in cases where inferences are held constant between expected and unexpected categories (Cohn and Kutas 2015). Thus, if a reader is at a Peak and expects a subsequent Release, incoming cues indicative of an Initial will trigger a reanalysis. A similar revision was evoked by unexpected categories that cued a break in the constituent structure. For example, in Figure 2.6, the *Peak-Peak* bigram of panels five and six should be unexpected because they do not follow the order of the canonical narrative schema. Thus, the second Peak should trigger a new constituent (Cohn and Bender 2017)—in this case, a return to the "upper level" matrix constituent of narrative schema in the higher part of the tree structure—or a conjunction where the repeated panels combine within a common grouping (Cohn and Kutas 2017). Indeed, P600s have suggested structural revision occurs in response to both reanalysis of violated constituent structures (Cohn et al. 2014) and to unexpected sequencing patterns like conjunction (Cohn and Kutas 2017).

Structural revision is also apparent in measurements of how long readers spend on panels. Like in situations where we observe P600s, readers take a longer time viewing panels that violate the expectations of narrative categories (Cohn 2012b, 2014c). Readers also spend longer viewing panels that follow a break in the constituent structure compared to panels prior to the boundary (Cohn 2012b). Disruptions of constituent structure also lead readers to spend more time viewing panels, both at panels immediately after a disruption and at panels several positions later in the sequence (Cohn 2012b). This implies that revision of structure occurs when incoming information probabilistically deviates from structural predictions, and such reanalysis may influence processing further downstream in the sequence.

2.5 Characteristics of Visual Narrative Processing and Proficiency

To summarize, I have proposed a common flow of processing across layout, semantics, and narrative structures within visual narrative sequences. Front-end processes guide a comprehender through the extraction of information in the visual surface of a panel. This input allows for the accessing of information (panel positioning, semantic memory, narrative categories) which can contribute to the building of a cognitive structure (assemblage structure, situation model, narrative structure). This accessed information may allow for probabilistic predictions on the basis of stored or contextual knowledge. As new information is then accessed, it is checked against prior context, which may trigger an update to revise the constructed model. Overall, such stages operate in parallel with potential interfaces between levels of representations.

This flow of processing across structures involves negotiating both bottom-up information extracted directly from the engaged features of a particular domain, and the top-down information of the context and stored knowledge. Both of these types of elements contribute to the overall whole of constructing a model for a given domain. This information is summarized in Table 2.2 across all three types of structures.

As much of the rest of this book will discuss how cultural variation and proficiency factor into the processing of visual narratives, it is worth considering which aspects of processing may be most affected by expertise. We might speculate that the ability to use top-down information may rely

TABLE 2.2 Bottom-up and top-down information involved in the processing of the layout, semantic structure, and narrative structure. Use of (*) indicates the cognitive structure constructed in the online processing of a given domain

Structures	Bottom-up information	Top-down information
Layout	Alignment and proximity of panel edges Layout devices (trails, numbers, balloon placement)	* Assemblage structure Perceptual Gestalt constraints Rule-based ordering Cultural layout schemas
Semantic structure	Semantic features within images (objects, events) and their associations	* Situation model content Event schemas Story specific schemas (Lucy's football)
Narrative structure	Semantic cues within images	* Constructed narrative structure Narrative schemas Cultural narrative patterns

on proficiency, particularly in the capacity to construct an appropriate cognitive structure for a given level of representation (i.e., assemblage structure, situation model, and/or narrative structure). If one is proficient in reading comics, we would thus expect comprehension to be more guided by various expectations for layouts, meanings, or narrative structure than a person less familiar with these structures.

For navigating a page layout, comprehenders with more comic reading experience should be motivated to construct a coherent assemblage structure, and thus would be guided by the constraints of this top-down cognitive structure. In contrast, less experienced comic readers would rely more on the bottom-up spatial alignment or proximity of panels to guide their linear route through a sequence. This would align with observations that more experienced comic readers have smoother eye-movements through page layouts, with fewer regressions (Bateman, Beckmann, and Varela 2018; Martín-Arnal et al. 2019; Nakazawa 2002a; Zhao and Mahrt 2018), showing that they have an easier and more committed reading path through a layout.

Layout actually provides an example of the effect of fluency that might be recognizable to some readers. Imagine (or recall) if you only have experiencing reading American comics, where the layouts predominantly use rule-based constraints of the Z-path with left-to-right and down directions. These rules place top-down constraints on the predictions you might have of how to navigate a comic page. Now consider being confronted with the layout of a Japanese manga that uses the opposite navigation, with a right-to-left and down "S-path." If you had little experience with manga and their layout conventions, it may be demanding to switch your expectations of how to navigate such pages (at least at first). In turn, it should lead to increased cautiousness in terms of where to go and further updating following each choice (manifesting in exploratory and regressive eye movements). This disconcerting nature is a matter of *fluency* in the conventions of one particular system over another.

We might imagine a similar top-down preference for the processing of the content. Expertise in visual narratives like comics may afford greater reliance on constructing a narrative structure, and thus processing could benefit more from using such a structure. Less fluency would increase reliance on semantic processing, because inexperienced readers would not have sufficiently acquired the patterns involved in constructing a narrative structure. There is some evidence that this is the case. Measurements of expertise typically correlate with aspects of processing related to narrative structure, not with semantics (Cohn et al. 2012; Cohn and Bender 2017; Cohn and Kutas 2015). In fact, at present no ERP study has *yet* shown correlations between comic reading experience and the N400, although correlations have appeared between measures of expertise and anterior negativities and P600s (Cohn et al. 2012; Cohn and Kutas 2015, 2017; Cohn and Maher 2015).

In addition, familiarity with specific narrative patterns from comics has been shown to evoke greater combinatorial processing (resulting in anterior negativities), while less familiarity evokes greater updating processes (resulting in P600s) (Cohn and Kutas 2017). That is, experience evokes processing more associated with combining structures together, as would be expected if expertise is associated with model construction. In contrast, updating processes would be consistent with less familiarity, as comprehension could not rely on top-down knowledge. Instead it would require more backward-looking operations to check a previous context given the new information. Thus, at least some evidence suggests that the building of a narrative structure would be involved with increased fluency.

2.6 Visual Narrative Processing and Other Domains

Finally, Visual Language Theory posits a similarity between the mechanisms involved in processing visual narrative sequences and language. Thus, it is worth addressing this comparison. Indeed, the growing literature on sequential image comprehension has suggested connections between the neural mechanisms at work in visual narrative and verbal language, thereby implicating domain-general processing (Cohn 2013b; Magliano et al. 2013;

Magliano, Higgs, and Clinton 2019). Behavioral research has implied an overlap between language and visual narratives in the working memory resources involved in inference generation (Magliano et al. 2015) and in how people segment visual sequences (Magliano et al. 2012). Brain imaging has also broadly observed similar activation in brain areas across written, oral, and visual narratives (Gernsbacher and Robertson 2004; Robertson 2000). More specifically, brain regions like Broca's and Wernicke's areas, which are classically associated with language processing, have been shown to activate during online processing of visual narratives (Cohn and Maher 2015; Nagai, Endo, and Takatsune 2007; Osaka et al. 2014; Schlaffke et al. 2015).

Research using ERPs provides further evidence of similar brain responses across visual narrative and language processing. Over years of research, recurring ERP effects have become reliably associated with different types of neurocognitive functions, particularly in language processing. Many of these components have already been discussed earlier: N400s, (left) anterior negativities, and P600s were all first discovered in the context of sentence processing.

The N400 has long been established as an index of semantic processing across domains (Kutas and Federmeier 2011). Although it was first observed in response to anomalous or unexpected words in sentences (Kutas and Hillyard 1980), N400 effects have also been evoked by anomalous and/or unexpected information in visual narratives, as in Figure 2.5a (Cohn et al. 2012; Cohn and Kutas 2015; West and Holcomb 2002). As discussed earlier, the N400 is not modulated by the presence of narrative structure, indicating separate processes for narrative and meaning (Cohn et al. 2012). In addition, the context of a visual narrative sequence can modulate the N400s evoked by words which replace a climactic event (*Pow!*), suggesting cross-modal semantic resources (Manfredi, Cohn, and Kutas 2017).

As discussed, in understanding a visual narrative, semantic information aggregates in a growing situation model, which becomes updated when dimensions like characters or events change. Such updating appears to be indexed in ERPs by a P600 (Brouwer et al. 2016; Kuperberg 2013). P600s in visual narratives have been shown to occur in response to congruous and incongruous changes of characters across images (Cohn and Kutas 2017, 2015), as well as cues signaling incongruous events (Cohn and Maher 2015). In general, greater situational changes appear to result in greater P600s (Cohn and Kutas 2015). Such findings are consistent with observations of P600s in response to referential discontinuity in language contexts (Burkhardt 2007; van Berkum et al. 2007), and with the idea that P600s belong to a family of brain responses indexing updating processes (Donchin and Coles 1988; Leckey and Federmeier 2019; Van Petten and Luka 2012).

Shared neurocognitive resources are also suggested in the ERPs evoked by the narrative structure of sequential images and the syntactic structure of sentences. Violations of syntactic structure have elicited two different ERP components: anterior negativities often with left lateralized distribution on the scalp, associated with combinatorial processing, and P600s associated with updating or revision of a structure (Hagoort 2017; Kaan 2007). As discussed earlier, ostensibly similar ERP components have been observed in studies of visual narrative in response to the violation of constituent structures and narrative patterns (Cohn et al. 2012; Cohn et al. 2014; Cohn and Kutas 2015, 2017). The similarities between ERPs in response to language and visual narratives parallel observations of shared neurocognitive mechanisms in the processing of language and music, where lateralized anterior negativities and P600s have also been observed as reactions to violated musical sequencing (Koelsch et al. 2005; Patel 2003). These similarities across domains persist despite involving different representations (words, images, notes), implying more abstract mechanisms of sequencing not tied to any particular modality or behavior.

Thus, there are growing findings that the brain uses similar mechanisms to process both the semantic and grammatical aspects of visual narratives as it does to process such levels of representation in sentences. Further experimentation is necessary to explore the degree to which these modalities draw on the same or overlapping neural resources. However, such findings provide direct support for Visual Language Theory's proposal that spoken and visual languages involve similar structure and processing.

2.7 Conclusion

This chapter has discussed how readers process visual narrative sequences and has posited a similar flow of information across layouts, semantic structures, and narrative structures. With regard to mechanisms of comprehension, these structures appear to evoke neurocognitive mechanisms similar to other domains, such as language.

Overall, these findings carry several implications: First, visual narrative processing is not uniform, and involves several interacting mechanisms. Second, among these, distinguishable brain responses index separate processing of meaning (e.g., N400) and combinatorial structure (e.g., anterior negativities, P600). Third, these cognitive resources do not appear unique to visual narratives and resemble those involved with sequencing in language and music. Fourth, given the implied multifaced and domain-general characteristic of these mechanisms, they do not strictly appear to be related to perception or event cognition alone, as one might presume under the Sequential Image Transparency Assumption. Rather, the similarities of the neurocognition of visual narrative processing to that of language (and other domains) supports the hypotheses of Visual Language Theory.

As we will see in further chapters, even if visual narratives rely on processing that is also involved in verbal language and music, fluency in the graphic modality is still required to access these domain-general processes.

This too is presumably similar to language: although the linguistic system appears to involve domain-general mechanisms, fluency in specific languages—whether spoken or signed—is required to elicit such processing and late acquisition or lack of fluency can be consequential on its development (Mayberry et al. 2011). Thus, the operations involved in visual narratives described here, both front-end and back-end processing, may rely on fluency acquired by exposure to cultural systems across a developmental trajectory.

CHAPTER THREE

Cross-cultural Diversity of Visual Languages

If we are to ask about the universality of visual language *comprehension*, then we first need to ask about how universal the *structure* of visual language might be in the first place. What are the properties of the visual narratives being comprehended? One facet of the Sequential Image Transparency Assumption appears to be an underestimation of the complexity of the structure of visual narratives. Accessible and transparent understanding carries with it the implications of simple and uniform sequencing across different types of visual narratives. However, if visual sequencing is patterned in diverse ways, such as across cultures, then it might require accounting for such diversity in the cognitive structures of those who comprehend them. In other words, if different visual languages manifest around the world, it requires readers to have fluency in those different systems.

Clearly, sequential images with different "styles"—i.e., different visual languages—appear across the world's history and cultures. Some of these diverse historical contexts include ancient Egyptian wall paintings, Japanese and Chinese scrolls (Kunzle 1973; McCloud 1993; Petersen 2011), early Indian Buddhist sculptures (Dehejia 1990), medieval European tapestries (Díaz Vera 2013a, b), pre-Colombian Mayan pottery (Wichmann and Nielsen 2016), Mesoamerican Codices (Navarrete 2000), and many others. All of these examples, like contemporary comics, picture stories, and storyboards use spatially sequential layouts. Temporally sequential visual narratives also persist in systems like Australian Aboriginal sand narratives, where stories are drawn over time in a single space (Green 2014; Munn 1986; Wilkins 1997/2016).

The ubiquity of visual narratives across cultures and history reinforces the perception of their universality. The ability to produce meaningful visual sequences is clearly unconstrained by cultural boundaries and appears to be a basic facet of human communication and cognition. Yet, it should be clear that graphic systems vary across cultures and historical time periods, at the least with regard to their graphic structure (i.e., their "visual style"). Yet, differences between their strategies of sequencing are less apparent on the surface. The question then is, to what degree are the sequencing methods of visual narratives uniform across cultures?

3.1 The Visual Language Research Corpus

To analyze the diversity of structures across various visual narratives, we here analyze the visual languages in comics specifically. Compared to other visual languages, like those used in instruction manuals or illustrated picture stories, the visual languages used in comics appear to be more complex and sophisticated across many levels of structure. They thus make for robust systems in which we can analyze various structures. Our approach is an empirical one: We seek evidence of diversity through a quantitative analysis of properties of the visual languages used in comics, rather than a qualitative analysis describing or speculating about such traits based on intuitions and/ or exemplars. This provides a data-driven analysis consistent with research from linguistics using a corpus—a collection of data—to investigate the properties of languages of the world.

Our analysis here consists of structures coded within 290 comics, amounting to roughly 36,000 panels across over 6,000 pages. This dataset comprises the Visual Language Research Corpus (http://www.visuallanguagelab.com/vlrc), summarized in Table 3.1. These comics were annotated by nine independent coders[1] who all received extensive training in Visual Language Theory and completed pre-coding assessments to ensure reliability in their annotation abilities prior to coding for the corpus. Roughly 70 percent of the books in the corpus were independently coded by two coders and were checked for intercoder reliability. Each comic was coded for the full book if it was the standard length of an issue or chapter (i.e., twenty to thirty pages). If a whole book was not annotated, coders analyzed twenty-five pages or one-hundred-twenty panels (rounded to the nearest page), whichever came first. A full listing of the books comprising the VLRC appears in Appendix 1.

Coded works in the VLRC span a number of different countries, genres, and publication dates. This variety occurred because many of the works were intended for specific targeted studies, some of which have since been subsequently published, some not. Other works in the corpus were less specifically targeted.

Our coded comics from Europe had a range of genres. Swedish comics mostly were cartoony children's comics, while the French bande desinée were primarily albums in the adventure and drama genres. Dutch and Flemish comics spanned 80 years from the 1940s through 2010s and mainly came from the adventure and humor genres. German comics were fairly diverse, including both dramatic and adventure comics, as well as some works from more underground independent creators.

TABLE 3.1 Analyzed comics within the Visual Language Research Corpus

Country/Type	Years	# of books	Total pages	Total panels	Panels/Page
Swedish	1980–2011	20	232	1,436	6.33
French	1985–2014	21	497	3,359	6.91
German	1987–2009	10	281	1,525	5.63
Dutch (classic)	1940–1978	20	449	2,745	7.26
Dutch (modern)	1980–2016	20	358	2,982	8.87
Flemish (classic)	1946–1978	20	316	3,040	10.32
Flemish (modern)	1981–2016	20	311	3,057	10.59
USA Mainstream (classic)	1940–1978	20	524	2,860	5.55
USA Mainstream (modern)	1981–2014	30	647	2,960	4.59
USA Indy	2002–2014	12	409	1,611	5.02
USA manga (OEL)	1991–2014	16	372	1,687	4.52
Japanese (shonen, seinen)	2003–2014	35	674	3,483	5.24
Japanese (shojo, josei)	2007–2014	20	483	2,308	4.90
Korean	1987–2010	15	326	1,324	4.19
Hong Kong	2002–2015	11	279	1,434	5.13
Total		**290**	**6,157**	**35,809**	**6.34**

Mainstream comics from the United States spanned the stereotypical superhero and power fantasy genres from the 1940s through the 2010s, as analyzed in prior studies (Cohn, Taylor, and Pederson 2017; Pederson and Cohn 2016). The corpus here expands on those prior works, primarily with additional comics between 1990 and 2014. Other books from the United States were Independent, or "Indy comics" which were primarily "graphic novels" with stories outside the mainstream superhero genre. "US manga" were considered as Original English Language (OEL) manga, created by English speakers but ostensibly drawn using the Japanese Visual Language

(JVL) stereotypical of manga (Brienza 2015). These works followed the influence of the mass importation of Japanese manga into the American comic market in the 1990s and 2000s (Brienza 2016; Goldberg 2010). We included OEL manga in this corpus to provide a way to investigate whether the structure used by these authors might be more similar to that of their culture (in the United States) or the visual language of the manga they associate with (JVL). It should be noted that many of the contemporary authors included in the Indy genre are likely influenced by manga, though they might not claim the label or associate with manga overtly (Mazur and Danner 2014).

Within our analysis of manga from Japan, we examined four different types of comics, typically delineated by demographics of an intended audience, which are shonen, shojo, seinen, and josei, which supposedly aim towards boys, girls, men, and women, respectively. Despite the supposed audiences labeled for these works, shonen manga is favored by all audiences over other types of manga and are the bestselling, while shojo manga typically are not read by boys (Allen and Ingulsrud 2005). In line with this popularity, shonen manga are often perceived as the stereotypical genre of manga both within and outside of Japan (Allen and Ingulsrud 2005). Given that these different types have recognizable variations in their styles (Schodt 1983, 1996), they could be argued as constituting different sub-dialects within the broader abstract, generalized Japanese Visual Language shared across many authors of manga and which would span across these demographic types (Cohn 2013b; Cohn and Ehly 2016). Here, we group these demographics by gender (shonen/seinen vs. shojo/josei), but more fine-grained analyses could certainly be warranted to examine their potential differences.

Our additional analyses of comics from Asia also included those from Hong Kong and Korea. Manhua from Hong Kong primarily came from action comics (martial arts and sci-fi). The manhwa from Korea had a mix of action and drama. As we did not have enough materials from various genres from each these countries (as we did for Japanese manga), we here collapse across any such variation in genres to have categories solely for Hong Kong manhua and Korean manhwa.

The primary unit of analysis for each comic was the panel, and we recorded a variety of dimensions for each panel in a book. For a given dimension, we calculated the number of panels manifesting that property and divided them out of the total number of panels in a given comic. That is, we derived the proportion that a property appears in a comic. These averages per book were then used in our subsequent analyses.[2]

3.2 Cross-cultural Diversity in Comics

As described in Chapter One, the visual languages used in comics involve several different structures. All of these components could potentially be investigated for their cross-cultural variability. For example, within individual images, aspects of morphology have been examined in European comics (Forceville 2011; Forceville, Veale, and Feyaerts 2010; Tasić and Stamenković 2018), American superhero comics (Juricevic 2017), and Japanese manga (Cohn and Ehly 2016; Shinohara and Matsunaka 2009). As the focus of this book is primarily on the comprehension of image *sequences*, here we will focus on sequential structures. Specifically, we focus on aspects of page layouts and two elements involved in narrative structure: the framing of panels and semantic changes across panels. Framing and semantic changes combined can also be informative about narrative patterns, and evidence of cross-cultural differences between such narrative patterns has been done using data from the VLRC (Cohn 2019b). For the sake of brevity, reporting of these more complicated patterns will be excluded from this chapter and will be explored in future works.

It is worth noting the importance of what systematic findings in cross-cultural research can imply. If patterns appear within and between the comics of cultures, it provides evidence for different visual languages of the world. Such systematic variation in structure would mean that these patterns would be encoded in the long-term memories of their authors. This would contrast with views which posit no patterns stored in memory, or where all comic creation amounts to unconstrained choices of a creator (e.g., McCloud 2006) or "cultural" influences operating on those choices (McCloud 1993). Thus, if patterns do arise in systematic ways within or between cultures, it provides evidence for differential encoding of structures in the minds of their authors, and potentially of their readers.

3.2.1 *External Compositional Structure (Layout)*

Page layouts are one of the most overt features of comics' structure. Indeed, work with machine learning has shown that features of page layout are among the most distinguishing of comics of different types (Laubrock and Dubray 2019). Here, we analyze select features of this external compositional structure within the VLRC. As not all books in the VLRC included coding of layout, we here report a subsection of the corpus with these annotations. Some of this data was previously reported (Cohn et al. 2019) in an analysis of sixty comics (ten in each type), but we here expand the number of works analyzed. The properties of books in this analysis appear in Table 3.2. We here exclude additional annotations of page layouts in mainstream US comics dated prior to 1990. As only comics from the United States were analyzed for page layout with publication dates prior to 1980, we felt it was inappropriate to include them in a cross-cultural comparison. Properties of layouts for older US comics (1940–1990) are reported in another section later.

When bearing in mind the whole corpus in Table 3.1, the average panels per page differed across countries/genres. This primarily manifested in more

TABLE 3.2 Subsection of the VLRC reported here for properties of page layout

Country/Type	Years	# of books	Total pages	Total panels	Panels/ Page
Swedish	1980–2011	20	232	1,436	6.33
French	2002–2014	11	293	1,823	6.31
US Mainstream	1990–2014	15	326	1,418	4.32
US Indy	2002–2014	10	250	1,304	5.23
Japanese (shonen)	2003–2014	11	195	1,022	5.26
Hong Kong	1989–2015	10	253	1,273	5.04
Total		**77**	**1,549**	**8,276**	**5.41**

panels per page used in comics from Europe than those from other cultures. Pages from comics from the United States or Asia had fewer panels per page, typically between 4.5 to 5.2 panels per page. This higher proportion of panels per page in European books may come from a difference in formatting of the pages themselves. European books typically have larger printed pages than American or Asian comics, as they appear in "album" formats. This larger space may create a flexibility to include more dense panels without compromising the readability of the content (Lefèvre 2000a), or conversely, the relatively smaller pages of other comics require proportionally larger panels to maintain a readable size. However, format itself does not mandate how many panels go onto any page, and any number of panels could hypothetically fill any page size. Further research could thus investigate whether panels have some sort of optimal sizing on actual printed pages or to their relative proportions on pages.

Given that the Z-path imitative of alphabetic writing systems (left-to-right and down) is largely taken as the default navigational order for comic page layouts (Cohn 2013a), we next wanted to confirm whether this prominence appeared across cultures. We therefore first analyzed the spatial relationship between panels as indicated by their relative directions in a page layout. To do this, coders approximated the centerpoint of a panel in relation to the centerpoint of the preceding panel in the narrative sequence. The direction of the resulting vector between these points was coded in terms of one of eight directionalities (*right, left, up, down,* and in-between). For example, a standard two-by-two grid would be ordered using a left-to-right and down Z-path, thus being coded with directions of right, down-left, right.

Directions were always coded for a panel relative to its preceding panel, and thus the starting panel on a given page was not assigned a directionality. Also, the overarching reading directions might differ between cultures' page layouts, with a left-to-right direction in Western books following the Latin alphabet and a right-to-left direction for various Asian books, following their native scripts. If we compared these books for their specific directions, proportions of left versus right directions may be misleading. In our final analysis, we therefore collapsed across these surface directions to create categories of *lateral* (left, right), *down-diagonal* (down-left, down-right), and *up-diagonal* (up-left, up-right) in addition to *down* and *up*.

Our cross-cultural results are depicted in Figure 3.1. In all comics except for those from Hong Kong, lateral directions were used more than all other directions. This was most pronounced in Swedish, French, and Indy comics from the United States, which all used lateral directions at or above 40 percent of the time. The next most-used direction differed between populations. In Swedish, French, and Indy comics, down-diagonal directions

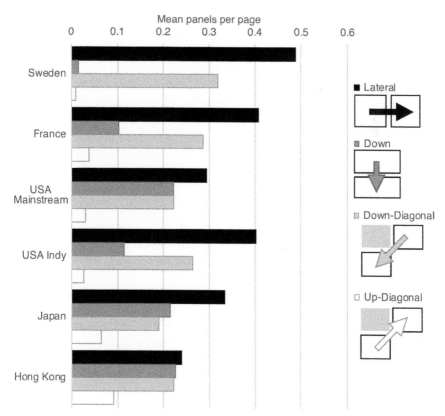

FIGURE 3.1 *Distribution of spatial directions between panels in page layouts across comics of different cultures.*

were also used at high proportions, followed by straight downward directions. This combination of lateral and down-diagonal directions thus implies a Z-path in a row-based structure. In contrast, mainstream American comics, Japanese manga, and Korean manhwa all used nearly equal amounts of downward and down-diagonal directions. Layouts from Japan and Hong Kong also used roughly double the amount of upward-diagonal directions. Together, the combination of downward and upward-diagonal directions imply alternative panel arrangements to the Z-path.

Why different layouts may or may not have upheld the directions of the Z-path were suggested by specific panel arrangements. These configurations are modulated by the alignment and/or proximity of panels' borders with each other (Bateman et al. 2016; Cohn 2013a; Pederson and Cohn 2016). To narrow these analyses, here I focus on four specific arrangements (as in Figure 3.2), but further analyses can be found in Cohn et al. (2019).

A *pure grid* is the most basic and iconic arrangement of panels, whereby all of the horizontal and vertical borders of panels are aligned to create rows and columns. A *horizontal stagger* maintains the rows of a grid but alters the vertical alignment of panel borders between rows (see Figure 3.2 for a visual depiction). A similar *vertical stagger* can be created by maintaining the vertical borders but misaligning the horizontal borders, but it is excluded from analysis here as it constituted less than 1 percent of all panel relations per page. If a single panel constituted a *whole row*, it extended from one side of the page to the other (just as a whole column, excluded here, would extend from top of the page to bottom). Finally, a *blockage* arrangement stacks a column of panels next to a single longer panel, making it an embedded vertical column within a horizontal row of panels.

Figure 3.2 depicts our findings related to these panel arrangements. Pure grids were used most by mainstream comics from the United States and in Swedish comics, both of which used pure grids in over 40 percent of panel relationships. All the other comics used pure grids near 30 percent of the time. A row structure was further maintained by high proportions of horizontal staggering in comics from Sweden, France, and Indy comics from the United States. These arrangements further account for the high proportions of directions corresponding to the use of Z-path (lateral and down-diagonal) in these comics.

This focus on grids and horizontal staggering would thereby increase the salience of a row-based structure in European and American comics. In the case of European comics, this salience may be an influence for why French theories of page layout place emphasis on the "strip"—i.e., rows—as a unit of page layout (Chavanne 2015; Groensteen 2007). For example, Chavanne's (2015) theory provides a notation for the number of panels involved in vertical and horizontal arrangements (grids, blockage), yet this theory remains largely constrained to relations within strips/rows, without explaining how they link together into a broader hierarchic structure (as in Cohn 2013a, Tanaka et al. 2007, etc.). Speculatively, this theoretical stance

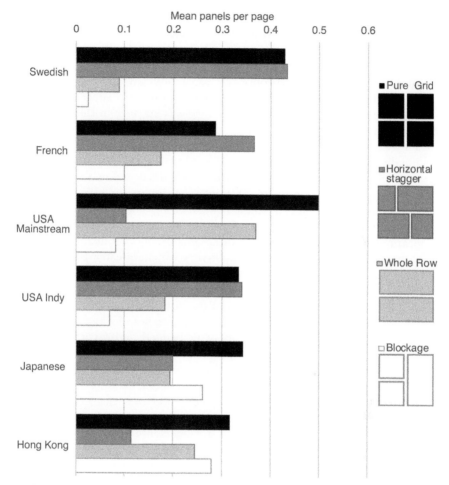

FIGURE 3.2 *Distribution of spatial arrangements between panels in page layouts across comics of different cultures.*

may be a result of these scholars being more familiar with European layouts that emphasize rows, with less consideration of layouts from other cultures that vary in their layouts in other ways, as discussed later. That is, issues of scholars' fluency for comics of a particular type may in turn influence the theories they create about visual narratives in general.

In contrast to grids, arrangements that support a departure from the Z-path (downward, up-diagonal) are evident in whole rows and blockage. First, whole rows were most prominent in mainstream US comics, where they constituted 37 percent of panel relationships. No other comics came close to this proportion of whole rows, with most using around 20 percent of whole rows, except Swedish comics which used far less. This prevalence of whole rows in American mainstream comics accounts for the observation of the large proportion of downward directions (in the absence of up-diagonal directions). That is, successive whole row panels appear in vertically stacked arrangements. Despite this verticality, whole rows still maintain a primarily row-based layout—only here those rows are comprised of single panels. These data support observations that American superhero comics have moved toward using "widescreen" panels starting in the late 1990s (Mazur and Danner 2014), a point that will be discussed further below when we address change in layouts over time.

Finally, a greater departure from the Z-path is suggested by blockage arrangements, where a vertical column is embedded within a row, thereby flouting the solely horizontal navigation. Blockage in our corpus primarily appeared in Asian comics (Japanese manga, Hong Kong manhua), where it constituted roughly 25 percent of all arrangements, in contrast to its appearance in less than 10 percent of layouts in all other analyzed comics. This proportion of blockage is consistent with the greater prevalence of downward and up-diagonal directions in layouts in Asian comics (Figure 3.1). Note that this differs from the directions in mainstream American comics, which had high proportions of downward directions, but not up-diagonals, thus supporting the use of whole rows, not blockage.

Why might Asian layouts use more embedded vertical arrangements (blockage) than American or European books? One reason could be an influence of the direction of the writing systems. Traditionally written Chinese and Japanese both use vertical columns extending from top-to-bottom (although contemporary writing sometimes also orders them laterally in a Z-path). These vertical arrangements in the writing systems could thus subtly influence the vertical arrangements in the page layouts of the visual languages. Previous research has found that the directionality of writing systems can influence other aspects of spatial cognition, such as depicting temporal relationships (Chan and Bergen 2005; Tversky, Kugelmass, and Winter 1991), determining what order images should be arranged (Fuhrman and Boroditsky 2010), and the order of perceptually scanning spatial arrays (Padakannaya et al. 2002). Given that imagistic page layouts also contain the layout of written words to create a multimodal whole, it is not infeasible that one might influence the other.

Although these Asian layouts may use increased prominence of vertical directions and arrangements, they still predominantly use the lateral Z-path, like American and European books. Thus, within whole *pages*, Asian comics maintain layouts that use a conventionalized navigation path consistent with other cultures' comics, despite imbuing greater verticality into them. This may suggest that visual languages used in comics widely maintain a "horizontal-before-vertical" preference for their layouts, even when sub-structures may increase the likelihood of verticality.

One additional point should be mentioned related to the relative proportionality between cultures' use of blockage. In advocacy of how to design page layouts, American comic authors often recommend avoiding blockage, since vertically stacked panels preceding a large "blocking" panel" will create "confusion" for a reader (e.g., Abel and Madden 2008; McCloud 2006). The idea is that a reader will not know whether to proceed vertically within the column, or laterally using their default Z-path. In fact, experimentation suggests that comic readers are not confused by this layout, and they recognize that the vertical non-Z-path order is preferred (Cohn 2013a; Cohn and Campbell 2015). It may be that this advocacy of avoidance by American comics authors comes because blockage arrangements are infrequent within American comics, thereby amplifying the perception of their difficulty. That is, familiarity with the conventions of a particular type of layout—i.e., *a culturally specific fluency*—may motivate the assumptions for how those conventions are comprehended and, in turn, advocacy for how layouts should be constructed.

3.2.2 *Framing Structure*

Visual languages used in comics also differ from each other in how panels frame information. The content of panels can be differentiated between "active" information that is relevant for the narrative sequence and "inactive" information that might be meaningful, but has little overall influence on the sequential construal (Cohn 2013b). This difference in classification can be assessed with a "deletion test": omission of active information from a panel will noticeably alter or inhibit the sequential understanding, while omission of inactive information results in less information being lost. Modulation of the amount of active and inactive information in a panel is its *attentional framing*—how a panel might package the information in a scene to a reader. Variation in attentional framing of panel content can impact the ways in which a scene is conveyed by narrative structures. For example, using panels with only single characters could potentially increase the number of modifiers to a basic narrative sequence (such as in Environmental-Conjunction) and/or demand spatial inferences by not showing a whole scene, and only showing its parts (Cohn 2015, 2019a).

Panels can thus be classified by the amount of active or inactive information that they contain. *Macro* panels depict multiple interacting active entities (characters) within a scene, as depicted in Figure 3.3a. *Monos* show only single entities (Figure 3.3b). This framing transcends the "filmic shot" of the representation—any depiction of a single character's face and/ or body to convey their identity is a mono, regardless of whether it windows a full body, bust, or just their face. A *micro* then frames less than a single entity, typically with a close up on a portion of the face or any other body part (Figure 3.3c). Finally, *amorphic* panels depict no active entities, showing only environmental information (i.e., the outside of a building or

a) Macro    b) Mono    c) Micro    d) Amorphic

FIGURE 3.3 *Attentional framing types of different panels, categorized by the amount of active information in each frame, include: (a) Macro and (b) Mono example panels come from* Lady Luck *by Klaus Nordling (1949), and (c) Micro and (d) Amorphic panels come from* Doll Man *by Bill Quackenbush (1950). Public Domain.*

non-character scene information), as in Figure 3.3d. In our corpus analyses, panels that did not conform to these categories were coded as ambiguous (e.g., such as a fully black "null" panel or a panel with only text), although other panel types will be categorized in future works.

Earlier studies of attentional framing types compared these categories in American and Japanese comics. The first study examined ten comics from the United States and ten from Japan (Cohn 2011), and found that American comics used more macros (59 percent) than monos (32 percent) or micros (6 percent), while Japanese manga used near equal amounts of macros (47 percent) and monos (43 percent) and more micros (10 percent). A follow-up study subsequently found that mainstream American superhero comics did not differ from those in Indy comics, again with more macros (~46 percent) than monos (~40 percent), with few micros (~7 percent) or amorphic (~5 percent) panels (Cohn, Taylor-Weiner, and Grossman 2012). These again differed from Japanese manga, which used more monos (52 percent) than macros (26 percent) and increased numbers of micros (11 percent) and amorphic (11 percent) panels. Overall, these findings suggested that American genres did not substantially differ from each other in their framing, but they did differ from panels in Japanese manga.

These initial findings raised questions about the degree to which panels in comics from across the world might vary in their framing, and the degree to which subgenres might differ within a culture's comics. We have now analyzed attentional framing of panels in all 290 comics coded within the VLRC (Table 3.1). The proportions for panel types across these works are depicted in Figure 3.4.

First, a clear difference is apparent between the pattern of framing types between comics from the United States and Europe compared to Asia.

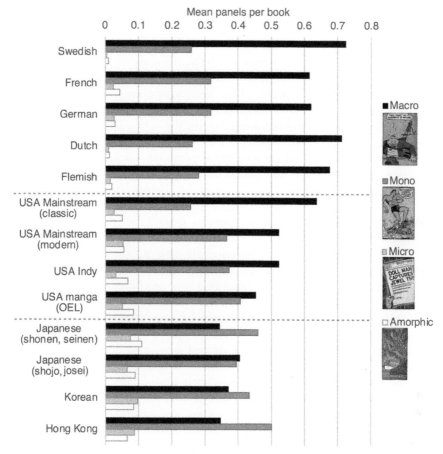

FIGURE 3.4 *Distribution of attentional framing categories across comics from Europe, the United States, and Asia.*

Consistent with the prior studies, American and European comics used more macros than monos, with few micros or amorphic panels. This was most pronounced in European comics and "classic" mainstream American comics (i.e., from prior to the 1980s), where macros appeared more than monos, micros, and amorphic panels combined. This ratio became somewhat less pronounced in modern American comics (1980s to 2010s) and Indy comics, which featured a larger proportion of non-macro panels, although macros still constituted over 50 percent of the panel types. Consistent with our prior study, mainstream and Indy US comics did not differ (Cohn, Taylor-Weiner, and Grossman 2012). The difference between classic and modern mainstream comics will be discussed further.

Framing in Asian comics was noticeably different from that in comics from the United States or Europe, yet were also fairly consistent across manga, manhwa, and manhua. These works used more monos than macros, with substantially greater proportions of micro and amorphic panels (~8–10 percent each). These findings also align with previous corpus analyses (Cohn, Taylor-Weiner, and Grossman 2012), showing that Japanese manga frame a whole scene (macros) less often than they frame component parts of a scene. While the precise macro-mono proportions are somewhat different between manga of different demographics (shonen/seinen versus shojo/josei), these differences did not differ statistically. Our additional analysis of manhwa from Korea and manhua from Hong Kong further suggested this relative proportionality of framing types extended outside of Japan. This consistency between Japanese manga with other Asian comics may reflect that manhwa or manhua are influenced by and/or use Japanese Visual Language (Lent 2010).

Why might the framing types of panels from Asian comics use such a different trend than European and American comics? There are several potential explanations, but let us entertain two possibilities here.[3] First, these differences could simply arise because they are different conventionalized systems, with deviating developments over time. Although Japanese manga was initially influenced by early American comics and cartoons (Gravett 2004), and more recent American comics have in turn been influenced by manga, they have had separate developments across the mid-twentieth century, which would have in turn created structural differences. Indeed, given that European, American, and Asian systems have other conventionalized disparities, such as in their morphology (Cohn and Ehly 2016; Forceville 2011; van Middelaar 2017), variance could also have manifested in panel framing structure. Thus, just as spoken languages may differ in systematic ways, visual languages too may simply have arbitrary variation in their structures.

A second possibility entertained in previous work (Cohn 2013b; Cohn, Taylor-Weiner, and Grossman 2012,), is that variance between Asian and Western framing relates to disparities in how individuals from different cultures direct their attention. Eye tracking studies have observed that individuals from the United States tend to focus on the primary objects of a visual scene, while Asians will fixate on primary objects and the surrounding environment (Masuda and Nisbett 2001; Nisbett and Masuda 2003). In terms of paneling, Western authors might unconsciously presume that readers will attend to the primary objects of their panels when presenting a whole scene (i.e., macro panel), and then only vary the framing to provide focus (monos, micros, amorphics) for narrative salience. In contrast, Asian authors would have less reliability that focus would be drawn in the intended ways in depicting a whole scene, since both the surrounding environment and primary figures might be attended to. Thus, Asian authors might directly individuate the relevant objects (monos, micros) and environmental information (amorphics) in each panel to better direct a reader to the important elements of the scene. The result would be that panels would effectively simulate the attention of how a viewer might shift their gaze across a scene. While such an explanation would link observations that panels serve as "attention units" (Cohn 2013b) on the information in a scene to mechanisms of actual attentional selection, this explanation has yet to be substantiated experimentally.

Another way to examine this cross-cultural difference is in the framing types displayed by the Original English Language (OEL) "US manga" from the United States. These comics had framing types that were halfway between the framing of American and Asian comics. This implies that these works are not fully following the properties of the works they imitate most (i.e., Japanese manga), despite their salient influence, and that they also retain properties similar to other comics from that culture (i.e., other US comics). Rather, these works may reflect more of a hybrid consequence of "language contact," blending properties of the comics from American and Japan (more on this below).[4] Given that Japanese manga accelerated in their influence in the 1990s (Brienza 2016; Goldberg 2010), I also analyzed whether our analyzed OEL manga showed trends for becoming more or less like Japanese manga over time. No such trends appeared across these comics, although continuing to track the properties of non-Asian manga would be interesting further research. Such analysis could examine the ways a visual language develops outside of its native environment and the degree to which "global manga" (Brienza 2015) uses the Japanese Visual Language or reflect cross-cultural variants of it.

A particularly salient feature of this analysis is the overall trade-off between the proportions of macros and non-macros, particularly mono panels. When collapsing across cultures, a decrease in the usage of macro panels is highly correlated with an increase in all other panel types. Monos, micros, and amorphic panels were all positively correlated with each other, suggesting that these framing types all increase as macros appear less frequently. This trade-off is most visible between macro and mono panels, as depicted in Figure 3.5. A high proportion of macros and a low proportion of monos (bottom right) is most apparent for European comics (circles). Meanwhile, systems using fewer macro panels and more mono panels (Asian comics: triangles), accompany other framing types, hence the more dispersed distribution in the upper left of the figure.

Overall, this implies that as visual languages move away from depicting full scenes, they use more diverse types of framing. This type of framing also has consequences on comprehension. If a visual sequence depicts panels with only single characters (monos), close ups (micros), or environmental information (amorphic panels), a reader must infer the broader scene, since it is not provided overtly (Cohn 2015, 2019a; Kukkonen 2008). Thus, readers of visual narratives who habituate to visual sequencing that does not demand this type of inference (i.e., readers of American and European comics) might be challenged by reading sequences with so many framing changes (i.e., Asian comics). As discussed in Chapter Two, such costs may

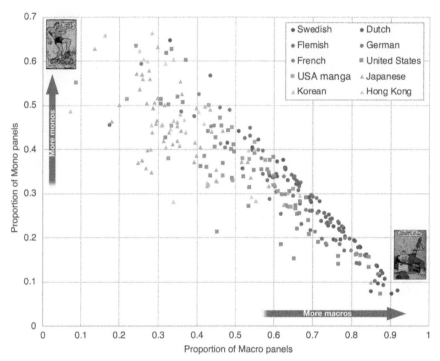

FIGURE 3.5 *Scatterplot of the mean proportion of macro and mono panels in 290 comics from around the world. Each datapoint represents the mean proportions of a comic.*

manifest as increased updating processes. Indeed, experimental evidence suggests that this is the case (Cohn and Kutas 2017).

3.2.3 *Semantic Changes*

Just as the framing of individual units varies across cultures, so might the meaningful changes between units. As discussed in Chapter Two, readers continually track semantic information across images while building a mental model of the scene. Discontinuity, like changes between characters or spatial location, evokes an update of the mental model, with smaller changes demanding more incremental updating and larger changes demanding greater updating (Huff, Meitz, and Papenmeier 2014; Loschky et al. 2018; Loschky et al. 2020). Starting with McCloud's (1993) analysis of the "transitions" between panels, many theorists have characterized inventories of how meaning changes across sequential images (Bateman and Wildfeuer 2014; Gavaler and Beavers 2018; Saraceni 2016; Stainbrook 2016).

McCloud's (1993) analysis of panel transitions was also one of the first to characterize differences in storytelling cross-culturally. He used his taxonomy of semantic changes between panels to compare the sequencing across comics from the United States, Japan, and Europe. McCloud observed that both American and European comics used more transitions related to conveying actions (~65 percent) than specifying changes in characters (~20 percent) or scenes (~14 percent). In contrast, Japanese manga used fewer actions (~42 percent) than American and European comics, while maintaining similar rates of scene changes (~10 percent) but greater rates of changes between characters (~30 percent) and also non-character aspects of the environment (~14 percent). These findings suggested that cultures might differ in the ways that meaningful information might flow across panels.

Since McCloud's analyses of panel transitions, no prominent works appear to have empirically investigated the changes in meaning across panels between cultures. In the VLRC, such changes have been coded across three primary dimensions discussed in theories of visual narrative and discourse coherence (Magliano and Zacks 2011; McCloud 1993; Zwaan and Radvansky 1998): changes between *characters*, between *spatial locations*, and between *states of time*. Our analyses considered semantic coherence changes to be non-mutually exclusive (i.e., panel relationships could have multiple semantic changes at the same time) and non-exhaustive (i.e., changes could be both full and partial). This type of analysis follows

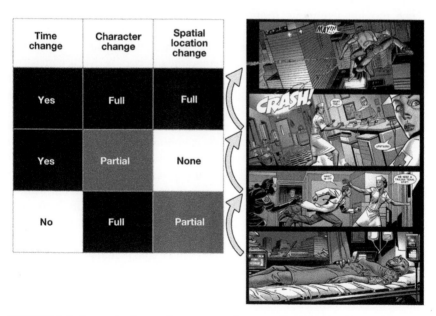

FIGURE 3.6 *Semantic changes between panels across dimensions of time, characters, and spatial location. Arrows go backwards, because semantic changes are backward-looking updates relative to a prior image.* The Amazing Spider-Man #539 *by J. Michael Straczynski and Ron Garney. Spider-Man* © *Marvel Comics.*

the psychological literature showing that meaningful change can be both incremental and full, and that greater changes in semantic types results in greater updating processes (Huff, Meitz, and Papenmeier 2014; Magliano and Zacks 2011).

Consider Figure 3.6, where the first panel shows Spider-Man bringing his injured Aunt May to a hospital. His unseen arrival is cued through the onomatopoeia "Crash!" (Cohn 2019a), which is heard by hospital staff in the second panel, who then run toward the room in panel three. Aunt May is then shown in a hospital bed in panel four, presumably in the room that the hospital staff runs towards. For both character changes and spatial location changes, coders of the VLRC distinguished between three types of shifts. Full shifts in characters between panels were coded as a "1" (i.e., two panels with different characters), while partial changes were coded as ".5" (i.e., one or more characters were held constant while others were depicted or omitted). The absence of a change between characters were coded as "0" (i.e., the same characters were retained). In Figure 3.6, the shift between panel one and two is a full change because all the characters are different, as is the change between panels three and four. However, only some characters in panel three also appear in the previous panel two, meaning this is a partial change.

Similarly, a full shift between locations was coded as a "1", while a partial shift was coded as ".5", such as changes within a common space, like the scene moving from one room in a building to another. Locations that remained constant across panels were coded as "0." Thus, in Figure 3.6, a full change occurs in between the first two panels, which shift from above a cityscape to within a hospital. No change then occurs between panels two and three, which feature the same hospital hallway. A partial change then occurs in the shift between that hallway, in panel three, and a different room, in panel four.

Finally, time changes were binary, coded as "1" for time interpreted as passing between panels, or "0" if time was ambiguous between panels. Note that the passage of time across panels was not taken as a default assumption and was only coded as passing if explicit cues signaled a change. In Figure 3.6, the shifts between panels one through three involve explicit clues about time changing ("crash," people running, etc.). However, the shift from panel three to four is ambiguous: It is unclear whether panel four occurs at the same moment as panel three or at a different moment. Thus, such a panel relation would be coded as ambiguous or "no explicit change."

Because semantic changes could be coded as incremental, they could be analyzed in two ways. First, an overall average was calculated across the coding of dimensions in a comic. This average reflects the amount of change for a given dimension across panels in a comic. A second analysis looked only at the number of panel relations that changed in only one dimension. Here, we look only at the average for changes that occurred in isolation, as this contrast gives a sense of what types of information might be singled out for change in a given system. In Figure 3.6, there are no isolated changes, since each shift between panels involves at least two types of changes in semantic coherence.

The results for our cross-cultural corpus analysis on semantic changes are graphed in Figure 3.7, divided between comics from Europe, the United States, and Asia. As with the attentional framing types discussed previously, we observe a clear difference in the patterns of panel relations in comics from Europe and the United States compared with those from Asia. On the whole, comics from Europe and the United States use more changes in time than those between characters or spatial locations. This is particularly noticeable in the data where only one semantic change was used between panels. European comics most often changed only in time between panels, with very few changes only between spatial locations or only full character

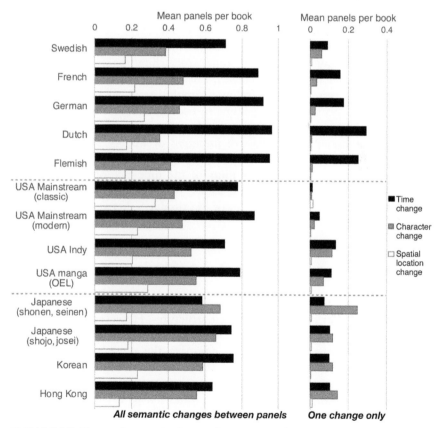

FIGURE 3.7 *Types of semantic changes between panels in comics of different types. The graph on the left depicts the proportions of all changes possible at a given time, while the graph on the right depicts the proportions of transitions when they are the only change happening.*

changes. Mainstream American comics seemed to use very few isolated changes at all, although the overall averages resembled European comics.

Again, Asian comics differed from these proportions, with time changes and character changes being much closer in proportion to each other. Shonen and seinen Japanese manga were the most extreme in this regard, using even more character changes across panels than time changes. This ratio also persisted when only one semantic dimension changed between panels. These findings are consistent with McCloud's (1993) observation of more "subject" or "aspect transitions" in Japanese manga than American or European comics (Note: "aspects" in McCloud's sense are covered by amorphic panels, which were shown above to be greater in Asian than American or European comics).

Here it is again worth comparing the proportions of semantic changes in OEL manga to those from the United States and Japan. Across all semantic changes between panels, OEL manga follow the patterning of other American comics, not like those of Japanese manga. This differs somewhat with the proportions of panels with only one semantic change though, where the patterns are slightly more like Japanese manga. This suggests that these authors may incorporate some storytelling habits from manga (especially greater character changes), but overall retain a style closer to other American comics. Again, follow-up analysis indicated that these OEL manga showed no trending over time to become more or less like manga. When taken together with the attentional framing results above, this suggests that, while these OEL manga are imitative of manga in their graphic structure (i.e., visual style), their storytelling remains fairly reflective of American comics but with some hints of the influence of JVL structure (discussed further later). However, as we will see, more nuance can be offered in response to this question of the similarity between comics from different places.

3.2.4 *Cluster Analysis*

The analyses discussed thus far have all focused on the ways in which cultures are similar or different in their structures. However, these analyses presuppose a categorization based on which cultures and/or genres they come from. Another method is to compare the data from each book regardless of cultural labels and see the ways in which this information might form clusters. Such clusters may or may not then align with the cultural categorization. This technique would tell us if cultures are fairly homogenous in their patterns, or if cultures and/or genres might actually have greater diversity in their structures than the labels imply.

I therefore conducted a "cluster analysis" of the framing structure, semantic structure, and panels per page, which are coded for all 290 comics within the VLRC. A cluster analysis of layout structures was conducted in

Cohn et al. (2019). This analysis partitions individual comics into similarly-structured clusters based on the relationships between their specified features. Here, books were partitioned into clusters nearest to the prototypical mean, which then gave values describing the distance from those means. I used a two-step cluster analysis specifying the number of clusters at three, given that three primary regions were analyzed in the VLRC (Europe, America, and Asia).

Figure 3.8a depicts the results of the cluster analysis, showing the proportion of books from different countries that group together. Cluster 1 includes most of the Asian comics (Japanese manga, Korean manhwa, Hong Kong manhua) and roughly half of the contemporary American comics (modern superheroes, Indy comics, OEL manga). The features of this cluster are reflective of the structures of Asian books in the cross-cultural analysis above, with high numbers of panels depicting individual characters (monos) and shifts between characters among time changes. As depicted in Figure 3.8b, the idealized structure of this cluster uses framing with more mono panels than macro panels, and high (~10 percent) proportions of micro and amorphic panels. This cluster also has near equal numbers of time and character changes, along with a fairly low number of panels per page (4.9). The similarities of these comics from the United States with the mostly uniform tendencies of Asian comics implies an influence from manga on these American comics.

The other American comics (modern and classic superheroes, Indy, OEL manga) are captured by Cluster 2, which also contains high proportions of German, French, and Swedish comics, with low overlap by Dutch, Flemish, and Korean comics (≤ 20 percent). This cluster is characterized by full scenes and shifts in time, but with moderate amounts of variation in framing. It uses twice as many macros as monos, and just a few micro (2 percent) and amorphic panels (4 percent), twice as many time changes as character changes, and an intermediate number of panels per page (5.8).

Finally, Cluster 3 is dominated by Dutch and Flemish comics, with additional overlap with German, French, and Swedish comics (20–30 percent). This primarily European cluster focuses on panels with whole scenes that shift in time across many panels per page. It uses almost three times as many macros as monos, with hardly any micros or amorphic panels (1 percent), and almost three times as many time changes as character changes. It also uses a much greater number of panels per page (8.9). Thus, Clusters 2 and 3—mostly made up of American and European comics—are fairly similar in structure, with Cluster 2 representing less exaggerated disparities between features and Cluster 3 representing the more extremes of these relations.

Overall, this analysis suggests that visual languages used in comics of the world have distinct structures that differ from each other in measurable ways. However, visual languages used in particular cultures may not be uniform, particularly given the influence of print cultures on each other. For example, contemporary comics from the United States appear to equally

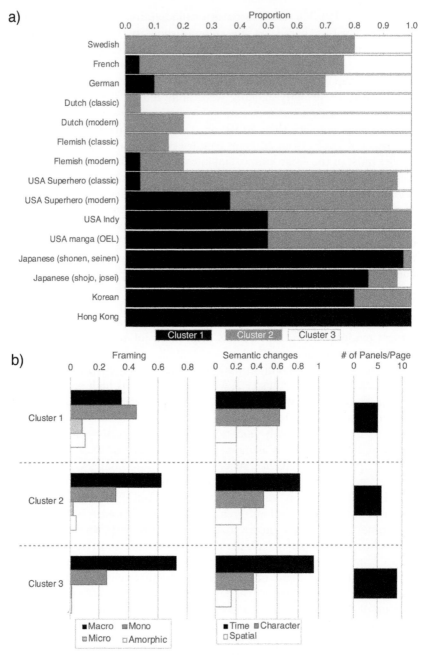

FIGURE 3.8 *Results of a cluster analysis identifying similarities in the data structures of 290 cross-cultural comics. a) A graph with the proportions of comics from different cultures that group together into three clusters. b) The structural properties of these clusters across dimensions of framing structure of panels, semantic changes between panels, and the average number of panels per page.*

share properties both with European comics or those from Asia. This is particularly interesting in comics here labeled as OEL manga, which ostensibly are using (or perhaps "influenced by") Japanese Visual Language. Here we find that roughly half of these books indeed share similar structure with Japanese manga, while half more resemble Euro-American storytelling styles.

While American comics seem split in their similarities between Asian and European comics, those from Europe remain similar only to each other. Save for a few comics, all European comics fall within Clusters 2 and 3. The inverse is true of Asian comics, which primarily group together (Cluster 1). Altogether, this implies that European and Asian comics are more homogenous in their structures, but comics from the United States are less uniform. As we will see in the section below, this characteristic of American comics is reflected in change that has occurred over time.

3.3 Change in Visual Languages Over Time

A second type of potential variation comes not between cultures, but across time, given that the properties of different systems may change and develop. Within the VLRC, there are only a few cultures with data spanning a sizeable range of dates. We have coded comics from the 1940s through the 2010s in both mainstream comics from the United States along with Dutch and Flemish comics. As will be discussed below, Dutch and Flemish comics have remained largely unchanged across time in many of the properties that we discuss below, and thus the focus here will be on changes in US mainstream comics.

3.3.1 *External Compositional Structure (Layout)*

Our first analysis of change over time in the structure of comics focused on the page layouts of US mainstream superhero comics (Pederson and Cohn 2016). I review some of these findings again here using the same corpus of forty comics, five from each decade, as was described in that publication. For a complementary analysis of page layout and narrative in a similar corpus, see Bateman, Veloso, and Lau (2019).

First, we noticed a decrease in the number of panels per page over time. This decline went from an average of 6.5 panels per page in the 1940s, to 4.2 by the 2010s (see also Table 3.1). Of more interest to us was the degree to which page layouts have retained or deviated from the grid pattern. A canonical grid can be considered the default layout structure, which invites a Z-path reading order of left-to-right and down inherited from the English writing system. Deviation in this structure, such as with embedded columns, would invite a different, vertical reading order (Bateman, Beckmann, and

Varela 2018; Cohn 2013a; Cohn and Campbell 2015). For our broader questions of variation in comprehension, layouts signaling a non-Z-path would mark a place that a default assumption might be confounded, thus potentially inviting a benefit from additional expertise.

Therefore, we first examined the directions between panels. In terms of basic directions, a Z-path order would be rightward directions punctuated by down-left diagonal directions ("left-to-right and down"). As depicted in Figure 3.9, both rightward and down-left diagonal directions have decreased across the 80 years of mainstream American comics in our corpus. In contrast, vertical directions straight downward have increased, particularly in the last two decades (2000s, 2010s). This suggests that orders using the Z-path have indeed reduced, supplanted instead by an increase in vertical directions.

Additional analyses of panels' spatial arrangements clarified the nature of these directional changes. We further analyzed how spatial arrangements may have changed across time, as depicted in Figure 3.10. Though grids of all types have declined, no change over time was shown for pure grids where both horizontal and vertical gutters were contiguous. This differed from arrangements using a horizontal stagger, where the row remains contiguous, but the vertical gutters between rows are not. These horizontal staggers showed a dramatic decrease in use over the 80 years analyzed in our corpus, as evident by the negative trendline in Figure 3.10. Given the cross-cultural findings above, this suggests that US comics have moved away from the traits more consistent with page layouts from European comics.

In contrast, panels spanning the whole length of a row saw an increasing trend, aligning with the observations of increased vertical downward reading orders discussed earlier. Another type of vertical ordering would be suggested by columns embedded into rows, a blockage arrangement. These arrangements were observed to be increasing over time, but did not reach the threshold of statistical significance.

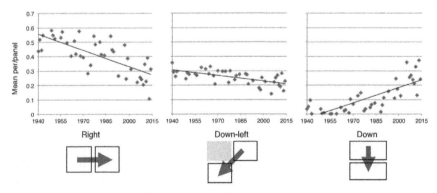

FIGURE 3.9 *Changes in directions of reading order between panel layouts in US mainstream comics from the 1940s through the 2010s.*

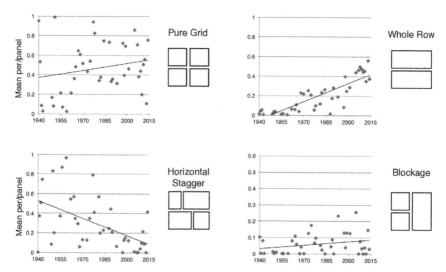

FIGURE 3.10 *Changes in various types of spatial arrangements in page layout in US mainstream comics from the 1940s through the 2010s.*

To further explore these vertical segments, we investigated the properties of whole pages (Pederson and Cohn 2016). This analysis showed that, though they are still the most used types, full pages with only grid-type layouts (pure grids, horizontal staggering) have been declining across the past 80 years. Pages with only one non-grid feature (blockage, overlapping panels, etc.) have been increasing, as have pages with only full rows. This suggests that the increase of vertical directions came more from stacked whole row panels rather than embedded columns (i.e., blockage). This provides further support that wide rectangular panels used in "widescreen" layouts have become particularly prevalent in American superhero comics in the 2000–2010s (Mazur and Danner 2014).

Altogether, these findings suggest that page layouts have changed over time in quantifiable ways. For our purposes, these patterns suggest that layouts have deviated from emphasizing rows with horizontal staggers (as found in European comics, discussed above), to filling rows with panels that span the distance of the page, along with other changes not mentioned here (see Pederson and Cohn 2016).

3.3.2 Framing Structure

Changes over time have also been observed in the attentional framing structure of panels of US mainstream comics (Cohn, Taylor, and Pederson 2017). As mentioned earlier, "classic" mainstream comics from the 1940s to 1970s emphasized macros far more than monos and other framing types,

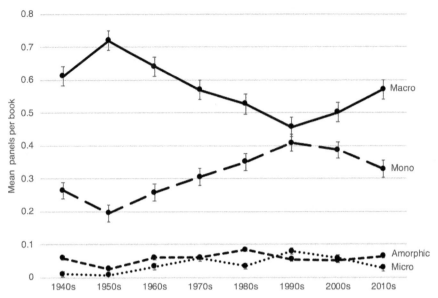

FIGURE 3.11 *Changes in framing structure of panels over time in US mainstream comics from the 1940s through the 2010s.*

consistent with the framing shown in European comics. In contrast, more recent mainstream comics from the 1980s through 2010s have reduced their use of macros, while still having a larger macro-to-mono ratio. The incremental nature of this change can be seen with more fine-grained analyses, as depicted in Figure 3.11.

As reflected in the group averages discussed earlier, macros have decreased over the 80 years of comics we have analyzed, while monos have increased. No change over time was observed for amorphic or micro panels, which have remained near or under 10 percent of all panel types. The changes in macros and monos appear gradual between decades, reaching an apex in the 1990s and then rebounding slightly into the 2000s. Such changes are consistent with differences in macro and mono proportions observed in earlier studies of framing in mainstream US comics between the 1980s to the early 2000s (Cohn 2011) and those only in the 2000s (Cohn, Taylor-Weiner, and Grossman 2012).

While comics from the United States have shifted in their framing structure from the 1940s through the 2010s, no such change was observed across a similar time frame for Dutch or Flemish comics (Dierick 2017). Rather, across the same 80 years, Dutch and Flemish comics maintained the same framing of twice as many macros than monos, with below 2 percent of micros and amorphic panels, as depicted in Figure 3.4. These proportions are consistent with those of older comics from the United States (pre-1960s), prior to the changes in their framing.

On this note, it is worth mentioning that Hollywood movies across the past 100 years have also been observed to have comparable changes: They have reduced in the number of characters per shot, decreased in the durations of film shots, and tightened the framing of the shot, i.e., from long shots to more close shots (Cutting 2015; Cutting and Armstrong 2018; Cutting, DeLong, and Nothelfer 2010). Thus, visual storytelling in the broader culture appears to have changed in the framing of information. However, it is difficult to assess whether the direction of such influence goes from film to comics, comics to film, or back and forth between the two. Indeed, comic artists often draw the storyboards that guide the filming and subsequent editing of films, meaning that there is less of a clear division between producers of these narratives than the differences in media may suggest.

3.3.3 *Semantic Changes*

The meaningful relationships between panels have also changed over time in mainstream US comics (Bateman, Veloso, and Lau 2019; Cohn, Taylor, and Pederson 2017). As depicted in Figure 3.12, mainstream US comics have maintained the same overall relationship between semantic changes as European cultures, with changes in time being the most prominent, then changes in characters, and then spatial location. This has only changed somewhat over time, with a marginal increase in character changes and an increase—and then decrease—in time changes between panels. Changes in spatial location appear to have decreased starting in the 1970s. In addition, as noted in Figure 3.7, relatively few semantic changes occurred on their own in US mainstream comics. Such isolated changes did not seem to appear until more recent comics in the 2000s and 2010s, where only time changes (~10 percent) and character changes (~6 percent) were used on their own.

These developments across 80 years imply that the storytelling of American superhero comics has shifted to keep scenes in one spatial location more often than switching between locations. The marginal shifts between characters overall combined with a slight increase in isolated character changes further implies that panels remain focused on the same characters over narrative time, even if depicting a single character, as implied by the increase in monos and micros in recent decades. Such changes support the idea that storytelling in American superhero comics has become "decompressed" in the last two decades (Mazur and Danner 2014). This term describes a narrative style using more panels to draw out scenes, rather than a terser "compressed" sequence. Indeed, we saw already that pages themselves have changed to have fewer panels, physically becoming less compact in their depictions. Fan and industry discourse describe decompression as "cinematic" storytelling, in part coupled with the concurrent increase of "widescreen" layouts described in the previous section. It also aligns with observations that these comics have shifted to

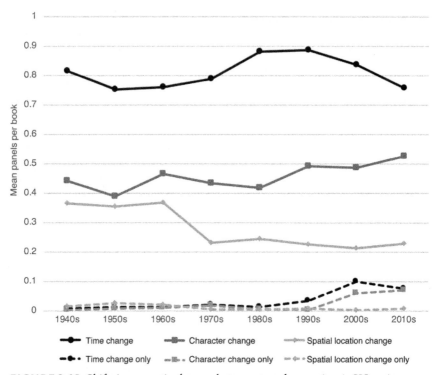

FIGURE 3.12 *Shifts in semantic changes between panels over time in US mainstream comics from the 1940s through the 2010s. Solid lines depict the proportions of all changes possible at a given time, while dashed lines depict the proportions of only one semantic change occurring between panels.*

conveying meaning more with images than with words (Cohn, Taylor, and Pederson 2017).

These shifts in storytelling in the past two decades in superhero comics have often been attributed to the influence of manga (Cicci 2015; Mazur and Danner 2014), which started arriving in the American comic market in the 1980s (Brienza 2016; Goldberg 2010), and escalated in the 1990s and 2000s. Some influence of manga may indeed be apparent in the isolated semantic changes between characters, which have increased only in the past two decades, along with the growing proportion of monos (Figure 3.11). Japanese manga are indeed distinguished from Western comics with higher proportions of character changes (Figure 3.7), and with greater prevalence of mono than macro panels (Figure 3.4). This is particularly true of shonen (boy's) and seinen (men's) manga, which were the works most commonly imported into the US market in the 1990s (which were followed by shojo manga more in the 2000s). This influence may be reflected in the half of the superhero comics that cluster with manga in Figure 3.8.

For mainstream American comics, the increase in character changes and decrease in time changes does seem to occur in the 2000s, while the increase in monos and decrease in macros reached an apex in the 1990s. These dates align with the influx of imported manga into the US market (Cicci 2015; Mazur and Danner 2014). It is therefore possible that narrative structures in American Visual Language, signaled by framing structure and semantic changes, were influenced by this increased exposure to the structure of Japanese Visual Language.

Nevertheless, the lasting influence of manga on American comics' storytelling during these decades may be more complicated. Our data suggest that while semantic changes have sustained in the 2000s, framing types have subsequently "rebounded" since the 1990s. This may reflect the anecdotal disparagement by contemporary fans and critics of the style of 1990s comics, and/or a further adaptation of the JVL structures into AVL following an assimilation period. In addition, the developments in framing types are not constrained to 1990–2000s, as in the semantic changes of time and characters. Rather, attentional framing structures seem to have gradually shifted the most between the 1940s and 1980s, which precedes the influx of manga into the American market. Thus, attentional framing has progressively shifted in American superhero comics, not just following manga's importation.

Other explanations might further account for these developments in storytelling in US comics. First, changes could have occurred because of the influence of particularly prominent comic creators or books. Our corpus does include annotations of works by widely accepted influential comic creators (e.g., Jack Kirby, Neal Adams, etc., also see Appendix 1). However, these authors' data were not outliers from their peers, although their influence might be found in ways not measured on these particular dimensions. Also, the changes in attentional framing at least appear gradual from decade-to-decade, suggesting that it was not due to a sudden innovation. Instead, creators from each decade appear to have built on the work of predecessors in prior decades, even when creators may have worked across the span of numerous decades.

Another possibility is that storytelling has changed because of developments in formatting and technology (Verano 2006). The earliest American comic books were compilations of earlier comic strips, which led to original short stories combined in 64-page anthologies. This gave way in the 1960s to issues featuring single stories, which aligned with developments in comics creation using physically larger pages, which would have allowed greater details in the same physical space (Moore 2003). If formatting shifts to longer pages-per-story allow for narrative structure to be more "decompressed" it could be reflected in the decrease in spatial location changes from 1960s to 1970s. Subsequent technological influence in contemporary works may be sensitive to the knowledge that single issues are often later compiled in book-formatted trade paperbacks, a trend that has also grown since the 1990s. Thus, the overall factors motivating changes in storytelling may be multifaceted.

Finally, we might ask: Are these types of changes in framing structure inevitable over time? Might they reflect the "evolution" of a system from starting with simple framing containing lots of macros (and storytelling), then progressing to more complex sequencing with more simple units (monos, micros)? While this seems apparent somewhat in American superhero comics, this does not occur in all comics. As noted earlier, Dutch and Flemish comics showed no such trends in their framing or semantic changes between the 1940s and 2010s (Dierick 2017).[5] Rather, their general distribution of framing reflects the average presented in Figure 3.4, and their semantic changes reflect that in Figure 3.7. Thus, compared to the developments across publication dates in American superhero comics, the relative paucity of change across Dutch and Flemish comics suggests that there is not necessarily an inevitable evolution or shifting of style across time.

3.4 Conclusion

Altogether, this research suggests that there is not one "visual language of comics," but rather that visual languages used in comics differ across cultures. This variation appears to be systematic, and our discussion here has been constrained to the contexts of visual languages in comics specifically. Despite the variation we have observed here, these visual languages may share substantial structure given their similar sociocultural context. Additional variation could exist in other genres and contexts, such as illustrated picture books or in more dynamic visual narratives like film. As is evident by cross-cultural and historical research, these visual languages differ further from other systems like the sand drawings of Australian Aboriginals (Green 2014; Munn 1986; Wilkins 1997/2016), the sequential images in paintings on Mayan pottery (Wichmann and Nielsen 2016), or the medieval European imagery on the Bayeux Tapestry (Díaz Vera 2013a, b). The extent to which underlying similarities exist between these varied contexts remains an open question for further corpus research. Nevertheless, it is clear that variation occurs across systems both within and outside the context of visual languages used in comics.

Given these findings about diversity in *structure* across systems, it then raises questions about the potential for diversity in *comprehension* of those systems. If a person is familiar with any type of visual narrative, does that mean they can understand all of them? Or, is familiarity required for the specific structures found in specific visual languages? For example: If a person grows up reading only American superhero comics, will they also be able to understand Japanese manga? Also, if a person grows up reading American superhero comics from the 1950s, will they have issues with the changes that have occurred in the structures since the 1990s or 2000s? It is unlikely that the visual languages used in comics are entirely mutually unintelligible, and the iconicity of images should allow for general understanding of the objects and events that they depict. However, there may be ways that specific fluencies affect the perception and processing of visual narratives.

If comics are still mostly understandable for comic readers across cultures, how might cross-cultural patterns create preferences for readers or differences in comprehension? A straightforward example was one I discussed in the previous chapter, of a reader who is used to American comics and then is confronted with Japanese manga that flip the surface directions of the layout. Now, instead of reading left-to-right and down in a Z-path (for American comics), they must read right-to-left and down for the manga. Any sense of difficulty or confusion arising from the differences in these rule-based systems is based on fluency in the cultural patterns of these different visual languages. Basic leftward versus rightward directions were not analyzed in this chapter, but if these simple rules can influence reading, might the various conventions that have been analyzed here do the same?

I have also already speculated on two aspects of fluency that might motivate the perception of page layouts by scholars and authors. First, the prevalence of row-based structures in European page layouts was posited as motivating French comic theorists to ascribe more salience to rows in their theories of layout (Chavanne 2015; Groensteen 2007). Second, American comic authors may be influenced by the relative paucity of blockage arrangements in American comics in their advocacy to not use blockage layouts (e.g., Abel and Madden 2008; McCloud 2006). In both cases, corpus data might be illustrative of the ways that culturally specific knowledge might inform the perceptions of the visual language(s) used in comics.

Some experimental findings more directly imply an influence of specific visual language proficiency. First, various conventions used in manga have been shown to be comprehended more accurately for college students in Japan than those in the United States (Nakazawa and Shwalb 2012). This implies that familiarity with manga specifically informs that understanding. Second, readership of manga has been shown to correlate with the preferences for the ordering of panels in a page layout (Cohn 2013a; Lee and Armour 2016). Third, neural responses to narrative patterns (Environmental-Conjunction) found more prevalently in Japanese manga than European or American comics (Cohn 2019b) were modulated by the frequency that participants read Japanese manga (Cohn and Kutas 2017). Such neural differences persisted despite all participants describing themselves as "comic readers" generally and the stimuli not actually being manga (they were *Peanuts* comics manipulated to have the narrative structure similar to manga).

More research is needed to fully assess the balance of general fluency in visual language comprehension (as discussed further in later chapters) and that of specific visual languages. Such research could include studies investigating not only comprehension, but the effect of fluency on sociocultural preferences. Because of their iconicity, visual narratives may often be more understandable across diverse systems, making any difficulties in comprehension seem more like a matter of "taste"—particularly if "comics" is perceived of as a uniform construct, with no conception of "visual languages" that might differ. That is, a person who is more familiar with European or American comics than manga may perceive their strained fluency with Japanese Visual Language as "bad storytelling" or just a dislike in personal preference.

Similar habituation to specific patterns might manifest in critiques of how a system might change over time from its state in prior generations. For example, familiarity with the structures of mainstream US superhero comics from the 1960s might render comics from the 1990s or 2000s as harder to comprehend, which in turn might manifest in critiques that these newer comics are worse in their storytelling. Such statements would effectively be a visual language version of statements like "kids today are ruining the language." Rather, such differences may be aspects of (visual) language change, possibly brought about by contact with structures from other systems (like the importation of manga into the United States and Europe). Thus, with any variance between structures—whether culturally or historically—we also need to ask how those differences might manifest in disparities in comprehension and likeability.

Overall, these findings of structural differences across systems encourage us to question several assumptions about the way "comics" are conceived of and treated. First, such diversity across visual languages calls into question the utility of referring to a monolithic notion of a "comics medium" at all. Rather, several distinctly patterned visual languages appear in visual narratives of the world, which differ in the ways that they manifest an abstract set of architectural principles. Second, this diversity should thus push us to ask two questions whenever we talk of visual narratives in their various contexts: 1) *Which visual language is it written in?* and 2) *What is the visual language fluency of the audience?* These questions persist in cases of visual narratives used as entertainment, but also when they are used as experimental stimuli or in educational or communicative contexts. Such questions maintain the knowledge that visual narratives are produced and comprehended by *people*, who have internalized these diverse patterns from the visual languages they have experienced.

CHAPTER FOUR

Cross-cultural Visual Narrative Comprehension

In the chapters so far, we have explored the structures that comprise visual languages (Chapter One), the mechanisms that guide their sequential understanding (Chapter Two), and the ways in which their structures may vary across diverse systems (Chapter Three). We can now ask: *Are visual narratives comprehended transparently?* To answer the question, this chapter turns to findings that challenge the Sequential Image Transparency Assumption that visual narratives are universally comprehensible. We focus here on studies with people from certain cultural backgrounds who may not spontaneously interpret images *as sequential*. As we will see, the challenges faced by these people come in construing fairly simple image sequences, without even approaching the type of complexity found in many comics across the world.

4.1 Experimental Methods Using Visual Narrative

Before addressing the literature on visual narrative fluency, it is first important to describe the prominent methods that inform these findings, which use wordless visual narratives in experimental tasks. In Chapter Two, we reviewed research on the cognition of visual narrative sequences, which integrated recent studies employing a wide range of behavioral and neurocognitive methods. Yet many researchers have used sequential images in tasks which do not necessarily aim at studying visual narratives themselves. As summarized in Table 4.1, these procedures often balance several characteristics and frequently they are used to study aspects of cognition like IQ, temporal cognition, Theory of Mind, or others. Only sometimes are such tests administered to test visual narrative fluency directly.

The most common method is the *picture arrangement task* (PAT), also called a *picture sequencing task*, which gives participants several images and

TABLE 4.1 Tasks involving visual narratives used in the psychological sciences and the methods involved in them. See the text that follows for references using each task and variations of them

Tasks	Arrangement	Narration	Inference	Recall	Questions
Picture arrangement task (PAT) Four panels are provided and then asked to be arranged in a sequence.	X				
Narrative elicitation task (NET) A participant reads a visual narrative aloud, or recalls it and then repeats the story.	?	X		?	
Sequential reasoning task (SRT) or Sequence completion task (SCT) A sequence is provided, and then participants choose a panel to complete the sequence.	?		X	?	
Fill in the blank task (FITBT) A panel is left out of a sequence, and the participant describes the missing content			X		
Narrative comprehension task (NCT) Participants read a visual narrative and then are asked questions about its contents				X	X

asks them to arrange them into a coherent sequence. Answers are then scored relative to an expected, "correct" target sequence. This task appears across many disciplines, including in general intelligence (IQ) tests (WAIS-IQ, WISC) and clinical assessments (Kaufman and Lichtenberger 2006; Wechsler 1981). Variants of the PAT have been created for specific purposes. For example, Cartoon Picture Stories is a PAT with different types of sequences intended to measure Theory of Mind (Langdon et al. 1997), where some of the sequences relate to the intentions or goals of the characters, while other sequences show simple "mechanistic" actions or occurrences. Another PAT variant claims to test temporal cognition with the *temporal card arrangement task* (TCAT), which also considers the spatial layout of the arrangement—i.e., in a horizontal row, vertical stack, circular shape, etc. (Boroditsky, Gaby, and Levinson 2008). The spatial layout of the arranged pictures is then taken as an indicator of spatial metaphors for how time may be understood, such as a vertically stacked layout being a proxy for a vertical spatial metaphor of how time is structured.

Other tasks ask participants to *infer* information about a sequence. This either comes as a *fill-in-the-blank task* to guess the content of a missing panel (Nakazawa and Nakazawa 1993a), or a *sequence completion task* (SCT), also called a *sequential reasoning task* (SRT), asking participants to select an image to be placed at the start, middle, or end of a picture sequence to complete the narrative (Brown and French 1976; Zampini et al. 2017). This same technique is used in assessments supposedly aimed at examining Theory of Mind, such as the Comic Strip Task (Sivaratnam et al. 2012) and the Story-Based Empathy Task (Dodich et al. 2015). Some of these tasks are preceded by exposure to visual narratives, often as PATs, introducing a *recall* component to the completion task.

Many fields use *narrative elicitation tasks* (NET), where participants describe the story in an image sequence (sometimes preceded by a PAT). The utterances elicited by these narrations are then analyzed for various linguistic and/or cognitive properties. There are many formalized versions of NETs, which include, but are not limited to:

- Frog Stories based on the Mercer Mayer picture books (Berman and Slobin 1994)

- Jackal and Crow (Carroll, Kelly, and Gawne 2011)

- Family Problems (Carroll et al. 2009; San Roque et al. 2012)

- Circle of Dirt (Eisenbeiss, McGregor, and Schmidt 1999)

- The Edmonton Narrative Norms Instrument (Schneider, Hayward, and Dubé 2006)

- The Multilingual assessment instrument for narratives (MAIN) (Gagarina et al. 2012)

NETs are assumed to be transparently understood, and/or engaging for children (Burris and Brown 2014) or native populations (San Roque et al. 2012). Although NETs are often used to assess other traits, like language ability or an assumed amodal narrative comprehension, the data generated from such tasks can be informative for how those visual sequences are understood in the first place.

Finally, some researchers have simply presented participants with visual narratives, and then followed a comprehension period with a battery of questions (e.g., detail questions, inferential questions, recall, recognition, etc.). These *narrative comprehension tasks* (NCT) typically measure overall comprehension of the visual sequences, comparable to reading comprehension tests for textual stories.

All of these methods are informative for the understanding of visual narratives. Nevertheless, their predominant use for informing *other* aspects of cognition may be problematic, as will be discussed throughout this and other chapters.

4.2 Cross-cultural Visual Narrative Comprehension

Cross-cultural research suggesting the non-universality of sequential images began emerging in the 1960s to the 1980s, when researchers sought to use wordless sequential images as a non-verbal method of communication, often in engagement with people from non-Western industrialized societies. This work was often motivated by practical, humanitarian, or educational efforts.[1] Nevertheless, sequential images often made for inadequate materials because various populations did not construe their expected meaning. These individuals typically lived in more rural communities, often with low literacy and with little or no exposure to sequential images in the form of comics or picture books.

A consistent finding across studies was that individuals from many communities appeared to not connect elements across panels—i.e., they did not recognize the *continuity constraint*—and instead interpreted each image as an isolated scene. A striking example came in a study in Nepal which sought to use wordless pictures to convey information about nutrition, hygiene, environmental concerns, etc. (Fussell and Haaland 1978). The respondents had difficulty discerning the meaning of individual images and less than 50 percent of respondents understood the need for a left-to-right order of the sequential images. Many respondents did not understand that images repeated the same characters across a three-image long sequence and in some cases only three percent recognized a juxtaposed pair of images as making a comparison between two event states.

A more recent study examined the comprehension of visual sequences by upland farmers aged 18 to 71 in the Philippines. Researchers sought to assess the comprehension of various visual techniques to communicate with the farmers about environmental protections (Gravoso and Stuart 2000). They found that visual sequences had only a 13 percent comprehensibility, which did not differ when arranged horizontally or vertically. However, comprehensibility was increased by connecting the images through arrows (20 percent) or through numbers (33 percent), although comprehension remained fairly low even with these additional connectors clarifying the sequencing.

Similarly, respondents in Papua New Guinea had difficulty construing sequences as conveying sequential (Bishop 1977) and/or temporal orders (Cook 1980). However, practice and familiarity with Western pictures and comics improved a sequential interpretation (Cook 1980). Comparable interpretations have been observed in more recent elicitation tasks, where Awiakay speakers from Papua New Guinea interpreted each image in a PAT as being a story on their own, and related experiences have been reported about Aboriginal Australian Umpila speakers (San Roque et al. 2012: 153).

Several studies from Africa report similar findings of challenges with referential continuity in sequencing (Brouwer 1995). An older study in Kenya found that respondents had trouble recognizing a sequence of images as being in a sequence, although they were somewhat better at construals of pairs of images (Holmes 1963). A study in South Africa found Bantu (Zulu and Tsonga) workers had difficulty recognizing the continuity between characters in pairs of images depicting "before and after" on industrial safety posters (Winter 1963), and rural Bantu populations interpreted continuity across sequential images less often than European counterparts, although this ability increased with age and acculturation (Duncan, Gourlay, and Hudson 1973). Similar observations have been made about differences in comprehension levels between native South Africans and their British counterparts (Liddell 1996, 1997), in studies with the Basotho people (Jenkins 1978) and a study in Botswana (Byram and Garforth 1980), with results modulated by exposure to graphics and literacy. This inclination to attribute individual images with more information is consistent with findings that children and adults from Rhodesia (modern Zimbabwe) and Zambia more often construed individual images as conveying intrinsic events than Canadian respondents (Deregowski and Munro 1974). A recent study using wordless comics to communicate about agricultural practices in Madagascar found most respondents understood the comics, although it was modulated by age and education (Stenchly et al. 2019).

Some picture arrangement tasks (PATs) are also illustrative. An older study of young men from the Ganda tribe (Uganda) showed fairly low proficiency on the PAT, despite proficient English and math skills (McFie 1961). More recently, lower PAT scores were found for illiterate Sudanese participants than for literate participants, but the authors also point out that 80 percent of participants "failed to respond adequately" to the PAT in a pilot study (Khaleefa and Ashria 1995).

Similar findings are reported from the temporal card arrangement task where the layout of a PAT (vertical, horizontal, circular, etc.) is claimed to inform about possible spatial metaphors underlying the construal of time (Boroditsky, Gaby, and Levinson 2008). The use of these tasks in native communities has been mixed. While industrialized participants are highly consistent in the sequencing of their layouts (Fuhrman and Boroditsky 2010; Levinson and Majid 2013; Spinillo and Dyson 2001), more variable layouts have been made by native individuals from cultures in Australia (Gaby 2012), South America (Brown 2012; Le Guen and Pool Balam 2012), and Papua New Guinea (Fedden and Boroditsky 2012; Levinson and Majid 2013), among others. Indeed, some Yucatec Mayan speakers even confounded the test itself, piling the pictures vertically rather than arranging them into a spatially juxtaposed linear layout (Le Guen and Pool Balam 2012). Again, construal of sequential images in these tasks has been attributed in part to participants' familiarity with written language (Gaby 2012; Le Guen and Pool Balam 2012; Levinson and Majid 2013). However, few of these studies report on comprehension levels of either arranged or unarranged sequences.

Finally, observations of unexpected interpretations of sequential images often go unreported. For example, in 2013, the linguist Rafael Núñez (personal communication) described fieldwork he conducted alongside linguist Kensy Cooperrider with the Yupno of Papua New Guinea (e.g., Núñez et al. 2012). They attempted to use four-panel sequences for an intended temporal card arrangement task. Sequences showed, for example, a banana at different stages of being peeled, and successive images of a person's beard getting longer. Their respondents construed the sequences as showing four different bananas and four different but related people (i.e., "brothers," because they looked similar). These experiences led Núñez and Cooperrider (2013: 225) to critique these tasks "because they presuppose familiarity with materials and practices that, in fact, require considerable cultural scaffolding."

The linguist Lauren Gawne (personal communication) also reported that using picture stories often did not go as planned with her research with Lamjung Yolmo speaking participants in Nepal. She used picture stories to elicit narration out of participants, intending for the language that they uttered to be analyzed for their linguistic properties. She describes one respondent who was "not literate in storybook conventions" (Gawne 2016: 144). In the first elicitation of a picture story, this respondent mostly described the images, but made few connections across images. In the second telling, the presence of juxtaposed panels led the respondent to interpret multiple birds, rather than a single bird across frames (Gawne 2016: 144). This participant was older, and younger participants did not make similar interpretations since they had learned "standard visual literacy" in formal schooling.

These reports via personal communication are important because many researchers use sequential images under the assumptions of transparency to study other aspects of cognition (e.g., Theory of Mind or temporal cognition) or use them as educational materials. In such contexts, when respondents do not perform as expected, the result is often perceived as a "failed" experiment which remains unreported in the scientific literature. It is thus unclear how widespread such findings may be.

Altogether, these studies report several cases where respondents did not construe sequential images *as a sequence*, where they confounded the expectations of a task involving visual narratives, and/or where they "misinterpreted" the individual images themselves (Duncan, Gourlay, and Hudson 1973; Fussell and Haaland 1978; San Roque et al. 2012). Across these examples, individuals did not seem to follow the continuity constraint and instead construed each image in isolation or as a type of visual list. It is worth emphasizing that most of the individuals in these studies lived in rural communities with little or no exposure to visual narratives (i.e., comics or picture books). Exposure to such materials, along with literacy and formal education, lead to greater likelihood of sequential construal.

Finally, it should be emphasized that there should be no implications here that lack of construing sequential images had anything to do with any aspects of the ethnicities of the respondents. In addition, several of these studies are fairly old, and may not reflect the current status of such populations' understandings given further adoption of Western culture (including comics and picture stories). Nevertheless, the implications persist: *Not everyone comprehends sequences of images as sequential.*

4.3 Diversity in Cross-cultural Visual Narrative Systems

The work described earlier suggests that a lack of exposure may contribute toward not construing static sequential images as sequences. However, an additional possibility is that comprehension of comic strip-like sequential images may compete with indigenous visual narrative systems, rather than manifest as a "lack" of comprehension or expertise. For example, Aboriginal communities in Central Australia have a rich system of narrative sand drawings that unfurl temporally in a single space (Green 2014; Munn 1986; Wilkins 1997/2016). In work with the Arrernte community, Wilkins (1997/2016) reports that respondents had difficulty construing comic strips as sequential events, instead interpreting each image as its own scene. These results are similar to the ones described earlier, where respondents were not exposed to sequential images, and thus could not construe the continuity constraint.

While such results could be interpreted as an inability to understand the content of the sequence, as above, the Arrernte use a rich and complex native system of sequential visual narratives which they *are fluent* in, yet they still construed images in comics as depicting independent scenes. Given that they clearly had fluency in visual narratives via their indigenous system, Wilkins posits that the spatially sequential layout in comics conflicts with the temporally sequential indigenous system. Such a difference in layout has ramifications on several levels of visual narratives' structure, including continuity (Cohn 2013b). Thus, this non-sequential construal does not arise simply because of "lack of a general visual narrative fluency" as perhaps hinted earlier, but from unfamiliarity with conventions between culturally specific visual languages. On this point it is worth stressing that visual language fluency is all relative, and people unfamiliar with the properties of the Arrernte visual language would also struggle to understand it as well.

Related to layout, several researchers have stressed that the ordering of sequential images relates to individuals' literacy in a written language. In picture arrangement tasks, left-to-right layouts correlate with literacy (Gaby 2012; Le Guen and Pool Balam 2012; Levinson and Majid 2013), and similar observations have been made with basic understandings of sequential images (Fussell and Haaland 1978). Literacy's influence may have nothing to do with content. Rather, both writing and visual narratives use spatially sequential layouts, making it conceivable that developing habits for linearly navigating a writing system may be transferable to linearly navigating a sequence of images.

The transference of directionality between written layout to visual narrative layouts guides the assumptions of card arrangement tasks, where it has been demonstrated experimentally that people arrange images into layouts similar to the order in their writing systems (Fuhrman and Boroditsky 2010). However, such a relationship between the navigation of spatial layouts of writing and visual narratives also occurs conventionally in comics: European and American comics follow the left-to-right order of alphabetic writing, while Japanese manga follow the right-to-left order of written Japanese. Indeed, experiments on people's preferences for the ordering of page layouts in comics have found that participants' reading orders may be modulated by their readership of Japanese manga (Cohn 2013a; Lee and Armour 2016). We also pointed to this as a fairly obvious source of conflict between visual language fluencies cross-culturally: Readers familiar with the directions of one system's navigation may have difficulties with systems using different directions.

Because both written and visual narratives use layout structures, for people inexperienced with visual narratives, borrowing the linear navigation of writing for their image sequences may in turn bootstrap the recognition of *content* as continuous. Another possibility is that literacy may accompany acculturation to visual narratives like comics, which also may go unreported in studies. Thus, visual narrative fluency in general is not reliant on literacy, but literacy may be beneficial for acquiring fluency in *certain visual narrative systems* given the shared layout structures and the ramifications of spatial juxtaposition on continuity.

4.4 Cross-cultural Visual Narrative Production

Additional insight comes not only from the comprehension of sequential images, but also from their *production*. This work is most informed by research by art educators Brent and Marjorie Wilson, who spent decades studying the properties of children's visual narratives across the world (see Wilson 2016 for a review). They administered a simple "Draw a Story" test in which they provided children with six empty frames and then asked them to draw a narrative about any topic.

Studies in the United States, Australia, Finland, and Egypt found that middle-class urban children (ages 9 through 12) produced comparable structures and themes (Wilson 2016; Wilson and Wilson 1984). In many cases, their visual narratives were imitative of comics (Wilson 1974). This influence is particularly apparent in the drawings of children from Japan, where manga are ubiquitous and immersive throughout culture. Nearly all Japanese 6-year-olds could produce comprehensible visual narratives, often with greater coherence and complexity than their counterparts around the world (Wilson 1988). Nearly all of the visual narratives produced by children in Japan imitated the properties of manga (Toku 2001a, b; Wilson 1999, 2016; Wilson and Wilson 1987).

A lack of exposure to visual narratives is most salient in the Wilsons' studies in Egypt, where they compared children's drawings from affluent and rural neighborhoods (Wilson 2016). Suburban Egyptian children (in Cairo) largely had comparable proficiency in drawing visual narratives as children from the United States, and these wealthier families had exposure to illustrated books and comics. These findings contrasted what they found in the drawings made by Egyptian children from a rural village (Nahia). These children had little access to such drawn visual culture, but they did have access to television, including programming with American cartoons, and they had proficient verbal narration abilities. Here, *only 4–8 percent* of village 9-year-old children drew coherent visual narratives where the contents of one image sequentially related to other images (Wilson 2016). They instead drew sequences of "frozen vignettes" with isolated objects or events (Wilson and Wilson 1987), with loose semantic relationships. Around 50 percent of the older village children (12-year-olds) drew coherent sequences, although their visual narratives appeared to just use step-by-step linear sequencing (Wilson 2016).

Overall, research on visual narrative production again implies a strong association between exposure to comics or picture books and proficiency. High levels of exposure to manga allows Japanese children to acquire complex narrative structures, even at young ages. In contrast, the isolated scenes produced by the young Egyptian children from a rural village resemble in production the inability to establish continuity across sequential images. Meanwhile, the step-by-step linear sequencing in older children's visual narratives maintains structurally simpler organizations than a robust narrative structure. That is, such sequences used linear grammars, not a narrative grammar, and Wilson (2016: 201) correspondingly attributed these step-by-step sequences to "commonsensical" notions than to "encounters with commercially produced visual narratives".

4.5 Conclusion

Altogether, in this chapter, we have reviewed cross-cultural findings that suggest a spatial sequence of images is neither universally construable nor producible. When sequences are not understood, they are interpreted as isolated scenes without continuity connecting them to other images. The fluency in order to understand and to subsequently produce these sequences appears to be modulated by exposure to Western-styled visual narratives, and possibly also with literacy. These findings overall go against the Sequential Image Transparency Assumption and suggest that the ability to comprehend a sequence of images requires experience with a visual language.

CHAPTER FIVE

Development of Visual Narrative Comprehension

If visual narratives are understood universally and transparently, the construal of sequences of images should "come for free" with basic cognitive processes. This implies no need for *development* or *acquisition* of specialized knowledge, since visual narratives could rely on event cognition; attention and perception; Theory of Mind; and other general cognitive mechanisms. Thus, according to the reasoning of the Sequential Image Transparency Assumption, so long as children have gained the ability to understand visual information, they should be able to understand a visual narrative sequence. Visual narratives are thus often assumed to be understood even by young children and researchers thus use them as materials in various experiments on the assumption of this comprehensibility. Indeed, in industrialized Western society, visual narratives in the form of picture books are often among the first exposure children have to reading and literacy.

As we have already seen, although visual narratives draw on domain-general mechanisms in their processing, they also involve culture-specific knowledge which requires exposure and practice with an external visual language. In terms of development, this implies a process beyond that of just perception and event cognition. Here then we ask the question: *How might the comprehension of visual narratives be learned and develop?*

While dedicated research programs on the development of sequential image understanding have yet to be established, many studies with children have used visual narratives in research, often with the intent to study other aspects of cognition. As will be demonstrated, despite this variety of intentions for research, consistent developmental trends emerge across these findings. Given the importance of exposure demonstrated in the previous chapter on cross-cultural understandings, the findings reported here reflect comprehension where we assume sufficient exposure is part of development, unless specified otherwise. These results come primarily from studies of children in Western, industrialized societies. We will thus examine the developmental trajectory of sequential images across both comprehension and production.

5.1 Development Research on Visual Narratives

Broadly, the developmental trajectory of sequential image understanding appears to progress incrementally (Bornens 1990; Trabasso and Nickels 1992; Trabasso and Stein 1994). While there is of course variation across individual children, we can generalize this trajectory as suggested by findings from developmental research. Children first recognize the referential information within individual images, like the characters and objects, and eventually recognize the events that those entities undertake, but without connecting across images (no continuity constraint). Eventually, they recognize the continuity and activity constraints across images for explicit information, and progressively learn to make inferences for unseen or missing information. This developmental trajectory is detailed further below.

5.1.1 Pre-sequencing (0–3 Years Old)

At early ages, children do not seem to comprehend the *sequence* of a sequence of images. Prior to age 3, children recognize that drawn images depict referential information, which may be modulated by the style of the images: more realistic depictions are recognized easier than cartoony images (Ganea, Pickard, and DeLoache 2008). In addition, despite 2-year-olds' attending to narrated elements in picture stories read by parents, their comprehension remains fairly poor (Kaefer, Pinkham, and Neuman 2017).

In experiments examining the continuity and activity constraints, children at or below the age of 4 do not construe characters repeated across images as the same referential entities (Bornens 1990). Children below age 4 also do fairly poor at picture arrangement tasks (Friedman 1990; Weist et al. 1997; Weist et al. 1999;), and they show little ability to accurately choose which panel might correctly end a sequence (Zampini et al. 2013; Zampini et al. 2017). Up until around age 4 or 5, children perceive each image in a sequence as an isolated event: Their verbal "narration" typically just describes the contents of each image, particularly the referential entities like characters, and sometimes events, but without integration of sequential information across images (Berman 1988; Poulsen et al. 1979; Trabasso and Nickels 1992; Trabasso and Stein 1994).

Despite this, children as young as 3 do seem to understand causal relations between image sequences of different drawn objects when no continuity constraint is maintained. For example, one study showed that children as young as 3 were able to recognize that a sequence of pictures showing *cup-hammer-broken cup* implies that the cup was broken by the hammer

(Gelman, Bullock, and Meck 1980). Such results imply that children may be able to recognize causal events at younger ages. Indeed, younger children (2–3 years) have been observed as recognizing event sequencing earlier than what is indicated by sequential image comprehension (O'Connell and Gerard 1985), and children as young as 3 will describe dynamic events in the stories that they tell (Berman and Slobin 1994). Thus, what appears to be lacking is not the knowledge of causation or event structure, but the establishing of continuity of referential elements across images.

5.1.2 *Sequencing (4–6 Years Old)*

After children recognize referential entities and events, they begin to construe the sequential aspects of narrative images. Such observations go back at least to research by the developmental psychologist Jean Piaget and colleagues (Krafft and Piaget 1925; Margairaz and Piaget 1925). They argued that around age 7 or 8, children recognize that characters occurring across images were the same character at different states, rather than numerous different characters—i.e., the continuity constraint. Subsequent work observed children around age 6 or 7 could better follow continuity when the images included consistent background information (Schweitzer and Schnall 1970).

Contemporary research has lowered this age substantially and with some degree of stability across studies. Around age 4, children begin to understand cross-panel continuity and activity cues, reaching full understanding between ages 5 and 6 (Bornens 1990). These ages align with the shift from children describing sequential images in terms of isolated image units, to descriptions of sequential events (Berman 1988; Karmiloff-Smith 1985; Paris and Paris 2003; Poulsen et al. 1979; Shapiro and Hudson 1991; Trabasso and Nickels 1992; Trabasso and Stein 1994). Children between 4 and 6 also show increasing ability to select accurate sequence-ending panels, but with a wide range of variance (Zampini et al. 2017). In addition, kindergarteners (5 years old) are only moderately good at discerning the causes or consequences of the main event of a sequence, but significantly improve between ages 7 and 10 (Brown and French 1976).

Ages 4 to 6 also appear to be the lower end for proficiency in the picture arrangement task (Consortium 2015; Fivush and Mandler 1985; Kato 2006). The PAT is difficult for children aged 2 and 3, but they become more competent by 5 years old (Bornens 1990; Friedman 1990; Weist et al. 1997; Weist et al. 1999). Some work has shown that 4-year-olds can better arrange a previously seen sequence from memory better than a random sequence (Brown and Murphy 1975), and although they are reasonably good at describing the content of images from a picture sequence, children at 4 retain fairly poor recall of those images (Poulsen et al. 1979). Also, kindergartners can reconstruct logically ordered sequences better than random visual sequences, although recall of them continues to increase through age 7 (Brown 1975).

The ability to infer missing content also appears to have a lower limit around 5 years old, when children start being able to proficiently infer omitted images of a sequence (Schmidt and Paris 1978; Zampini et al. 2013; Zampini et al. 2017). Inferencing may also be modulated by whether sequences maintain continuity of characters across images (Kunen, Chabaud, and Dean 1987), and is not predicted by general intelligence or cognitive flexibility (Zampini et al. 2013). In addition, 4-year-olds have a harder time inferring about depicted sequential event information than children between 5 and 8 years old (Shaklee 1976). Children between ages 4 and 6 also have increasing ability to discern the primary story elements of a narrative picture sequence (Hayward, Schneider, and Gillam 2009; Poulsen et al. 1979; Silva and Cain 2019). General improvements in retelling ability and narrative comprehension occur between 4 and 9 years old (Milch-Reich et al. 1999; Paris and Paris 2001, 2003; Schneider, Hayward, and Dubé 2006). This comprehension varies little for children of different ethnic backgrounds who speak different languages, but who live in the same culture (Verhoeven and Vermeer 2006).

Although comprehension of sequencing grows proficient between ages 4 and 6, fluency continues developing with age. PAT performance improves into later ages (Brown 1975), reaching peak accuracy by the low teens (Nakazawa 2005, 2016), as does understanding of narrative coherence (Bingham, Rembold, and Yussen 1986), recall for story content (Milch-Reich et al. 1999; Nakazawa 2016; Nakazawa and Nakazawa 1993b), and both making bridging inferences about missing content (Nakazawa and Nakazawa 1993a; Schmidt, Paris, and Stober 1979) and predictive inferences about future content (Pallenik 1986; Paris and Paris 2003). Frequency of comic reading experience may modulate these abilities into later life (Nakazawa 1997, 2004).

Neurocognitive findings further support that by adolescence, brain responses appear comparable to those observed in adults. In a recent study, adolescents between 11 and 15 viewed short visual narratives with either a congruent or incongruent final panel (Manfredi et al. 2020). Incongruent final panels evoked large N400 effects (semantic access), followed by P600s (updating of a situation model), consistent with observations in adults, as described in Chapter Two (Cohn 2020b). In addition, by ages 10 to 12, children appear to have similar eye-movements in response to incongruities in visual sequences as adults, although children have more fixations and regressions (Martín-Arnal et al. 2019). This work suggests that, while still developing, older children begin converging on similar comprehension abilities as adults.

This trajectory for visual narrative development may also be modulated by exposure to visual narratives and the cultural factors that influence that exposure. For example, Bornens (1990) reported that comprehension of the continuity constraint was modulated by children's socioeconomic status, with those from less "culturally privileged" environments not reaching proficiency until 5 to 7, as opposed to the 4 to 5 age range of more well-to-do children. As with the cross-cultural findings discussed in the previous chapter, the delayed development for less privileged children may be attributable to less exposure to visual narratives like comics. This may also explain the older ages observed in early studies by Piaget and colleagues (Krafft and Piaget 1925; Margairaz and Piaget 1925) for when children begin understanding the continuity constraint in (i.e., ~7 to 8 years old instead of 4 to 6). Variance in exposure may also explain diverse findings between children from different cultures (Weist et al. 1997), and why comics reading experience modulates image sequencing abilities even between college-aged students (Lee and Armour 2016; Nakazawa 1997, 2004).

It is also interesting that Australian Aboriginal children with high exposure to a very different visual narrative system (sand drawings) have a comparable developmental trajectory as outlined here. Wilkins (1997/2016) described that Aboriginal Arrernte children by age 3 will produce the basic visual vocabulary of sand drawings, but will recognize more than they can produce. By 5 years old, they have a relatively full vocabulary, can start producing more complicated scenes, and begin conveying sequential narratives. By age 10, they will create sequential narratives, although they will not incorporate all the conventions of sequential structure until their teens. Thus, the development of comprehending these temporally sequential narratives drawn in sand share characteristics with the learning of spatially sequential visual narratives like comics or picture stories.

Finally, it is worth remembering that these abilities do not arise in isolation. During these early ages of development, children manifest many cognitive abilities that may or may not contribute to the understanding of sequential images. For example, Theory of Mind develops prior to or coinciding with the ages implicated for sequential image construal (Wellman, Cross, and Watson 2001). Certainly, the recognition of characters' intentions and goals are necessary for understanding stories, although it is unclear whether it would be required to assess basic aspects of referential continuity. This is complicated by the fact that many empirical tasks of Theory of Mind with young children use sequential images (Baron-Cohen, Leslie, and Frith 1986; Sivaratnam et al. 2012), without sensitivity to the developmental trajectory of understanding these stimuli. Visual narrative development also coincides with verbal narrative abilities (Berman and Slobin 1994; Trabasso and Nickels 1992; Trabasso and Stein 1994), which warrants more careful examination of the development of each modality on its own and the capacities that these modalities might share, which are often conflated.

5.2 Development of Sequential Image Comprehension

To get a better sense of the consistency of how children come to understand sequences of images, I conducted an analysis aggregating the findings across

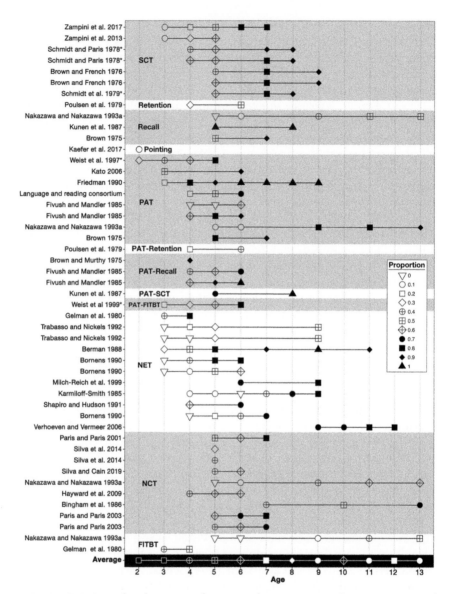

FIGURE 5.1 *Age-related aspects of sequential image comprehension aggregated from developmental studies using visual narratives, normalized into proportions and rounded (indicated by markers). All scores report unmanipulated sequence types (not including those using backwards, scrambled, or random sequences, etc.), and studies with mixed age groups here report the mean age per group (*). Grey and white bands and adjacent acronyms depict different tasks assessed (see Table 4.1 in Chapter Four). Repeated entries index different sub-experiments.*

various studies that could inform the development of sequential image understanding. I examined only the reported comprehension of "ordered" or coherent narrative sequences, excluding results involving manipulated sequences (scrambled, random, backward, etc.), and only the results for neurotypical populations (see Chapter Seven for research related to neurodiverse populations). When possible, I recorded the scores that were reported as proportions directly in the papers (usually "proportion correct" or "accuracy"). For papers providing only raw scores, I calculated proportions by dividing raw scores by total possible correct (as stated in their Results or Methods sections). For mixed age groups, I averaged the mean age per group. This analysis originally appeared in Cohn (2020a), where the raw data is provided in the Supplementary Materials.

Figure 5.1 summarizes the results of several studies using visual narrative tasks by transforming raw scores into percentages and rounding the numbers where needed. Despite the wide range of methods and inquiries, a consistent pattern of age-related effects can be observed. Overall, proficiency rises from age 2 through age 8, with a crucial shift occurring between ages 4 and 6. After this, average scores decline, partially because the complexity of these studies is adjusted based on the relative ages being tested. This age-related trajectory is also striking because many of these studies claim to investigate different aspects of cognition—narrative comprehension, sequential reasoning, temporal cognition, causal inference, etc.—yet the age-related task results remain consistent. This suggests that at least some aspect of the findings throughout is due to fluency in the visual narratives used in the tasks themselves, which is an interpretation offered by few of the many studies analyzed.

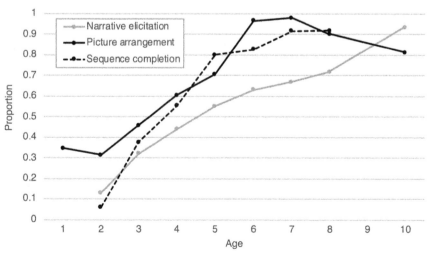

FIGURE 5.2 *Averaged performance on three tasks related to visual narrative comprehension (data in Figure 5.1) across different ages of children.*

This trajectory is further clarified by averaging the scores across studies for particular tasks. I therefore calculated averages for the scores in the most prevalent tasks from Figure 5.1: the sequence completion task (SCT), picture arrangement tasks (PAT), and narrative elicitation tasks (NET). Figure 5.2 plots these averaged values, which further highlights the consistent increase in proficiency across ages. As discussed earlier, the crucial period appears to be between ages 4 and 6 when children begin to respond more proficiently (passing 50 percent performance) and then approach peak performance in these tasks. Nevertheless, it should be apparent that most of these tasks have no "jump" in performance at any particular age, suggesting that a particular capacity suddenly "switched on." Rather, there is a gradual increase in proficiency across ages for each task, despite finally reaching more consistent performance in tasks after age 5. This suggests that recognition of continuity belongs to a process of ongoing development that progresses incrementally, rather than an ability that "switches on" at a particular age. As such, it is one part of a broader developmental trajectory for understanding (and producing) the various structures that comprise visual languages.

5.2.1 *Developmental Stages of Visual Narrative Comprehension*

While more dedicated research is needed to further clarify these findings, the results in these studies implicate various stages in the development of sequential image understanding. Speculatively, the learning trajectory described earlier implies that visual narrative comprehension develops in ways similar to the semantic aspects of processing discussed in Chapter Two. This prospective developmental trajectory is summarized in Table 5.1, along with its potential correspondence to aspects of cognitive processing.

At early ages (2–4), children first recognize referential and event information in individual images. Because this recognition involves identifying the relevant information in images and mapping this graphic surface to meanings, it may be characterized by the "information extraction" and "semantic access" stages of processing. Between 4 to 5 years old, when children begin to recognize the continuity and activity constraints, it implies further capacities for constructing a situation model by mapping information across panels. This further develops into the ability to update a model when confronted with discontinuous information, such as when inference is needed to resolve absent information in a sequence.

It should be noted that this timeline of development is at least somewhat similar to that of verbal narrative abilities (Berman and Slobin 1994; Trabasso and Stein 1997). This overlap implies the potential for domain-general mechanisms in narrative processing. However, given that much of the research on verbal narrative development has been based on elicitation tasks asking children to describe visual narratives (Burris and Brown 2014), understanding of verbal narrative development may be confounded by assessment tools using the visual modality. For example, one comparative study found that both kindergartners (mean age 5.58) and second graders (mean age 7.81) retold fewer story elements from purely pictorial stories than oral stories or those that combined pictures and an oral story (Schneider and Dubé 2005). In addition, similarities between verbal and visual narrative development would not explain the lack of the continuity constraint across *images* in early ages and its subsequent recognition between ages 4 and 6. These modality-specific affordances would thus still need to be developed, regardless of shared comprehension mechanisms across modalities. Therefore, teasing out the domain-general and modality-specific aspects of narrative development are necessary in future research.

It is also worth noting that, in this development, the continuity and activity constraints do not seem to arise from aspects of perceptual discrimination alone. Cognitive abilities related to the perception of real-world scenes develop substantially earlier than for picture understanding. Children are already able to discriminate basic percepts at birth and can perceive variation in visual features across objects within their first months (Johnson 2013). Scene contexts can aid visual attention by children's second year (Helo et al. 2017). Even by 15 months old, infants have been observed to be able to detect subtle referential *dis*continuity between objects in sequentially presented photographed scenes (Duh and Wang 2014). If visual narratives were grounded in processing of vision alone,

TABLE 5.1 Estimated developmental trajectory of visual narrative comprehension, along with corresponding aspects of processing

Age of onset	Comprehension abilities	Cognitive mechanisms
~2–3	Single image referential understanding entities and events	Information extraction (mapping form to meaning) and semantic access
~3–5	Single image referential relations and temporal events	Information extraction (mapping form to meaning) and semantic access
~4–6	Recognition of relationships across panels; continuity and activity constraints	Mental model construction and mapping (form-meaning mappings across images)
~5–12	Recognition of inferential relationships across panels	Mental model updating (inference)

such perception of spatial discontinuity would be the basis for the continuity and activity constraints. Yet, proficiency in these constraints does not become developed until age 4 at the earliest—several years after this perceptual discrimination—and these constraints appear to be modulated by exposure to visual narratives. This implies that recognition of drawn sequences of images require fluency and development beyond that of basic perception alone.

In the previous chapter, we discussed findings where adults from different cultures had difficulty comprehending the sequencing of sequential images. However, they could still mostly recognize the meaning of the content of the images. Relative to this developmental trajectory, this implies that such individuals reached the levels of picture understanding (although, see Arbuckle 2004; de Lange 2000; Goldsmith 1984) whereby they could do information extraction and semantic access. However, they did not reach the level of fluency where they could connect meaning across images and use this information to build a situation model.

The developmental progression discussed so far relates to how children come to construe meaning from a sequence of narrative images. As implied by Table 5.1, these properties largely relate to the processing of the semantic level of representation described in Chapter Two. However, as was argued before, a narrative level of representation functions to organize this semantic information. What then of the development of this narrative structure?

Developmental findings on narrative structural development (as defined in Chapter Two) is less forthcoming than that of semantic processing. This is because research has primarily targeted how children make meaning of visual narratives (semantics), rather than how they recognize the conventional patterns organizing those meanings (narrative). This is partially a consequence of much of the literature discussed earlier coming from studies that use visual narratives to ostensibly investigate other aspects of cognition (Theory of Mind, temporal cognition, etc.), rather than to examine the understanding of image sequences themselves. While these findings may implicate narrative structural development as well, such findings would be clearer if tasks like the PAT or SCT expressly coded or manipulated the properties of the narrative structure (e.g., Cohn 2014c).

Recent work has begun looking at comprehension of visual sequences characterized by their narrative structures. A study compared the eye-movements of children (10–12 years old) and adults in short comic strips which were characterized by Visual Narrative Grammar (Martín-Arnal et al. 2019). Strips compared climactic Peak or Release panels that were either coherent or incoherent, with characters switching in their thematic roles (i.e., the doer and receiver of actions became suddenly reversed). Overall, children looked more and longer at panels than adults in the coherent sequences and had more regressions within coherent Peaks than Releases. The number of fixations increased for both groups for incoherent panels of both types. Such findings suggest that fluent older children comprehend visual narratives comparably to adults, although such processing takes children longer than adults.

Despite the insights of this study, further research is needed into the development of narrative structure. As an alternative to looking for evidence of narrative structure development in studies of how children understand visual narratives, we can also look to studies of children producing visual narratives, where their acquisition of patterns may be more apparent. We turn to this next.

5.3 Development of Visual Narrative Production

How might we characterize children's development of producing visual narratives? While various studies have investigated children's ability to produce visual narratives, few have analyzed such creations in such a way as to generalize them into a developmental trajectory. This is compounded because comprehension and production skills may be asymmetrical—one may be able to read a comic, but not draw one (Stoermer 2009).

The production of sequential images must also be situated within the trajectory of drawing more broadly (for details, see Cohn 2012a; Willats 2005; Wilson and Wilson 2010). Within Visual Language Theory, "learning to draw", would characterize "acquiring a visual lexicon" by which a person can convey information graphically. That is, learning how to draw involves acquiring the various graphic patterns that constitute a person's drawing capacity. In general, children start with scribbling (1–3 years old) and using outlines to map drawn regions to conceptual volumes (3–8 years). These stages are often characterized by children creating what might appear to be odd images—figures with too many legs, "folded out" drawings showing all sides of a house at once, etc. These representations are guided by various conceptual heuristics, rather than attempts at showing visual realism (Wilson and Wilson 2010). Eventually, children no longer use lines to depict the border of regions, but rather to depict contours and edges (8–11 years old), characterized by T-junctions that imply one object is placed in front of another object (e.g., Willats 2005).

This trajectory may reflect development without factoring in cultural exposure to and practice with a graphic system. There appear to be no models of drawing development that yet take into account the influence of exposure and imitation (or lack thereof) to a visual language. Thus, ages at which various "stages" of drawing development occur may thus differ with such experience (Cohn 2012a; Cox 1998; Cox et al. 2001; Toku 2001a; Wilkins 1997/2016; Wilson 1988, 1999, 2016). Without exposure and practice, children's ability to learn to draw appears to stagnate around puberty, suggesting a critical learning period for drawing development similar to that of language development (Cohn 2012a).

These ages characterize the growth of how children become proficient in the graphic structures of creating individual drawings (a visual lexicon). As will be seen later, and hinted in the review of comprehension earlier, proficiency in creating *sequences* of images runs concurrent to these abilities to create individual images. This again suggests that these structures are organized in parallel, as in the model in Chapter One, rather than in a serial way (e.g., if skills for creating individual images preceded sequencing ability). This is also important because it implies that a child may develop these capacities independently and/or at different paces. Other than the need for at least a basic visual lexicon within a sequence, a child could potentially develop the ability to competently draw images without being able to string them together, or they could develop an ability to convey coherent sequences even without complex units (such as with stick figures).

Consideration of a developmental trajectory for drawing in the context of visual narratives is also important because unintelligible scribbles may still have meaningful intent. In dissertation research by Lauren Davi Silver (2000), she asked 3- and 5-year-olds to "retell" a videoed story through drawing with the intent to examine their capacities for creating visual narratives. Although many 3-year-olds produced what appeared to be incomprehensible scribbles, they still assigned them with intended meaning. Yet, in line with the comprehension findings described above, 3-year-olds largely draw an inventory of characters, rarely depicting them in events or including spatial locations. This content also was not connected across sequences, and with few cues of any progression of time. In contrast, 5-year-olds moderately depicted temporality in their images, with a mean of 1.44 panels per narrative, reflecting a higher rate of juxtaposing images than 3-year-olds, who produced a mean of 1.03 panels. Thus, both ages both produced fairly short sequences, if at all.

Differences in sequencing also appear between older groups. As described in the previous chapter, Brent and Marjorie Wilson studied children's ability to create narrative sequences of images around the world. Of most interest here is an analysis of Egyptian village children with minimal exposure to visual narratives. As described in the last chapter, when asked to draw a story into an empty six-panel grid, nearly all the 9-year-old village children produced unconnected isolated images, while only half of 12-year-olds produced visual sequences, although most with simple linear progressions (Wilson 2016).

Similar findings were reported in a study of 8-year-old Greek children, which found minimal examples of sequencing when asking children to draw a story, instead finding more drawings of individual images (Labitsi 2007). In exercises with 9- to 13-year-old children drawing visual narratives, Cox (1999) described that in early stages children had "fairly primitive" cohesive devices, and captions were necessary to maintain a "continuous narrative." Finally, an unpublished study by Durant (1981) found that 85 percent of the children aged 11–13 chose to draw a story-prompt using a single frame, while adolescents aged 15–17 chose equally between one, four, or six panel sequences (cited in Smith 1985). Altogether, these findings reinforce an interaction between age and exposure, here in the context of producing visual narratives.

The shift to sequencing pictures to tell stories occurs between 5 and 7 years old (Wilson and Wilson 1979a, 1982). With exposure to comics, children can produce complex conventions reproduced in visual narratives, like framing and narrative patterning (Wilson 1974). Wilson and Wilson (1979b) found that 9- and 12-year-old American children changed the framing of a scene (e.g., full view to a close up) on average about once in a six-panel story, although 6-year-olds rarely did, a trait attributed to exposure with reading comics. Greater exposure to and practice with visual narratives leads to earlier proficiency: Nearly all 6-year-old Japanese children can produce coherent visual narratives, and complex framing changes are observed across most panels drawn by Japanese 12-year-olds (Wilson 1988). Similar maturation in sequencing and layout has been observed from age 8 to 11 for a Korean child (Kim 2008).

Consider the sequences in Figure 5.3, which were made by a 7-year-old Japanese boy, clearly using the visual style of the Japanese Visual Language used in manga. The sequence in Figure 5.3a shows a consistent repeated composition and figures (i.e., continuity) with a clear narrative arc that climaxes in the final panel (where the mouse-friend of the boy smashes a piggy-bank, much to his surprise). The sequence in Figure 5.3b has much more complex framing and structures. The framing in each panel changes, with the first two panels showing the subjective viewpoint of the boy looking at the mouse through his camera. In the second panel, the viewpoint even zooms in to show the crumbs in the mouse's mouth that signal that he ate the boy's cake. Both sequences show clear narrative arcs. Note also that both sequences maintain a vertical layout, characteristic of Japanese yonkoma (four-panel) manga.

Compare these short sequences to those in Figure 5.4, which were produced by American-Dutch sisters living in the Netherlands, who also frequently read and draw comics. Both sequences maintain clear referential continuity, vary the attentional framing of the panels, crop information out of view, and use row-based grid layouts. Figure 5.4a was produced by an 11-year-old girl, with stylistic aspects of manga such as head-shapes and eyes. This sequence uses a clear narrative arc, but also uses distinct modifiers: The second row uses a type of conjunction listing off actions (Cohn 2015), which here shows the "llama causes drama" by creating mischief. This is a clearly defined narrative clause which is reinforced through the layout, by comprising its own row and using only lines to divide the panels, unlike the normative gutters separating the other panels. Thus, this sequence shows clear hierarchic constituency and narrative roles, along with interfaces between the narrative and layout.

Consider also Figure 5.4b, produced by a 9-year-old girl. Here, the graphic representations remain as simple stick figures, along with clear

FIGURE 5.3 *Comic strips drawn by a 7-year-old Japanese boy using sophisticated narrative structure.*

morphology like radial lines and upfixes. Yet, the structure again has a fairly lengthy and coherent narrative (of a man who almost steps on a littler person, who is then picked up and they become "BFFs!"). Again, the layout reinforces the content, evident in the smaller second panel for the smaller person, and the large final panel to emphasize the climactic outcome.

Overall, these examples from Figure 5.3 and Figure 5.4 demonstrate the complexity that can appear in children's visual narratives with exposure to reading and drawing comics. So far as I know, none of these children received active lessons in drawing comics. Yet, all of them maintain conventionalized features from comics (style, morphology), and all use a range of sophisticated narrative features. Such aspects of structure can appear even at relatively young ages given what research thus far suggests regarding when children can comprehend visual sequences (Figure 5.3). In addition, such proficiency for visual sequencing may be independent or parallel to proficiency for visual representations, as in the stick figures in Figure 5.4b.

Additional work has examined the production abilities displayed by children and adolescents when directly taught how to draw comics. This work shows that explicit instruction and guidance can enhance proficiency

FIGURE 5.4 *Single page comics using robust narrative sequencing drawn by American-Dutch sisters a) Kaylee Spenader (age 11) and b) Kiki Spenader (age 9). Reproduced with permission.*

seemingly beyond passive exposure (Bitz 2004a, b). In dissertation research by Mary Stoermer (2009), she found that 7- and 8-years-old students could develop complex stories with clear narrative arcs and developed backstories, although there was wide variability across students. Nevertheless, they often had to be "coached image by image in order for the comic to be readable" (Stoermer 2009: 191), particularly for correction of continuity errors across frames. In addition, they did "not 'naturally' understand or invent comic book conventions" (Stoermer 2009: 86), and using templates allowed students to bootstrap sequencing abilities beyond what they created without teacher intervention. Children were also observed to dissociate their drawing abilities for individual versus sequential images. For example, they sometimes abandoned the stylistic detail that they would use if drawing a single image in favor of even more simplistic drawings in sequential storytelling.

Extensive instructional research has been undertaken with children by Sylvia Pantaleo. Her case studies of students' visual narratives describe that 8- and 9-year-old children can adopt complex aspects of paneling from comics, such as manipulating the size, shape, and semantics of panel frames, and they may even play with meta-knowledge about frames, such as narratively breaking their borders (Pantaleo 2013b). Some children by age 12 can be observed to use fairly sophisticated narrative structure, such as using zoom panels as modifiers and alternation patterns that flip back and forth between elements in sequencing (Pantaleo 2015). They can consciously manipulate sequences' framing, point-of-view (Pantaleo 2012b, 2013a), and narrative "rhythm" (Pantaleo 2019), and they may also create complex embedding of metafictional narration (Pantaleo 2011, 2012a).

Altogether, while there are various interesting studies of how children create sequential visual stories, the developmental trajectory of visual narrative production remains understudied and a wide range of variability in proficiencies are observed across ages. This literature does suggest that greater proficiency comes either through non-explicit exposure or through direct instruction in the conventions of visual narratives. Such findings reinforce the importance of exposure to and practice with visual narratives on proficiency.

5.4 Conclusion

To summarize, the study of how children understand a sequence of images is scattered across a wide body of literature, mostly aimed at studying other aspects of cognition. Yet, when the insights from this research are combined, they suggest that visual narrative comprehension develops incrementally, with a crucial shift from understanding individual to sequential images occurring between roughly 4 and 6 years of age. Such developmental timelines may be modulated by a learner's environment, particularly their exposure to a visual language (i.e., the systems used in comics and picture stories that a child may gain experience with both through use and by having them demonstrated). The timeline for children's ability to produce a sequence of images is less forthcoming, but cross-cultural evidence again suggests a strong role of exposure in creating conditions for proficiency at younger ages. Further research exploring these issues is clearly needed to better understand these modality-specific developmental trajectories and how they interact with the development of other expressive modalities (like speech) and other cognitive processes (like Theory of Mind or temporal cognition).

CHAPTER SIX

Variation in Fluent Comprehenders

Thus far we've discussed how the understanding of narrative visual sequences requires exposure to and practice with visual narratives like comics or picture books, and this capacity for comprehension develops across a trajectory of learning. Such findings go against the Sequential Image Transparency Assumption, and instead imply the need for learning and development of culturally relative structures. Now we will further examine this fluency to ask: What is comprehension like among people who receive this exposure and development? Once a threshold is reached, is fluency stable, or is there variation among people who are already fluent? While most cross-cultural and developmental studies have done little to measure such expertise, two threads of research have designed procedures for examining visual narrative proficiency: the Chiba University Comic Comprehension Test (CCCT) and the Visual Language Fluency Index (VLFI). Along with other studies examining proficiency, these threads of research indeed imply that visual narrative fluency may be variable even among experienced readers of visual narratives.

6.1 Chiba University Comic Comprehension Test (CCCT)

Since the early 1990s, Japanese developmental psychologist Jun Nakazawa has examined manga comprehension and development, and founded one of the first, if not *the* first, dedicated psychological research program related to these materials. Nakazawa's battery of experiments include simply asking for interpretations of image-elements; questionnaires asking about recall and comprehension; a picture arrangement task using actual manga strips; and a fill-in-the-blank inference task asking for participants to say what happened in a narrative sequence where content was deleted. Participants' responses are compared with the original comics. Together, these tasks comprise the *Chiba University Comic Comprehension Test* (CCCT) by which Nakazawa has assessed general proficiency in sequential image understanding (for reviews in English, see Nakazawa 2005, 2016).

Nakazawa's studies consistently show that comprehension of sequential images increases with age, from kindergarteners (~5 years) through eighth graders (~14 years), in line with the findings discussed in the previous chapter. Even higher scores have been observed for college students than these younger people (Nakazawa and Nakazawa 1993a, b). However, studies with individuals ranging in age from their 20s through 60s suggest that age alone does not modulate performance, and frequent manga readers both within and between age groups demonstrated increased recall and comprehension (Nakazawa 1997). In addition, manga reading comprehension correlated with students' interest and achievement in language arts and social studies, but not with art classes (Nakazawa 2002b).

Higher CCCT scores also arose for individuals from Japan, where comic reading is ubiquitous, compared to those from the United States, where comic reading is less prevalent across the general culture (Nakazawa and Shwalb 2012). Panel sequencing has further shown dramatic differences between college-aged participants who had experience reading manga versus those who did not (Lee and Armour 2016). Nevertheless, given that the CCCT uses Japanese manga as materials, cross-cultural findings associated with the CCCT may also be crossed with comprehension of Japanese manga specifically, rather than general visual narrative fluency.

Finally, Nakazawa (2002a) conducted one of the first reported studies using eye-tracking to analyze comic reading processes by contrasting the eye-movements of an experienced and inexperienced manga reader. He observed that the experienced manga reader had smoother eye-movements across panels of a page than a less-experienced manga reader. In addition, despite having a higher rate of skipping over panels and balloons, the experienced reader had better overall story comprehension and recall than the inexperienced reader. By comparison, the inexperienced reader instead focused more on the text than the images, and overall spent more time reading the page than the experienced reader, even though it led to worse comprehension and recall.

Recent work has corroborated Nakazawa's findings. An eye-tracking study with twelve experienced and twelve inexperienced readers showed that experienced readers were more efficient and focused more on images than inexperienced readers (Zhao and Mahrt 2018). Inexperienced comic readers had more and longer eye fixations across wordless comic pages than experienced readers, Meanwhile, inexperienced readers comprehended multimodal text-image comics better than purely pictorial visual narratives. These results are also consistent with findings that children have more and longer fixations on the images in wordless comic strips than adults, along with an increased amount of regressive eye-movements, i.e., looks returning to previously viewed content (Martín-Arnal et al. 2019). Altogether, these studies imply that proficiency with comics leads to more efficient processing of the image content of visual narratives, with less reliance on the text within multimodal interactions.

In sum, Nakazawa's research marked an important start to investigating the role of experience in visual narrative understanding. This work suggested that both age and experience with visual narratives modulates the comprehension of sequential images, even among experienced readers.

6.2 Visual Language Fluency Index (VLFI)

In my own research examining visual narrative processing, we have designed measurements of comic reading frequency to assess proficiency. This began in a study of comic page layouts that I originally ran in 2004—what was in fact the first experiment I ever conducted. I had observed that collaborators of mine had difficulty knowing "which way to go" when navigating certain arrangements of comic page layouts. However, these confusions only seemed to occur for people who were infrequent readers of comics. This pushed me to examine whether a larger sample of people would order arrangements of panels in a page layout in similar ways, and whether their experience with comics influenced these choices. So, a simple measure of expertise was included within the study that asked how often participants read comics and manga. Indeed, I found that experience with comics modulated various choices for how participants chose to order the panels in layouts, as did their experience with American comics compared to Japanese manga (Cohn 2013a). These findings gave initial clues that experience might factor into the way in which comics are comprehended, and indeed, similar, albeit weaker, findings of expertise with regard to page layout also appeared in later studies (Cohn and Campbell 2015).

Based on these findings, I recognized the need for a consistent measure of expertise in my research on visual narrative comprehension. I thus developed the *Visual Language Fluency Index* (VLFI—pronounced "vil-fee") questionnaire, which asks participants about their frequency of reading and drawing comics both currently and while growing up. Participants are asked to rate their frequency of reading comic books, comic strips, graphic novels, and Japanese manga, frequency of drawing (1–7 scale), and ratings of comic reading and drawing expertise (1–5 scale). The VLFI questionnaire is depicted in Figure 6.1.

From these self-assessed ratings, a *VLFI score* is then computed, weighing the metric towards comic reading comprehension, giving an additional "bonus" for production, since more individuals typically read comics than draw them (as reinforced by answers on VLFI questionnaires). This formula is as follows:

$$\left(\begin{array}{l}\textit{Mean Comic Reading Freq.}\\ \times \textit{ Comic reading expertise}\end{array}\right) + \left(\frac{\textit{Comic Drawing Freq.} \times \textit{Drawing Ability}}{2}\right)$$

This formula yields a low fluency VLFI score around 8 or below, average around 12, and high around 22, although the maximum possible is 52.5. These idealized values are calculated by inserting various sample values into the formula—such as all middle values, or ratings where only one type of comic is at maximum and others are lower. Nevertheless, the VLFI scores indicated by most experiments support these values and have indeed yielded scores in the "average" range, which will be discussed further.

The VLFI first appeared in a publication with two experiments measuring response times and event-related brain potentials (Cohn et al. 2012), although it did not yet have a codified name or the acronym "VLFI." By the time of this first published account reporting the VLFI in analysis, well over a dozen experiments had actually included it in the experimental methods, and these studies were eventually published. VLFI scores have since been used as a standard protocol in the Visual Language Theory research program (Cohn 2013b), and resources for using the VLFI are available online at: http://www.visuallanguagelab.com/resources.html

While VLFI scores have not received any dedicated tests of their validity, they consistently correlate with many aspects of visual narrative processing, as described in Table 6.1. In behavioral research, VLFI scores correlate with both conscious decisions from participants (ratings, segmentation) and unconscious actions (accuracy, response times, reading times). When participants are presented with "upfixes"—individual images of faces with various elements floating above their heads (stars, gears, fish)—more experienced comic readers are more discriminating to unconventional visual morphology than less experienced readers (Cohn, Murthy, and Foulsham 2016). In tasks where participants were asked to divide a narrative sequence into subparts, greater experience correlated with various factors related to segmentation, including an easier perceived effort for making these segmentations, an advantage which diminished as more segmentations were made (Cohn and Bender 2017). In another study that presented panels of a sequence at rapid speeds, higher VLFI scores correlated with participants' ability to better tolerate sequences where panels incongruously switched positions in the sequence (Hagmann and Cohn 2016).

Experience might also lead to changes in the speed at which participants read or respond to image content within sequences. Experienced readers are faster to react to specific "target" panels within sequences when they search for particular panels in sequences that violate the narrative and/or semantic relations across images (Cohn et al. 2012). Similarly, correlations between faster viewing times of panels and higher VLFI scores implied that comic reading experience better enabled readers to infer prior missing content (Cohn and Wittenberg 2015). Other studies have similarly found that more experienced readers read particular comic panels faster and have an easier

1. Using the following scale, on average, how often per week do/did you…? (place a whole number in the square)

Never ----------------------------------Sometimes----------------------------------Always
    1   2   3   4   5   6   7

	Currently (mark 1 – 7)	While growing up (mark 1 – 7)	Which is your favorite? (mark with "X")
…read text-only books for enjoyment			DO NOT MARK HERE
…watch movies			DO NOT MARK HERE
…watch cartoons/anime			DO NOT MARK HERE
…read comic books			
…read comic strips			
…read graphic novels			
…read Japanese comics (manga)			
…draw comics			

2. How would you rate your expertise with reading comics (of any sort)? (Mark "X" once in each row)

	Above average (5)	Slightly above average (4)	Average (3)	Slightly below average (2)	Below average (1)
Currently					
While growing up					

3. How would you rate your drawing ability? (Mark "X" once in each row)

	Above average (5)	Slightly above average (4)	Average (3)	Slightly below average (2)	Below average (1)
Currently					
While growing up					

4. How old were you when you began reading comics? _____ Drawing comics? _____

FIGURE 6.1 *The Visual Language Fluency Index questionnaire. Resources for the VLFI are available online at: http://www.visuallanguagelab.com/resources.html.*

time comprehending them (Foulsham and Cohn forthcoming). In contrast, another study examining motion lines showed that experienced readers viewed panels in a sequence slower when they contained anomalous motion lines (Cohn and Maher 2015), implying that the violations were more impactful when participants were more familiar with comics' conventions.

As in the studies comparing groups of experienced and inexperienced comic readers, VLFI scores have also been shown to interact with readers eye-movements. In a study comparing participants' eye-movements across a variety of comic pages with layout arrangements of varying complexity, participants with higher VLFI scores were reported to have more consistent reading paths than lower-scoring VLFI participants (Bateman, Beckmann, and Varela 2018). An additional marginal effect was shown for higher VLFI scores associating with larger saccades within panels, particularly for the reading of text (Kirtley et al. 2018). Finally, in our study of eye-movements (Foulsham, Wybrow, and Cohn 2016) a correlation between VLFI and regressions went unreported in the published manuscript (it was discovered in exploratory analyses after publication). We found that in the contrast between wordless normal and scrambled sequences, participants with higher VLFI scores had fewer regressions (looks backward), suggesting again that they better tolerated the incongruities of the sequence than less frequent comic readers.

Beyond behavioral research, VLFI scores have been observed to correlate with direct measurements of the brain using event-related potentials (ERPs). In these cases, we found that VLFI scores correlated with the brainwave responses to the contrast *between* different types of stimuli (i.e., the differential ERP "effect"). For example, higher VLFI scores led to greater differences in the brain responses between people who viewed fully scrambled sequences and those with only a narrative structure but no meaning (Cohn et al. 2012). Larger brainwave amplitude differences were also associated with larger VLFI scores for contrasts involving interactions between narrative and inferential processing (Cohn and Kutas 2015). VLFI scores also modulated brain responses to panels where actions used different types of motion lines (Cohn and Maher 2015), specifically suggesting that more experienced comic readers had an easier time processing the actions in panels where motion lines were omitted (or conversely, that processing by less experienced readers were further aided by normal motion lines and further impaired by anomalous lines).

Finally, recent research has hinted that structures found in particular visual narrative systems can modulate processing beyond the "general fluency" suggested by the overall aggregated VLFI score. An ERP study examined processing of a narrative pattern—i.e., Environmental-Conjunction—that appears more frequently in Japanese manga than in

TABLE 6.1 Published studies on visual narrative processing reporting interactions between scores from the Visual Language Fluency Index questionnaire and behavioral or neurocognitive measures

Paper reference	Measure	Processing type	Effect of fluency
(Cohn et al. 2012)	Reaction times	Narrative and semantic structure	Faster RTs for greater fluency
	ERP effects	Narrative structure	Larger amplitude ERP effects for greater fluency
(Cohn and Kutas 2015)	ERP effects	Narrative and inference	Larger amplitude ERP effects for greater fluency

Paper reference	Measure	Processing type	Effect of fluency
(Cohn and Kutas 2017)	ERP effects	Narrative patterning	Different ERP components for familiarity with narrative pattern
(Cohn and Maher 2015)	ERP effects	Morphological incongruity	Larger amplitude ERP effects for greater fluency
	Self-paced viewing times	Morphological incongruity	Longer viewing times to anomalies for greater fluency
(Cohn and Wittenberg 2015)	Self-paced viewing times	Inference	Shorter viewing times for greater fluency
(Foulsham and Cohn forthcoming)	Self-paced viewing times	Narrative comprehension	Faster viewing of panels and easier comprehension for greater fluency
(Cohn and Bender 2017)	Segmentation choices	Narrative segmentation	Greater fluency correlated with segmentation properties and ease of segmentation
(Hagmann and Cohn 2016)	Accuracy	Narrative structure	Greater tolerance of incongruity for greater fluency
(Cohn, Murthy, and Foulsham 2016)	Ratings	Morphological familiarity and interpretations	Less tolerance of incongruity for greater fluency
(Cohn forthcoming)	Ratings	Narrative comprehension	More fluency associated with higher coherence ratings
(Bateman, Beckmann, and Varela 2018)	Eye movements	Layout	More fluency associated with more consistent reading paths across panels
(Kirtley et al. 2018)	Eye movements	Text-image relationships	Larger saccades within panels for greater fluency

comics from the United States or Europe (Cohn 2013b, 2019b). Across all participants, this narrative pattern evoked neural responses related to both combinatorial processing (anterior negativities) and mental model updating (P600) (Cohn and Kutas 2017). A regression analysis then found that the only significant predictor was participants' frequency of reading Japanese manga "while growing up" and these ERP effects varied based on this experience. These results implied that participants' specific reading experience modulated their response to this pattern, beyond general exposure.

6.2.1 Aggregated Analysis of VLFI Scores

Given that VLFI scores have been used across studies of visual narrative comprehension for over 10 years, analysis of these questionnaires themselves can offer insights beyond just their relations to behavioral and neurocognitive measurements. Here, I analyzed the VLFI questionnaires of 1,927 participants, aggregated across thirty-two studies, including participants from both published and unpublished works. These participants came from in-lab studies in the United States (Boston, San Diego) and Europe (United Kingdom, The Netherlands), and from participants worldwide in studies run on the Internet. This sample contained an even number of participants who identified as female (949) and male (949), along with 29 who identified as "other" or did not provide a response. Participants had an average age of 26.72 (SD = 9.96), with a range from 18 to 78 years old.

Overall, participants had an average VLFI score of 15.16 (SD = 9.6), which is indeed in the predicted "average" range of the measurement, idealized to fall between 12 and 20. The highest VLFI score was a 50 (with 52.5 being the highest possible), and the lowest was a 1.5 (with 1 as the lowest possible). Participants identifying as male had a slightly higher average VLFI score (Mean = 17.8, SD = 9.97) than those identifying as female (Mean = 12.6, SD = 8.3), but still within the average range.

The initial findings of note are relationships between VLFI scores and various age measures. First, a positive correlation between participants' VLFI scores and age, as depicted in Figure 6.2a, suggested that older participants have greater self-rated expertise with comics and a higher frequency of reading them. Further aspects of age-related expertise are illustrated by breaking apart the VLFI score into its subscores for both current reading habits and while growing up. These subscores are calculated with the average of participants' ratings of expertise (1–5) multiplied by ratings of frequency of reading comics (1–7). This yields a score from 1 to 35. As depicted in Figure 6.2b, these scores for adulthood and while growing up highly correlate with each other, indicating that greater expertise/experience with comics while growing up leads to subsequent expertise while in adulthood. Phrased another way, people who more frequently read comics while growing up are more likely to also read them later in life.

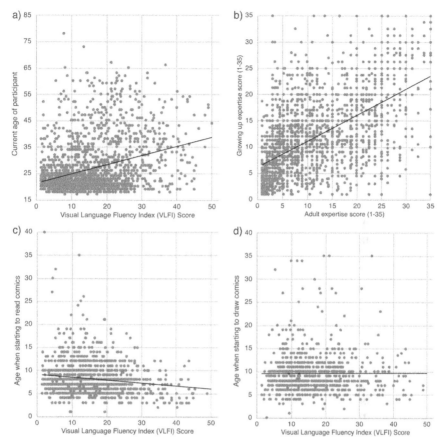

FIGURE 6.2 *Relationships between a) VLFI scores and age of 1,927 participants from experiments on visual language, and c) age that participants started reading comics and d) drawing comics. Separately, (b) shows the relationship between their subscores for expertise and frequency currently compared to while they were growing up.*

Nevertheless, participants consistently showed a drop off in their "current" reading habits from those "while growing up." When examining the reported scores for both comic books and comic strips, participants dropped a whole rating point from 4 to 3 in their reading frequency along a 7-point scale (a 14 percent decrease) between childhood reading habits and adulthood. It is noteworthy that, in contrast to this, frequency of reading manga actually increased across ages, with a slight .15 rating increase between age groups. This implies that manga inspire more consistency in reading habits as people age than comic books or strips.

The VLFI questionnaire also asks at what ages participants began reading and drawing comics. On average, participants started reading comics at age

8.24, with the lowest age often described as being "as early as I can remember." The average age for starting to draw comics was slightly later than this, at age 9.46. Roughly 35 percent of participants who responded for their age at drawing comics said that they never drew comics. It is noteworthy that these ages line up well with the developmental trajectory discussed in the previous chapter. There, it was argued that, given exposure, children typically become proficient in understanding a sequence of images by around age 6. So, an average age of 8 for starting to read comics implies a slight delay between gaining basic fluency and then engaging in comics, possibly preceded by other types of visual narratives like picture stories. Similarly, an average age of 9.5 for drawing comics implies that children gain experience comprehending the structures in comics before producing them.

Nevertheless, strong positive correlations between raw scores for comic reading experience and for drawing suggested that the more people read comics, the more likely they are to also draw them. Similar correlations between comic reading frequency and drawing ability suggested that people who read comics frequently (and thus draw more) also have a higher assessment of their drawing abilities.

The VLFI questionnaire also asks about habits for consuming other media, specifically books, movies, and cartoons. In fact, all ratings for engaging these media were roughly one-rating point higher than all scores for engagement with various types of comics. So, comics are the least consumed of all media questioned. However, as with comics, frequency of reading books and watching movies or cartoons also decreased by one rating point from consumption "while growing up" to their "current" frequency. It is also noteworthy that the frequency of all other media positively correlated with VLFI scores and individual comics-type frequency ratings. This implies that people who read comics frequently are also more likely to consume other media.

To further assess the relationships between the elements in the VLFI questionnaire, I entered the elements of the VLFI formula and associated questions into a Principal Component Analysis. This procedure informs us which elements might cluster together to form "principal components" that characterize the relations between variables.

This analysis revealed four principal components, which are depicted in Figure 6.3. The largest component (RC1), which accounts for most of the variability in the data, appears to involve the reading habits of comic books, strips, and graphic novels, along with age and ratings of current comic expertise. A second component (RC2) appears to cluster around participants' drawing habits, including all of their self-assessments of drawing ability and the rate at which they draw comics. The relative independence of this component is interesting in that it implies drawing habits do not interact much with comic reading habits. The third component (RC3) involves manga reading habits, both current and while growing up. Interestingly, this

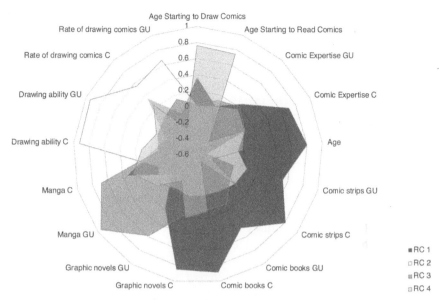

FIGURE 6.3 *Results from a Principal Component Analysis of 1,927 participants'*
VLFI questionnaires. "C" indicates assessments of current habits or expertise, while
"GU" indicates habits or expertise "while growing up."

component also included the rate at which participants read graphic novels
while growing up, implying there may be "book formatted" reading habits
across both manga and Western comics. Finally, a fourth component (RC4)
involved just two primary variables of the age that participants started to
read and draw comics.[1] All components were positively correlated with each
other.

Altogether, this analysis implies that certain aspects of comic reading
form identifiable relationships. These appear to be 1) general reading of
comics (books, strips) across the lifespan, 2) drawing habits, 3) manga
reading, and 4) the age at which one begins reading or drawing comics. As
illustrated by the other preceding analyses, these elements appear to have
relationships with each other as well. As further research progresses within
the Visual Language Theory research program, further assessment and
refinement of VLFI scores can be made, especially accounting for these
types of relations between reading habits and age.

6.3 Conclusions

Overall, this research shows that proficiency modulates processing even
among competent readers of visual narratives. This can vary across age and
frequency of reading comics. These offline, self-rated measurements of

frequency of comic reading are even capable of capturing differences across individuals' unconscious brain responses, which are direct measures of their cognitive processing. Such results imply that "exposure" to visual narratives is measurable and reliable for characterizing expertise effects even with surveys comprised of self-rated assessments.

While the CCCT and VLFI have been proven to be predictive measures of visual narrative proficiency, future research can better refine these measures. First, the VLFI form may be limited in its questions and aggregate scores. For example, the VLFI currently asks questions about only a few genres and culture-specific comics reading. Yet, research suggests that readership of culturally specific visual narratives (e.g., Japanese manga versus American superhero comics) may modulate comprehension beyond general fluency (Cohn and Kutas 2017). This implies that more specific questions related to other cultures' comics may be needed, as well as methods to balance these culture-specific fluencies with a general VLFI score.

Second, despite findings of age-related variance to comprehension, the VLFI asks about reading habits at different ages but does not incorporate such numbers into its formula (e.g., as multipliers for high versus low frequency periods of readership). These limitations to the VLFI suggest that changes to the VLFI algorithm and/or questionnaire might be able to capture even more nuance in the proficiency levels across participants. This is reinforced by the Principal Component Analysis, which identified the age of starting to read/draw comics as a distinct component, while also incorporating current age into the first component.

An additional limitation of the VLFI is that it measures participants' self-reported reading habits, and thus may vary from actual cognitive proficiencies. Given the generally stated nature of the measures, some people might over-estimate their frequency of reading habits and/or expertise levels, while others might under-estimate them. A remedy for this would be the development of a simple test battery, like the CCCT, that people could take to assess their fluency. Such a battery would run participants through a sequence of short experiments, the performance on which would aim to reliably generate a score to assess visual language fluency. Such a test battery would be useful if participants had little exposure or experience with comics and visual narratives specifically (low VLFI score), but still acquired fluency through contextual and cultural exposure. Or, the reverse: if high exposure to comics (high VLFI score) still yielded a fluency with divergent comprehension abilities (for example, due to neurodiversities, as discussed next chapter). A behavioral battery could also compensate for over- or under-estimation of expertise and readership of visual narratives, as in the VLFI.

Development and use of these metrics for visual narrative fluency are important for researchers to better assess the proficiency of their participants. For example, if studies are done about comics or visual narrative understanding, measures like the VLFI or others should be essential. This extends further to other studies using visual narratives to study other aspects of cognition, such as tests of Theory of Mind (Baron-Cohen, Leslie, and Frith 1986; Sivaratnam et al. 2012), sequential reasoning (Zampini et al. 2017), temporal cognition (Boroditsky, Gaby, and Levinson 2008), or discourse comprehension (Gernsbacher, Varner, and Faust 1990), among others. Without such measures, such experiments could face confounds in confirming the validity of their measures. However, with such measurements, we can further assess how visual narrative fluency interacts with these various other aspects of basic cognition.

Such measures are also helpful for assessing the degree to which comics and visual narratives may be useful in educational contexts. Visual language fluency may modulate how much children vary in whether they benefit from comics or multimodal visual narratives as educational materials. Fluency might also influence whether they like or dislike the materials in the first place. Without such measures, it may otherwise be harder to identify why children struggle or dislike what may be perceived as something beneficial for them. (However, fluency may be one of many reasons for why children may struggle or dislike something, but at least lack of fluency has an identifiable solution: teach them to become fluent.)

Indeed, one of the important questions related to visual language fluency is: Just what exactly is fluency modulating? It is likely that proficiency affects various aspects of basic cognition and various levels of structure across visual narrative processing. Teasing apart these factors can better help us understand the structure and processing of visual narratives themselves and in relation to other aspects of cognition. Such findings then also open up the door to investigating the potential benefits of visual language fluency on other domains. Does fluency with visual narratives lead to better reading comprehension abilities or spatial memory? Better reasoning or critical thinking skills? While some studies have begun to investigate this type of cross-domain transference, better understanding of visual language fluency, guided by measures of it, can propel such research forward.

CHAPTER SEVEN

Visual Narrative Comprehension in Neurodiverse and Cognitively Impaired Populations

The discussion so far suggests that typically developing humans have the capacity to understand and produce sequential images, but this ability is contingent on developing a fluency through exposure and practice with visual narratives in a culture. Under what circumstances then might this fluency be disrupted, such as among individuals who are not "neurotypical"? One reason to study neurodiverse individuals is that their processing styles can inform about how the comprehension system as a whole might be structured. For example, if people with a certain type of neurodiversity faces challenges with the comprehension of multiple modalities—such as both spoken and visual language processing—it can point towards domain-general mechanisms operating on both modalities. Conversely, if certain neurodiverse people struggle with normative language processing but retain typical visual narrative processing, it might show how these modalities differ.

By and large, much research on neurodiverse populations has assumed this latter situation, where visual materials, particularly visual narratives, are thought to circumvent deficits with verbal language. Cognitive psychologist Emily Coderre has described this idea as the *Visual Ease Assumption* (for review, see Coderre 2020). Because of this assumption, visual narratives have often been used with neurodiverse populations as a way to avoid known comprehension problems with language. However, the Visual Ease Assumption is a corollary of the Sequential Image Transparency Assumption (SITA), and thereby presumes that visual narratives require no expertise or proficiency to decode. As we have seen in the prior chapters, the SITA is unfounded, and indeed visual narratives require proficiency that is acquired from exposure to an external system. In addition, in studies of neurotypical adults, this proficiency seems to involve multifaceted neurocognitive machinery also implicated in other domains, particularly language processing.

Because of both the Visual Ease Assumption and the SITA, visual narratives have been a staple of clinical assessments. This is especially true of the picture arrangement task (PAT) which is included in general intelligence (IQ) tests (WAIS-IQ, WISC) and thereby also clinical assessments (Kaufman and Lichtenberger 2006; Wechsler 1981). Along with narrative elicitation tasks (NET), the PAT and variants of it are prevalently claimed to test a number of cognitive deficits, including from social intelligence, Theory of Mind (ToM), and sequential or causal reasoning, among others.

Indeed, several neurodiverse populations have demonstrated difficulties with visual narrative processing in these tasks. For example, poor performance on the PAT and/or NET is shown by individuals with:

- Dyslexia (Helland and Asbjørnsen 2003)

- Down's syndrome (Baron-Cohen, Leslie, and Frith 1986)

- Parkinson's disease (Beatty and Monson 1990; Tinaz, Schendan, and Stern 2008)

- Multiple sclerosis (Beatty and Monson 1994; Ouellet et al. 2010)

- Williams syndrome (Farran and Jarrold 2003; Gonçalves et al. 2010; Marini et al. 2010; Reilly et al. 2004; Stojanovik, Perkins, and Howard 2004)

As the PAT and NET are widely used, the overall number and scope of performance difficulties on these tasks is beyond what can be covered here. It is worth noting upfront that, like in the cross-cultural and developmental studies discussed in the previous chapters, rarely are the struggles with visual narratives attributed to proficiency with these materials themselves. Rather, in lieu of recognizing that visual narratives demand complex patterns and processing, difficulties with their comprehension are typically explained as related to generalized cognitive functions like those discussed earlier (possibly also reinforced by confirmation bias that these materials test the assumed cognitive function they aim to test).

Nevertheless, it is worth further examining a few populations documented to have challenges with processing both spoken/written language and visual narratives. Examining these populations is important given the arguments by Visual Language Theory that visual language and verbal language processing involves shared cognitive mechanisms. Below I highlight findings related to visual narrative processing particularly for individuals with neurodiversities such as Autism Spectrum Disorder (ASD), Schizophrenia Spectrum Disorders (SSD), and Developmental Language Disorder (DLD, formerly Specific Language Impairment), in addition to examining results from individuals with damage to their brains, as in aphasia.

7.1 Autism Spectrum Disorder

One particularly rich area of research using visual narratives has investigated individuals with Autism Spectrum Disorder (ASD), which is a neurodevelopmental disorder manifesting in deficits across domains, but often characterized by challenges with social communication and interaction, as well as with repetitive or restricted interests or behaviors. Deficits often manifest across other domains and individuals with ASD have also been observed to struggle with aspects of language processing, although it is no longer considered as diagnostic. For example, as many as 65 percent of individuals with ASD have been assessed as having challenges with reading comprehension (Jones et al. 2009; McIntyre et al. 2017). These "challenges" often manifest as difficulties identifying the main ideas of a text rather than specific details, and generating inferences that require integrating world knowledge (Happé and Frith 2006; Nuske and Bavin 2011). Individuals with ASD also have difficulties taking the perspective of characters in a text, which relates to broader challenges with ToM, which is the ability to recognize that other individuals have thoughts that are separate from one's own (Premack and Woodruff 1978).

Despite the documented issues with language processing, individuals with ASD have been said to do better with visual stimuli. Yet, theories of autism have often implicated general processing strategies which should not differentiate between modalities. For example, autism has been hypothesized as connected to a focus on more local information than a broader, global integration (Happé and Frith 2006), or to deficiencies with predictive processing more generally (Pellicano and Burr 2012; Sinha et al. 2014). Neither of these potential explanations should in principle vary between modalities, as they characterize domain-general aspects of processing.

Although motivated in part by the Visual Ease Assumption, advocates have argued that comics might confer an advantage to reading comprehension for individuals with ASD (Rozema 2015). Indeed, while anecdotal evidence comes from individuals with ASD who report greatly enjoying and reading comics, only a few studies have examined the reading habits of individuals with ASD and included comics. One survey found that individuals with ASD enjoyed fiction more than nonfiction, and comics and manga were included in this "fiction" category (Davidson and Ellis Weismer 2018). However, this study did not provide relative preferences for these visual narratives compared to non-multimodal textual works. Another survey using parental questionnaires reported that children with ASD enjoy reading comics more than neurotypical children—with over 90 percent of children who have ASD with language disorders reported as enjoying comics and

~80 percent of ASD children with normal language, compared to ~60 percent of neurotypical children (Lucas and Norbury 2018). In fact, comics were the only type of reading material (versus fictional and factual books, websites, and periodicals) which children with ASD preferred more than neurotypical children.

A recent analysis may shed more light on comic reading habits by individuals with ASD. When participants complete our studies, my collaborator Emily Coderre collects data from both the VLFI questionnaire as well as the Autism Quotient (AQ), a self-report measure of autistic traits (Baron-Cohen et al. 2001). Both of these measures yield scores, which were aggregated across the participants of several studies, resulting in forty-five individuals with ASD and sixty-six neurotypical individuals. She found that over the entire group, VLFI scores and AQ scores were positively correlated, suggesting that higher levels of autistic traits were related with greater comic reading fluency. A sub-analysis of the component scores of the VLFI provided further insight. Here, neurotypical participants overall reported reading text-only books (mean = 3.9 on a 1 to 7 scale) more often than individuals with ASD (M = 3.2), but the reverse was true for reading of various types of comics. While the numbers overall indicated low comic reading frequency, individuals with ASD more frequently read comics (averaged across types, M = 2.67) than neurotypical participants (M = 1.36). Combining all participants together also showed that these subscales correlated with AQ scores: Textual-book reading negatively correlated with AQ scores, while all types of comic reading were positively correlated with AQ scores. In other words, individuals who scored higher on having autistic traits were more likely to read comics and less likely to read textual books. Overall, these analyses suggest that individuals with autistic traits may have preferences for reading multimodal narratives like comics more than neurotypical individuals.

Is there evidence that visual languages might benefit comprehension for individuals with ASD? Some aspects of the visual vocabulary of visual languages may assist understanding. Individuals with ASD have been shown to have an easier time understanding the emotions of cartoony faces than photographs of faces (Rosset et al. 2008; Rosset et al. 2010), possibly because such drawings use a patterned visual vocabulary for conveying emotions. This would allow individuals to recognize the encoded "visual lexical item" for emotions, rather than need to assess the complexities of an actual human face. In addition, children with ASD can be taught to recognize that thought bubbles are representations of characters' thoughts (Parsons and Mitchell 1999), and these children subsequently scored better on false belief tasks that assess aspects of ToM (Wellman et al. 2002). Such a finding implies that thought bubbles within comics have the potential to aid people to recognize that others' have thoughts more generally. Comics may have other beneficial effects, as research has demonstrated that comics can help decrease loneliness and increase social interaction for individuals with ASD (Pierson and Glaeser 2007).

Nevertheless, research on the comprehension of visual narratives by individuals with ASD does not necessarily support that visual sequences confer the advantage of processing implied by the Visual Ease Assumption. This is first implied by picture arrangement tasks, where individuals with ASD have been observed to do worse than neurotypical individuals (Baron-Cohen, Leslie, and Frith 1986; Johnels et al. 2013). Indeed, low PAT scores are among the most consistent findings for individuals with ASD on IQ test batteries (Siegel, Minshew, and Goldstein 1996). Adults with ASD also do worse at PATs than children with ASD (Siegel, Minshew, and Goldstein 1996), and worse than children with other language deficits (Allen, Lincoln, and Kaufman 1991). In addition, individuals with ASD do worse at the PAT than individuals with learning disabilities related to arithmetic, but better than those who have learning disabilities related to reading (Goldstein et al. 2001).

Individuals with ASD also manifest difficulties in tasks requiring an inference of information about a visual sequence. For example, participants with ASD had difficulty "filling in the blank" for a missing image in an event sequence (Davis et al. 2007) and were less accurate for predicting the final image of a visual event sequence than neurotypical controls (Zalla et al. 2010). Children with ASD have also been observed to provide shorter narrations of picture stories than typically developing children (Tager-Flusberg 1995).

One way that researchers have interpreted these findings of challenges understanding visual sequencing is to attribute them to deficits with ToM. Individuals with ASD often struggle with ToM, and the visual narratives used in experiments often show people with intentions doing activities. Indeed, in the first study using PATs as diagnostic of ASD, sequences involving ToM were arranged less accurately by individuals with ASD, but sequences that did not require ToM were arranged comparably to those of other groups (Baron-Cohen, Leslie, and Frith 1986). Thus, interpreting visual narratives may be difficult overall if an individual with ASD cannot recognize a character's goals. This reasoning has underscored the use of wordless comic strips as diagnostics for testing aspects of ToM more generally, especially for individuals with various neurodiversities (Baron-Cohen, Leslie, and Frith 1986; Dodich et al. 2015; Sivaratnam et al. 2012).

To further assess these behavioral findings, I analyzed the results of tasks in studies with neurotypical participants and individuals with various neurodiversities: Autism Spectrum Disorder (ASD), Schizophrenia Spectrum Disorder (SSD), and Developmental Language Disorder (DLD). These latter two populations will be discussed further in the next sections. In each study that I examined, I recorded the proportion of correct responses out of the total possible responses. In total, there were twenty-four studies using picture arrangement tasks (PAT) and sequence completion tasks (SCT). A table with the full data is provided in Appendix 2, but these averaged results are depicted in Figure 7.1.

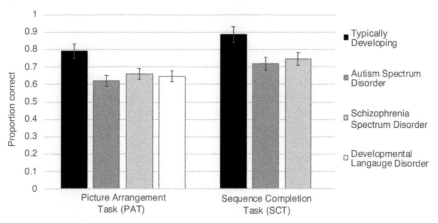

FIGURE 7.1 *Results of an analysis averaging the proportion of correct responses for typically developing participants and individuals with Autism Spectrum Disorder (ASD), Developmental Language Disorder (DLD), and Schizophrenia Spectrum Disorder (SSD) in picture arrangement tasks (PAT) and sequence completion tasks (SCT). Data is in Appendix 2.*

There are two primary insights from this analysis that are worth highlighting. First, as depicted in Figure 7.1, individuals with neurodiversities, including ASD, scored lower in both PATs and SCTs than typically developing participants. Scores in both tasks fell roughly 15–20 percent lower for individuals with neurodiversities and interestingly, these proportions were roughly equal with those for individuals with ASD, SSD, and DLD, discussed later. It is worth pointing out that these scores included both tasks targeting ToM and those that did not specifically depict scenarios involving characters' intentions, suggesting a broader deficit.

Second, although the neurodiverse populations in this analysis scored lower than neurotypical populations, on average the overall scores are not substantially low as to show a complete inability to comprehend the image sequences. This does not suggest a "deficit" that fully inhibits or impairs comprehension. Rather, the scores were only 15–20 percent lower than neurotypical individuals. This suggests that these neurodiverse individuals do maintain the primary systems necessary to comprehend visual narratives overall, even if aspects of those systems may differ from neurotypical individuals.

For individuals with ASD, some hints about which systems may be impacted comes from neurocognitive research. In research with Emily Coderre and colleagues (2018), we measured the brain responses of adults with ASD and neurotypical controls (ages 18 to 68) when presented with short written narratives and six-panel-long visual narrative sequences. These narratives had either a congruous or incongruous final word or image. Here, individuals with ASD were shown to have an attenuated response to their semantic processing, as measured by the N400 ERP effect, for incongruities in both verbal and visual narratives compared to neurotypical controls. That is, individuals with ASD displayed a reduced ability to process the incongruous meanings of both the verbal and visual narratives. These findings implied that a common mechanism pervades deficits of semantic processing in both verbal and visual sequential domains.

A second analysis in this study suggested that this was not merely about the processing of incongruous information. We also analyzed the brain responses at each image in the sequence, panel-by-panel, where there were no incongruities. Neurotypical adults in this study showed a similar response as in other studies: The N400 response at the first image was greatest, and then reduced or remained consistent across each image in the sequence, suggesting that sequential context made semantic processing easier at each position (Cohn et al. 2012). However, the brain response for individuals with ASD was already reduced at the first panel of the sequence, and this pattern persisted at this level throughout the sequence. This implied that the individuals with ASD were not processing each image in such a way as to build up meaning across the sequence.

A similar experimental design was undertaken with Mirella Manfredi and colleagues (2020), where we examined the brainwaves of both adolescents with ASD and neurotypical adolescents (ages 9 to 15). Participants viewed both three-panel-long visual sequences or heard three-word-long spoken sentences that had either a congruous or incongruous final panel or word, respectively. Here, differences in the brainwaves were not observed for the N400, but rather adolescents with ASD had reduced amplitude brainwave effects in later time windows (500–700 milliseconds after viewing the images or hearing the words), such as a late negativity (sentences) or P600 (visual narratives). Given that earlier (N400) and later (late negativities, P600) neural responses are connected processing mechanisms (Baggio 2018; Brouwer, Fitz, and Hoeks 2012; Cohn 2020b; Tanner, Goldstein, and Weissman 2018), these later differences suggest that these younger participants had more challenges with processing stages subsequent to the access of semantic memory, such as integrating or incorporating these meanings together.

These findings of comparable impairment in semantic processing imply a closer link between verbal and visual sequential processing in ASD than might be expected in the Visual Ease Assumption. Does this mean that visual narratives are actually *not* beneficial for individuals with ASD? Some research has provided an interesting counterpoint to these findings.

In dissertation research by Alexander Blum (2019), adolescents with and without ASD were presented with narratives as comics or as text, each of which required some type of motivational or evaluative inference to be understood. Blum examined how much respondents integrated their world knowledge with the information provided in the narrative to inform their inferential thinking, a measure he called Integrated Inferential Reasoning (IIR). In the text-only format, the respondents with ASD presented deficits in IIR, confirming previous reports of difficulties with inferencing in verbal narrative comprehension, as depicted in Figure 7.2. With the comics, respondents with ASD as a whole still presented deficits in IIR, just like in the verbal texts. However, their responses also were modulated by their self-rated frequency of reading comics. Most notably, autistic participants with the highest level of comic experience *performed comparably to their neurotypical peers.*

It is also worth mentioning that comic reading experience did not only benefit the autistic participants, but neurotypical participants as well. As depicted in Figure 7.2, typically developing (TD) respondents also performed better in IIR when they had greater expertise reading comics. However, this advantage was substantially more pronounced for respondents with ASD. With increasing self-rated comic experience, these participants with ASD had up to an equivalent of a 37 percent increase in scoring into a higher level of inferential thinking. These findings suggest that fluency in the visual language used in comics aids the ability to integrate world knowledge into inferential thinking, and this fluency benefits individuals with ASD even more than neurotypical individuals.

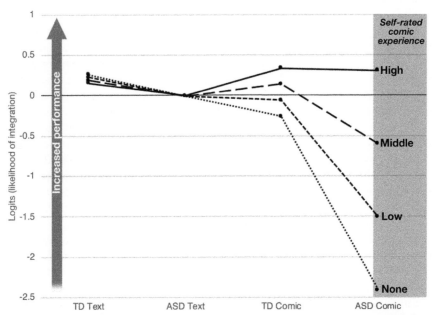

FIGURE 7.2 *Performance of participants who were typically developing (TD) or with autism spectrum disorder (ASD) on tasks measuring integration of world knowledge to make inferences for stories that are purely textual or as a comic. Participants are divided by their self-rated level of comic experience (high, middle, low, none).*

We now have two sets of findings that may seem to contrast each other. On the one hand, individuals with ASD seem to have challenges in comprehension of visual narratives, and their brain responses indeed show comparable deficits in semantic processing to sequences of images as to sequences of words. Yet, we have also seen survey data that suggests individuals with ASD read and enjoy comics to a greater degree than textual books, and Blum's research described earlier indicates that comic reading frequency can boost comprehension abilities for comics to levels comparable of neurotypical individuals. How might we reconcile these findings?

First off, it should be noted that these results imply that visual narratives as an expressive modality alone do not provide a panacea for comprehension by individuals with ASD. The key seems to be about gaining *fluency* in this modality, which is where there indeed appear to be benefits for comprehension. One possibility for why fluency facilitates comprehension can connect back to the PINS model presented in Chapter Two. There, it was proposed that processing involved a semantic level of representation that was connected in parallel to a narrative level of representation. I posited that proficiency enabled comprehension to further rely on the top-down patterns involved in the narrative structure. In contrast, less proficiency was proposed to be more associated with the bottom-up properties of the semantic level of representation.

The studies of visual narrative processing discussed above seem to imply that semantic processing is disrupted in individuals with ASD, as evident in the attenuated responses to the N400 (in adults) and/or subsequent P600 (in adolescents). While further testing of narrative processing would be required, it is possible that fluency enables individuals with ASD to draw on the top-down, stored patterns in the narrative structure rather than the bottom-up semantic associations that otherwise pose challenges to processing. Such narrative patterns could only be acquired through fluency developed by experience reading visual narratives. If this is the case, visual narratives could indeed provide a benefit to comprehension for individuals with ASD, but only after acquiring sufficient proficiency in their structural patterns.[1] Future research can better explore such interactions between visual narrative comprehension and fluency.

7.2 Schizophrenia Spectrum Disorder

Schizophrenia Spectrum Disorder (SSD) is a neurodiversity arising from biological abnormalities in the brain, typically becoming apparent in young adulthood. SSD is often characterized by deficits in the attribution of intentions and beliefs, which can involve sensory experiences like hallucinations or delusions. These experiences may be connected to an inability to monitor other people's beliefs, as in ToM (Frith 1994). Although there are several sub-types of SSD, disorganization of thought and speech are primary characteristics (Kuperberg 2010). Because speech is affected, it again has motivated researchers to use wordless visual narratives in an attempt to circumvent these language deficits, in line with the Visual Ease Assumption. Yet, like autism, theories of schizophrenia's pathologies do not necessarily differentiate between modalities, such as the idea that SSD is related to faster and further activation spreading throughout semantic memory (Manschreck et al. 1988; Spitzer et al. 1993), or to an inability to build up and use context, particularly related to working memory and executive function (Cohen and Servan-Schreiber 1992).

Similar to other neurodiverse populations, individuals with SSD show noticeable deficits in picture arrangement tasks compared with neurotypical control groups (Heaton, Baade, and Johnson 1978). PATs have become a staple for studying SSD, particularly with the creation of tasks which contrast sequences intended to test ToM (scenarios involving characters' intentions) with more event-based situations. Correspondingly, much of this work has emphasized the challenges that individuals with SSD have at arranging the ToM-related sequences specifically.

Individuals with SSD indeed have lower accuracy for arranging pictures into an expected sequence if they relate to ToM when compared to neurotypical controls, and they often take longer to complete these tasks (Brüne 2005; Brüne and Bodenstein 2005). Other work has found that this varies between groups. While most individuals with SSD have deficits in PATs involving ToM (e.g., false belief scenarios), some have more severe deficits in arranging picture sequences of all types that cannot be accounted for by impairment with ToM alone (Brüne et al. 2007; Brüne et al. 2011; Langdon and Ward 2008; Langdon et al. 1997; Langdon et al. 2001; Zalla et al. 2006). Indeed, some individuals with SSD have shown deficits in picture arrangement broadly, including changes in states or locations, which have little to do with characters' mental states (Beatty, Jocic, and Monson 1993).

An additional popular measure of individuals with SSD has been sequence completion tasks. Individuals with SSD are consistently less accurate than neurotypical controls at choosing the appropriate sequence-ending panel that represented characters' intentions (Sarfati, Hardy-Baylé, Besche, et al. 1997; Sarfati, Hardy-Baylé, Nadel, et al. 1997; Sarfati, Passerieux, and Hardy-Baylé 2000). However, the types of errors they make are not simply about attributions of intentions, and sometimes these errors even lack congruity with a sequence (Brunet et al. 2003; Sarfati, Hardy-Baylé, Besche, et al. 1997). In addition, individuals with SSD have been shown to take longer to choose a sequence-ending panel than neurotypical controls, even for sequences related to physical causality that did not involve attribution of intentions (Roux et al. 2016). This study also found that individuals with SSD looked longer than neurotypical controls to critical regions of interest in sequences that required an attribution of intention, but also did so to sequences related to physical causality.

It is noteworthy that individuals with SSD have a harder time than neurotypical controls to complete sequences with pictures than with verbal text (Sarfati et al. 1999; Sarfati, Passerieux, and Hardy-Baylé 2000). In addition, completion scores for both verbal *and* pictorial sequences were lowest for individuals with SSD characterized by disorganized thought and speech compared to non-disorganized patients and controls (Sarfati et al. 1999). Performance on sequence completion for individuals with SSD also appears to be correlated with poor verbal referential communication (Champagne-Lavau et al. 2009). Further meta-analysis of twenty-nine studies of SSD, many using PATs or SCTs, further suggest deficits to subtypes characterized by disorganization (Sprong et al. 2007).

Overall, these studies use visual narratives in contexts specifically to study ToM. While individuals with SSD consistently showed deficits in the ToM-related stimuli compared to controls, their impairments were not isolated to the attribution of intentions. This is further reflected in the analysis across studies conducted for this chapter (Appendix 2, Figure 7.1), where performance on PATs and SCTs yielded scores roughly 15 percent lower for individuals with SSD than neurotypical participants. In addition, comparable results were shown in visual and verbal stimuli, where they often did worse with visual stimuli than verbal stimuli, contrary to the Visual Ease Assumption. These findings imply that deficits exhibited by individuals with SSD may also apply to the comprehension of sequential images more generally and are not just constrained to sequences related to ToM.

7.3 Developmental Language Disorder

Additional connections between visual and verbal language processing are implied by studies of individuals with Developmental Language Disorder (DLD, previously known as Specific Language Impairment, SLI). This condition is a diagnosis given to children who have delayed language development yet perform typically on "non-verbal" intelligence tests and have no problems with their hearing or physical abilities. The traits of DLD vary greatly across individuals, but a consistent feature is problems with acquiring grammatical structure (Leonard 1998), in contrast to other deficits such as pragmatics or reading abilities. However, the heterogeneity of characteristics of DLD may mean it is not a singular condition across individuals.

Some theories have posited that DLD is not linguistic in origin but has to do with a more domain-general capacity for sequencing. For example, Ullman and Pierpont (2005) posit that DLD is involved with a deficit to procedural memory in general. Such a view would therefore predict that sequencing outside of verbal language would also be affected, such as the sequential images in visual narratives.

Because children with DLD have difficulty with language, experiments often require tasks that motivate children to speak, including elicitation tasks where they describe picture stories. Children with DLD have broadly been observed to have limitations with this type of narration. For example, both monolingual and bilingual children with DLD produce and/or comprehend fewer elements of story structure in elicitations of a visual narrative than neurotypical children (Kupersmitt and Armon-Lotem 2019; Tsimpli, Peristeri, and Andreou 2016), and this is true of elicitations in both languages for bilinguals with DLD (Fichman et al. 2017). One study showed that children with language impairment did poorly with elicitation of narrative elements for a four-image picture story both for an initial elicitation and a retelling of the same story, although they were able to improve after an intervention (Hayward and Schneider 2000). Another study showed that children with language impairment were able to recant fewer aspects of stories when they were presented only in pictures or pictures combined with oral storytelling than after hearing oral stories alone (Schneider, 1996). That is, these children comprehended picture stories worse than spoken language, despite being identified by their "language impairment".

Children with DLD describe fewer aspects of picture stories than typically developing children (Ukrainetz and Gillam 2009; van Daal, Verhoeven, and van Balkom 2004, 2007; van Daal et al. 2008), children with "pragmatic language impairment" (Botting 2002), and children with focal brain legions (Reilly et al. 2004). These deficiencies in narrative elicitation for children with DLD compared to typically developing children occur despite also showing similar age-related improvements (Schneider, Hayward, and Dubé 2006).

While elicitation tasks have a verbal component, and thus could be attributed to problems with speech, individuals with DLD also score lower on non-verbal picture arrangement tasks. For example, in a study of a family affected with genetic language impairment, PAT performance was found to be lower for both those affected by and unaffected with DLD (Watkins, Dronkers, and Vargha-Khadem 2002). However, worse performance was shown for the affected family members than the unaffected ones, which was attributed to educational backgrounds (i.e., possibly including exposure to visual narratives). Children with DLD do worse on the PAT than neurotypical controls (Baker 2013; Holmes 2001), though not always (Brizzolara et al. 2011), and PAT performance for children with DLD has correlated with frontally distributed EEG activation (a measure of the electrical activity of the brain), particularly with the alpha spectral frequency (Nenadović et al. 2014). PAT performance for children with DLD has been observed as similar to that of children with ASD (Loucas et al. 2013), and better than children with Williams syndrome (Stojanovik, Perkins, and Howard 2004). The analysis across studies reported here (Appendix 2, Figure 7.1) suggests indeed that individuals with DLD struggle with this task in ways comparable to individuals with ASD or SSD.

Additional research implies that challenges faced by children with DLD for visual narratives are dissociated from non-verbal IQ. In one study, children with DLD were proficient at non-verbal IQ tests, but they struggled with answering questions about pictorial narratives to the same degree that they struggled with questions about verbal narratives (Bishop and Adams 1992). Patterns of errors for these children did not seem to have to do with articulation of verbal responses, but rather of encoding details about the visual stories. Follow up work again found similar deficits in the encoding and recall of information in photographed image sequences compared to neurotypical children, again beyond the relative competency shown in tasks assessing non-verbal IQ (Bishop and Donlan 2005).

Overall, this research with individuals with DLD further implies overlapping cognitive mechanisms between linguistic and visual narrative systems. These deficits with visual narratives appear to be disconnected from the assessments of non-verbal IQ, showing again that visual languages are not merely reducible to general spatial or perceptual reasoning abilities.

7.4 Aphasia

A final population that can inform the relationship between visual narratives and language processing comes from individuals with neurological damage caused by stroke or head injury. This aspect of research further allows for questions about whether the neural mechanisms involved with the processing of language are similar to those involved with visual narratives. Indeed, the understanding of language's neural processing began with studies of aphasics in the nineteenth century.

As discussed in Chapter Two, studies of electrophysiology measuring event-related brain potentials (ERPs) in neurotypical healthy adults have implicated similar neural responses in visual narratives to those shown in language processing (Cohn 2020b). In addition, in studies of healthy adults, imaging techniques have shown activation of brain areas for the processing of visual narratives that overlap with those typical of language processing (Cohn and Maher 2015; Nagai, Endo, and Takatsune 2007; Osaka et al. 2014; Schlaffke et al. 2015; Tinaz et al. 2006). These include regions in the left hemisphere such as "classically recognized" language areas like Broca's area (BA44/45: inferior frontal gyrus) and Wernicke's area (BA22: superior temporal gyrus), and the anterior temporal lobes, among others. As we now move to discuss aspects of neural architecture, it is worth noting that brain areas involved in language processing are not necessarily static, discrete modules. Rather, processing unfolds in time and across cortical connections whereby the flow of activity between brain areas may be of equal importance to the activated nodes in that network (Baggio 2018).

Given the limited neuroimaging research examining the brain areas involved in visual narrative processing directly, studies of neurological damage can thus inform us about these neural origins. However, overall findings from this literature are not straightforward. In general, frontal lobe damage impairs performance in the PAT, even in studies dating to the 1950s (e.g., McFie and Piercy 1952), and some work suggests that damage to the right frontal lobe appears to impair this task worse than left frontal damage (McFie and Thompson 1972). This is consistent with other findings showing PAT deficiency for patients with broad right hemisphere damage, who often have greater deficiency than for left hemisphere damage (Huber and Gleber 1982; Marini et al. 2005; Wallesch et al. 1983).

Although studies vary in their findings, difficulty with the PAT does not appear constrained to the right hemisphere. Other studies suggest that both right and left hemispheric damage can impair performance on the PAT, depending on the particular characteristics of the visual sequence (Veroff 1978). Struggles with the PAT appear to patients with genetic mutations associated with left frontotemporal and anterior parietal lobe damage (De Renzi et al. 1966), with broad left hemisphere damage (Fucetola et al. 2009), and with Wernicke's aphasia (Huber and Gleber 1982). Poor PAT performance was also worse for aphasics with heterogenous left hemispheric damage than non-aphasics with language disorder, although both groups showed impairments (Baldo et al. 2015). Strikingly poor PAT scores also appeared for a patient with a left basal ganglia lesion, who also had impaired language production abilities (Crescentini et al. 2008). Nevertheless, expressive aphasics with left hemisphere damage from strokes did better on the PAT than individuals with genetic language disorders (Watkins, Dronkers, and Vargha-Khadem 2002).

Research using sequence completion tasks are also illustrative. Again, patients with right hemisphere damage appear to be generally worse at choosing a coherent and humorous sequence ending compared to patients with left hemisphere damage (Bihrle et al. 1986). However, patients differed in the types of errors they made: Patients with right hemisphere damage chose structurally well-formed but not coherent endings, while patients with left hemisphere damage chose coherent but less structurally intact endings. In terms of the PINS model presented in Chapter Two, this implies a difference between impairments related to semantics (damaged right hemisphere) and narrative structure (damaged left hemisphere). In another study, the recognition of the congruity of a sequence-ending image was less accurate and took longer for a patient with Wernicke's aphasia than patients with conduction aphasia or anomia (Stead, Savage, and Buckingham 2012).

Altogether, damage to a diverse range of brain areas lead to impairment in performance in tasks using visual narratives. In many cases, these brain areas overlap with those involved with language processing. Nevertheless, these findings are not straightforward, given that damaged areas result in diverse and sometimes opposing findings related to performance on tasks. For example, sometimes right hemisphere damage impairs PATs worse than left hemisphere damage, but not consistently or uniformly. These findings should perhaps not be surprising and are an important reminder that visual narrative processing itself is complex and non-uniform (as discussed in

Chapter Two). Damage to different brain areas may be impairing diverse aspects of that complexity. While use of visual narratives as diagnostics in tests of aphasia are informative, they remain difficult to interpret without parallel investigations into the neural areas involved in processing visual narratives in neurotypical adults—all while being sensitive to participants' relative fluency.

7.5 Conclusions

Altogether, in this chapter, I have described how proficiency of visual narrative comprehension appears to be impaired across individuals with Autism Spectrum Disorders, Schizophrenia Spectrum Disorders, Developmental Language Disorder (Specific Language Impairment), and aphasia. The empirical literature suggests all of these conditions affect the comprehension of visual narratives. In addition, as suggested in the analysis across studies presented in Figure 7.1, this deficit manifests in roughly equivalent ways across individuals with ASD, SSD, and DLD. It is worth emphasizing again that, while all populations show roughly a 15–20 percent drop in performance, it is not so severe as to be below 50 percent or lower. Thus, while visual narrative comprehension appears impacted, it is not eliminated, and enhanced fluency may in fact compensate for such deficits (Blum 2019). Given the varied profiles and deficits shown in these neurodiversities and impairments, sequential image processing may be affected in heterogenous ways, again supporting the multifaceted and complex nature of visual narratives.

In addition, as individuals with these neurodiversities and brain damage often have difficulties with language processing, it implies connections between the mechanisms of processing visual narratives and language. There are several ways that this relationship could play out. One possibility is that these findings suggest that verbal language and visual narratives involve overlapping neural mechanisms, thus leading impairments to affect both modalities. However, these modalities could maintain independent neural systems, but impairments are so general as to affect modalities in similar ways. Finally, it could be that substructures within these modalities may overlap or remain separate, and these substructures respond to impairment in heterogenous ways (for example, semantic processing overlapping across modalities and being impaired, or grammatical processing overlapping and being impaired). Further disentangling these options requires tasks that more carefully target the substructures of verbal and visual language to better assess which aspects of processing might be affected.

Dedicated study of visual narrative comprehension is required both for interpreting these clinical results, and also for assessing what is indexed by tasks using visual narratives. As discussed, visual narratives are often used as a proxy for investigating other aspects of cognition. Yet, in many cases, it remains unknown just what aspects of cognition these tasks implicate. Consider the picture arrangement task. Because of its inclusion in intelligence (IQ) tests and clinical assessments (Kaufman and Lichtenberger 2006; Wechsler 1981), the PAT has been a staple of diagnosing brain damage (Breiger 1956; De Renzi et al. 1966; Huber and Gleber 1982; McFie and Thompson 1972), and many other cognitive disorders (Beatty and Monson 1990, 1994; Beatty, Jocic, and Monson 1993).

Yet, questions have long persisted about what the PAT indexes, including claims that it tests social intelligence, Theory of Mind, logical reasoning, temporal cognition, and narrative comprehension (Campbell and McCord 1996; Ingber and Eden 2011; Lipsitz, Dworkin, and Erlenmeyer-Kimling 1993; Ramos and Die 1986; Tulsky and Price 2003). In addition, studies that include the PAT *never include measures of visual narrative reading experience*, despite longstanding findings that proficiency on this sort of task is modulated by cultural background (Breiger 1956), as well as age and experience with visual narratives (Brown 1975; Fivush and Mandler 1985; Friedman 1990; Nakazawa 2016; Weist et al. 1997; Weist et al. 1999).

Additional confounds arise because the PAT is scored relative to an expected "correct" order, although multiple well-formed sequences can arise in picture arrangement when accounting for the structure of visual narratives (Cohn 2014c). For example, as discussed in Chapter Two, the content of some panels may allow them to function coherently as multiple narrative categories. This was evident in a PAT when participants consistently chose to arrange the same panels in positions where they would function as either Establishers and Releases, and the reversal of these categories did not lead to costs in viewing times (Cohn 2014c). This was unlike reversals of Initials and Peaks, which were more rare in the PAT, and incurred greater costs in viewing time when moved around a sequence. Thus, by scoring PATs related to a "correct" sequence alone, it may be ignoring alternate well-formed narrative structures.

Such findings suggest that, while assessments like the PAT *may* be useful for diagnoses of clinical conditions, just what such tasks index remains unknown.[2] This may be why many of these tasks show impairments across populations: these tasks are not testing uniform aspects of neurocognition, because they do not explicitly target uniform structures within visual narratives. Indeed, sequential image comprehension is a complex system, and deficits in processing may be heterogeneous in nature across populations. Such complexity underscores the necessity of dedicated research on the structure and fluency of visual narratives.

CHAPTER EIGHT

Graphic Narratives versus Filmed Narratives

Thus far, we have discussed the comprehension and proficiency of sequential images in the context of drawn visual narratives, such as comics or picture stories. However, contemporary society also is immersed in the dynamic visual narratives of film—on television, in movies, and now ubiquitously on the internet. Given this prevalence, it is worth asking about the relationship between drawn, static visual narratives and dynamic, filmed visual narratives. In particular, to what degree might film involve similar issues of proficiency as static visual narratives? To what degree might film provide the requisite fluency for us to understand or produce drawn visual narratives? Is there a transfer between the comprehension of filmed visual narratives and drawn visual narratives?

To address these questions, in this chapter we will first explore the relationships between the static, drawn visual narratives in comics and picture stories, and the dynamic, moving visual narratives in film. This will involve a survey of the ways in which these modality differences manifest in aspects of structure and comprehension. Then, following on the previous chapters, we will explore findings related to cross-cultural comprehension and development of film understanding, and compare these findings to those already discussed for drawn visual narratives. Finally, related to the broader questions of this book, we will address whether proficiency in filmic narratives allow for proficiency in understanding static visual narratives.

8.1 Drawn versus Filmed Narratives

The question of how we understand sequences of communicative images applies equally to static sequential images—as in the visual narratives found in comics—and to moving sequential images—as in the visual narratives found in film. Many assume that similar underlying principles of comprehension apply across both static and moving images, although they present information in ways that clearly deviate from each other (Cohn 2016a; Loschky et al. 2020; Magliano et al. 2013; Magliano, Higgs, and Clinton 2019).

First, how does film relate to static visual narratives? Recent research has emphasized that film comprehension taps into general cognitive resources for event perception and attention (Levin and Baker 2017; Smith 2012; Zacks 2014; Zacks and Magliano 2011). For example, cognitive psychologist Jeff Zacks has emphasized that the ways that comprehenders understand film draws upon the same recognition of discontinuities across frames as in event cognition (Radvansky and Zacks 2014; Zacks 2014), whereby greater discontinuity between film shots triggers the recognition of the need for segmental boundaries (Magliano and Zacks 2011). A similar position is taken in the Scene Perception and Event Cognition Theory (SPECT) which was discussed in Chapter Two (Loschky et al. 2020). This model of visual narrative understanding argues that basic aspects of how we understand visual scenes well adapts to visual depictions in film and comics, including tracking information across film cuts (Smith 2012). SPECT is also consistent with Zacks' arguments about the meaningful discontinuities triggering segmentation of a film sequence.

These theories and others have largely stressed the ways that film comprehension, and the development of film editing techniques, have adapted to general cognitive processes related to attention, perception, and event cognition (Berliner and Cohen 2011; Levin and Simons 2000; Smith 2012; Zacks 2014). If film comprehension relies only on such general cognitive mechanisms, then presumably people should have a more universal understanding of film than of drawn visual narratives. As demonstrated throughout this book, drawn visual narratives involve considerable proficiency to comprehend; might the Sequential Image Transparency Assumption apply more to film than to drawn visual narratives then?

Nevertheless, two points should be remembered before ceding people's understanding of film to general perceptual and event cognition. First, using only such general mechanisms would also imply that the cognition of film is minimally different than how we experience daily life. Yet, films are clearly distinguished from everyday experiences (Cutting 2005; Hochberg and Brooks 1978). As opposed to the constant unfurling experience of events, films are divided into *shots* edited together in a temporal sequence. These shots can jump in time or space, omit events, or show different views of the same information, unlike the everyday experience of events. Furthermore, we clearly recognize narrative films *as narratives*— they tell a story—which gives them some differentiating structures from lived events which are not necessarily narratives while they are experienced (although they may be converted into narratives when recounted). In that they have narrative structure, films make use of patterned sequencing constructions that are not aspects of daily experience (Bateman and Schmidt 2012).

Second, these sequencing patterns found in films are similar to those found in visual narratives like comics. There's a good reason for this overlap: Drawn visual narratives typically precede the filming process. *Storyboards* are drawn visual narratives that provide the initial guidance for the visual storytelling of film, which is carried out in shooting and editing. In fact, often times creators of comics also work to produce these storyboards. They are similar to comics, often using a uniform panel shape (the shape of a screen) with a simple grid layout and incorporating a visual vocabulary specific to filmmaking (such as arrows notating zooming-in or panning with a camera), although, they often remain wordless (or dialogue is set below), without integrative text-image relationships like speech balloons or thought bubbles. These drawn static visual narratives form the basis of filmic storytelling—i.e., the application of a cognitive narrative structure—which may be altered in the shooting and editing process. Thus, *static, spatially juxtaposed drawn visual narratives form the basis for what becomes the dynamic moving images sequenced in film.*

The fact that films often begin as storyboards is particularly important to remember when discussing filmic structure. For many decades, scholars have detailed the various patterns of sequencing used in filmic storytelling, including conventions like establishing shots, shot/reverse shot patterns, cross-cutting alternation patterns, among others (for review, see Bateman and Schmidt 2012). However, such sequencing patterns in film are not a consequence of comprehension processes, but of *production.* Since they often start as drawn narratives, it raises questions about the degree to which such film sequencing patterns should be considered "filmic" in origin.

This process of using drawn visual narratives to guide filmic storytelling should make sense: Film is fairly demanding to produce. If one is going to shoot extensive footage to be edited together, it is much easier to have a drawn guide than to hold all this information in memory and/or shoot it ad hoc, with its sequencing to be decided on later in editing. There may also be reasoning connected to the modality itself. Film is a new, technologically mediated phenomenon (i.e., it requires a camera and/or editing equipment), and one cannot "produce" film in a natural way from one's body as a natural expressive modality. This is different than drawings, including sequential drawings, which go back many millennia as a basic human ability to convey thoughts visually. Film thus takes the natural visual narrative structures enacted through storyboarding (i.e., the production of a natural visual language) and altered through the editing process, and combines them with natural percepts to form a *hybrid* form of visual narrative. Such a structure would be reflected by the parallel architecture in Figure 8.1, modified from that in Chapter One for drawn visual narratives like comics.

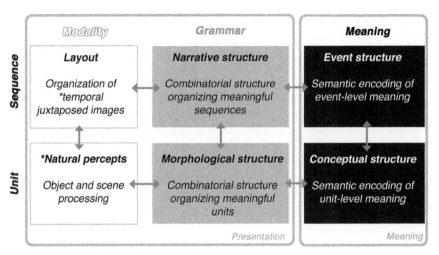

FIGURE 8.1 *Parallel architecture of the moving pictures in film.*

Like drawn visual narratives, the moving images of film also can be described as composed of six structures. Its units use a modality (general perception) that is organized into units of film shots (morphological structure) to convey meanings (conceptual structure), and these units are displayed in a temporal juxtaposition (layout) of patterned sequences (narrative) that convey sequential meanings (event structure). These six structures outline the component parts of filmed visual sequences. However, films in full are multimodal experiences, incorporating the moving images with speech, gesture, music, and more. A complete characterization of film comprehension would need to incorporate all of these multimodal elements (Wildfeuer 2013).[1] Here we focus on the visual relations specifically to better address our overarching questions of unimodal sequential image transparency and proficiency.

Given this architecture, we can now explore questions related to the differences between visual narratives that have static versus moving images. Within Visual Language Theory, the *Principle of Equivalence* states that the mind/brain involves similar structure and cognition of expressive modalities, given modality-specific constraints (Cohn 2013b). Thus, the prediction would be that differences between static and dynamic visual narratives will arise from the affordances offered by how the modalities themselves structure information. This is consistent with theorizing that static and drawn narratives would diverge the most in the front-end processes guiding how a comprehender engages with the modality, rather than the back-end comprehension mechanisms (Magliano et al. 2013; Magliano, Higgs, and Clinton 2019). Below, I therefore discuss various aspects of these divergences between the structure of static drawn visual narratives (like comics or picture stories) and moving filmic narratives.

8.1.1 General Percepts versus Drawings

An overt difference between static visual narratives and filmic narratives is the modality itself. Static visual narratives are typically drawn, while films usually capture natural percepts with a camera (and now often supplemented with naturalistic-*looking* digital effects). The act of drawing is a biological capacity exhibited by typically developing humans with exposure to graphics, and children will draw unprompted from infancy, tempered by the graphic patterns in their cultural environment, just like the expression of language (Cohn 2012a; Willats 2005; Wilson 1988). Drawn visual narratives thus use a visual lexicon of patterned graphics, which may demand proficiency to decode the graphic representations (for review see Arbuckle 2004; de Lange 2000; Goldsmith 1984). In contrast, film does not use such produced patterns of the modality itself (drawings), and instead relies on technology to mediate both its production (using a camera to capture percepts and tools to edit that film) and its presentation (a screen and technology to show it). Film thus bypasses any patterned visual representations stored in memory to have a direct interface with general perception. The exception to this is of course animation, which then uses a visual vocabulary that is drawn (or computer generated from drawn designs), but still reliant on technology for its presentation. Thus, where drawn visual narratives use a natural expressive modality, films use a technologically mediated expressive system.

Similarly, in that film uses natural percepts instead of a visual vocabulary made of graphic patterns, it typically does not use the morphological elements of visual languages. These elements like speech balloons, motion lines, or other conventionalized visual patterns (Cohn 2013b) provide further expressivity to the visual representation than the iconicity of characters and objects. In general, films do not use these graphic patterns unless they are animated or attempt to reference the style of comics, such as in the film adaptation of the comic *Scott Pilgrim vs. the World*.

An additional trait typical of film is that of *motion* across a temporal dimension. A recognizable unit within a filmic sequence is the *shot*—a duration of filmed information that spans across time demarcated by "cuts" which segment it from other filmic units. In contrast to the units of (mostly) static drawn visual narratives (i.e., "panels"), shots have a temporal span, as characters and objects move in the events they undertake. In addition, the viewpoint itself can move, with panning or zooming. Yet, while movement goes along with natural percepts, this again is a feature that can vary based on context. Digital comics might introduce subtle animations (often loops) into the static images, while film might use freeze frames. Animations combine both of these features, where drawn (or generated) visual representations introduce motion and temporality. Some animation uses minimal movement (often to save production costs), panning across an otherwise static frame or moving just portions of an image (such as only a mouth moving to talk while everything else remains static). The converse is also possible: Naturalistic percepts without motion appear in genres of photo-comics. Thus, the presence of motion and the type of visuals (natural percepts, drawn) are complementary yet independent features of visual narrative's modalities.

These aspects of the filmic modality—naturalistic percepts, motion, and temporality—create the primary affordances for how filmic narratives differ from static narratives. As will be shown below, these traits can impact differences in other aspects of structure and comprehension.

8.1.2 *Temporal versus Spatial Layout*

Temporality can characterize the units of filmic narratives, but also the nature of its *layout*. Filmed narratives typically progress temporally in a single space, while static visual narratives typically juxtapose units spatially, dividing up the space of a canvas. This means that film often lacks the tension between the dually holistic (page) and linear (sequence of panels) nature of a spatial layout (Molotiu 2012) and might not toggle the shape or size of the frame on a unit-by-unit basis. It also means that film requires no additional knowledge structures for how to navigate through such a spatial arrangement (Cohn 2013b; Cohn and Campbell 2015).

Exceptions here exist as well, since some films may play with "split screens" or complicated framing devices to divide a film screen into component "panels" (Bateman and Veloso 2013). These "filmic panels" differ from those in static visual narratives like comics because the content is often implied to occur simultaneously, or these frames appear onto a screen in their own temporal sequence. In static visual narratives, content alone determines whether juxtaposed images depict simultaneous events (such as in narrative conjunction, discussed in Chapter Two). Also, as there are few navigational structures operating on filmic panels, there is no "reading order" independent of their content. Rather, the order of such divided panels on a screen might depend on their content, the order that they appear, if they move around the screen, sound cues, and other attention-grabbing filmic techniques.

A byproduct of this difference in temporal versus spatial layouts is the relative control over the pace by which a narrative may be experienced (Magliano et al. 2013; Magliano, Higgs, and Clinton 2019). In temporal layouts used in film, a comprehender has little control over the pace of receiving the sequence of narrative units, as the temporal unfolding of the film persists with little influence of a comprehender (save for rewinding or fast-forwarding). This means that a comprehender must maintain attentional focus on the flow of information in order to follow along, and filmmakers use explicit devices to direct comprehenders' attention within shots (Smith 2012). In contrast, static visual narratives allow a comprehender to set their own pace while engaging images in succession across a page. This in turn requires consciously directed attention for both the navigation of layouts and the acquisition of content.

Some empirical work might inform these aspects of attention and pacing. One study of static visual narratives has contrasted layouts where participants viewed each panel one at a time compared to seeing all panels in a whole three-by-two grid (Foulsham, Wybrow, and Cohn 2016). Participants largely looked at the same content of panels in both layouts, but they spent slightly longer viewing each panel in the one-by-one layout than the spatial layout, likely reflecting a recognition that they would have no ability to go back and check that content again (or, conversely, that in a spatial layout they *could* regress to adjacent panels). In another study asking participants to compare a comic and animated film of roughly the same content (a Batman story), participants had more discrepancies remembering the events of the story when the film version was viewed second than when the static version came second (Magliano et al. 2018). Again, this may have been because of the lack of control of the pacing in the temporal sequence of the film compared to the static sequence of the comic. Thus, the manner in which sequences are presented can introduce different demands on the comprehension system.

8.1.3 Meaning Across Units

The persisting time and motion in filmic shots compared to static drawn panels also results in differences in the sequencing of their content. The predominant form of "continuity editing" of film pushes there to be contiguous motion maintained across film shots (Berliner and Cohen 2011; Smith 2012; Zacks and Magliano 2011), to the point that many cuts between shots remain imperceptible (Smith 2012). For example, consider a scene showing a person walking behind a tree moving left-to-right across the screen, and then coming out the other side from the left side of the screen. With continuity editing, a cut would be placed where the person went behind the tree, so it would seem smooth and seamless when they emerged out the other side. A discontinuous edit would instead cut before the person reached the tree, with the second shot being them coming out the other side. This cut would thus make it seem like the person disappeared mid-stride only to reappear behind the tree. Such shots are believed to be jarring and less coherent because of their deviation from the expectations of perceptual contiguity (Berliner and Cohen 2011; Smith 2012; Zacks and Magliano 2011).

Drawn sequences seem to require less explicit image-to-image continuity of the drawn actions that take place in them. Consider the first two panels of Figure 8.2. By film standards, the shift between panel one and two would render a discontinuous cut, as the paper airplane and arm "jump" from one position to the next. The airplane and arm have no incremental, fluid change

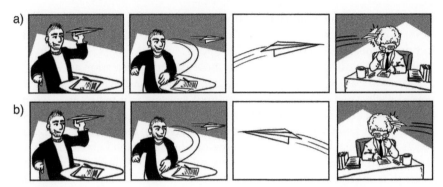

FIGURE 8.2 *Visual sequence where the motion of the paper airplane a) remains continuous along a left-to-right direction across panels, or b) becomes discontinuous in the final two panels.*

between positions, and the motion is only inferred, facilitated by the cues of the motion lines (Cohn and Maher 2015). Static drawings may allow for more discontinuity of this nature because they show only discrete moments, and actions taken by characters in static visual narratives are not actually in motion, leaving their motion to remain conceptual in nature.

Nevertheless, some static, spatially juxtaposed images sequences do allow for figures in one panel to "flow" into the next based on the interaction of the internal composition of the panel contents and the external composition of panels in the spatial layout. Consider Figure 8.2a, where the path of the paper airplane maintains a continuous left-to-right direction across all four panels. In contrast, Figure 8.2b reverses the left-to-right motion in the first two panels to a discontinuous right-to-left direction in each of the last two panels. This discontinuity does seem to impact the comprehensibility. Note that both cases depict the same basic events, while only the laterality of their graphic composition changes. This suggests that, although they are separate structures, layout and content may interact in static visual narratives. In addition, there may be an analogy between the temporal continuity of motion across film shots and the inferred continuity of motion across static, spatially juxtaposed images.

An additional difference between static and moving sequences comes with how much they demand a reader to maintain referential continuity. As we have discussed in prior chapters, the continuity constraint in drawn visual narratives requires that a reader be sensitive to visual features that persist across panels, whereby similarity of features provides cues that entities are the same identity across images. That is, the recognition of graphic cues for facial and bodily features, aspects of clothing, and other identifying traits reinforce that a character in one panel is the same entity as in other panels. Differences between these graphic features, such as those suggesting a change in characters, triggers an updating process in the comprehension of static visual narratives, where such character changes are noticed as less congruous (Cohn and Kutas 2015, 2017).

In contrast, incongruity of referential continuity often goes unnoticed in filmed sequences. In several classic experiments, film viewers were shown to be fairly insensitive to noticing when actors and/or their clothing changed across film shots (Levin and Simons 1997, 2000). Indeed, such "blindness" to change extends to viewers not recognizing when such details change in daily interactions (Simons and Ambinder 2005; Simons and Levin 1997). For instance, one such study showed that customers did not notice the change if an employee they were talking to ducked under a table but a different person came back up! Such cases may even support a "tyranny of continuity" in film whereby the expectation of continuity persists even in the absence of perceptual evidence to the contrary (such as an actual change of a person).

Thus, maintaining continuity across a *static* sequence of images appears to be more demanding than across a filmic sequence (or daily perception!). As with the continuity of motion, such maintenance of referential continuity may be more taxing in static visual narratives because such connections require a low-level inference—i.e., "mapping" in a situation model (Loschky et al. 2020). This is a consequence of the affordances of the static, graphic modality whereby static images repeat across a spatial layout. These drawn representations need to be decoded and mapped across images, with various different graphic features recognized as each indexing the same conceptual knowledge. That is, despite depicting lines and shapes in different configurations across frames, we must understand them as indexing the same characters. In contrast, the natural percepts in film (excluding animation) demand only basic object recognition, while movement and editing can facilitate continuity between shots (Smith 2012), even when the visual features might incongruously change (Levin and Simons 1997, 2000).

8.1.4 Tension Between Units and Sequences

As discussed before, motion is a primary way that moving images differ from static, drawn images. In film, this can manifest either as the motions of elements within a shot, such as characters and objects moving around, but it can also manifest in the motion created by the viewpoint itself. Here, a camera may pan (moving side-to-side or up-and-down) or zoom (moving in or out) from an object, thus giving motion to the perspective of a viewer of that film. While panning, a viewpoint will continuously shift between locations in a space while only showing a select portion of a scene at a time.

Drawings allow no such motion overtly, but they can attempt to simulate such movement, such as with "divisional" panels that divide a singular background into separate units, as in the sequences in Figure 8.3 (Cohn

2014a). When this segmentation retains an object persisting throughout each position in the broader background, it creates an illusion of motion across the space, such as the bee "moving" across panels in Figure 8.3a. Yet, unlike panning, the drawn form will always retain physical segmentation because the units do not inherently move. In addition, while panning renders only a portion of the space visible, the full space of divisional framing persists in view regardless of which particular unit the eyes are on. This again displays the tension between the holistic canvas and the sequenced units in a static visual narrative (Molotiu 2012). This spatial perseverance may be why eye movements largely do not differ between divisional panels of a scene and a contiguous, non-segmented single panel of that same representation (Cherry and Brickler 2016).

These differences between panning and divisionals create interesting contrasts in terms of the affordances created by a modality with or without

Figure 8.3 *Divisional panels dividing single spaces into multiple segments. In a) the bee flying across a space gives the illusion of motion, while in b) each character is given a different panel.*

motion, but they also reveal tensions between units and sequences. Although the prototypical units in drawn visual narratives are panels, while those in film are shots (Magliano et al. 2013), motion complicates this unitization. In divisional panels like Figure 8.3a, each panel is clearly segmented as a unit, although it is also recognized as belonging to a Gestalt of a broader image which is divided up across the sequence. With panning in a film, this difference is less apparent. Panning shows only a portion of a scene at a time, but this segment does not create a distinct unit as a "shot" marked by a cut, and it is contiguous with the additional space that is panned across.

Consider how divisionals and panning might vary if each selected space showed a different character. In Figure 8.3b, the divisional panels each show a particular character in the scene. Here, a spatial inference would be required to understand that they belong to a common environment, but this inference is alleviated by the persisting background of the divisional framing. If a similar scene was filmed using a pan, each character would appear in the frame one at a time, but the frame would contiguously move to subsequent characters with no distinct cut. Because multiple characters would never be in the same frame all at once, any inferential demand would be dampened by seeing them as contiguously belonging to the same space with no overt segmentation. This would all constitute a single shot, but would be composed of contiguously framed information showing only a portion of the overall space. Thus, because a camera allows for motion of the viewpoint itself, it creates a potential tension between units and sequencing that is less apparent in drawn form.

A similar tension occurs with zooming. In a film, a person's whole body may be framed in a shot, but then the viewpoint might rush forward to zoom into just their eyes. This single shot would thus start with a broad amount of information and transition contiguously to a focal part of that whole. In static visual narratives, this zoom may be accomplished with two (or more) panels: first a panel of a whole body, then a second of an eye. This zoom thus modifies the broader view to bring "refined" focus or attention to the character and/or a specific body part (Cohn 2015, 2019b). Again, in drawings, the base (full view) and the modifier (zoom) would be discrete, but film allows for these states to be contiguous. Does the convention of the zoom itself mark them as separate units, despite no explicit cut?

This same type of tension would occur with shifts in the perspective of a single object that may not change in time. In a static sequence, this would involve a series of individuated panels that show the same object from different viewpoints, thereby requiring a comprehender to link these separate representations to the same referential entity (i.e., the continuity constraint). In a film, this could potentially be done with a single shot, as with the famous "bullet-time" shot from *The Matrix* where the "camera" sweeps in a circle around Neo, who moves minimally.

Across all these examples, motion of the viewpoint allows for a single unit that achieves what would be required of multiple units in a static, drawn narrative. These motions themselves might mark the representations as involving a tension between units and sequencing.

8.1.5 Narrative Structure

The motion within the temporality of a film shot can also affect sequencing in more basic ways related to the narrative structure. Because a film can just present a continuous shot without cuts, the temporality of events may not be segmented into distinct units. Such a continuous shot would just show the general perception of events, which have their own segmental structure (Zacks et al. 2001). Yet, if cuts provide cues for *narrative* structure, as described in Chapter Two, continuous single shots may not use those events to cue lower-level narrative categories.

Consider Figure 8.2, where the first two panels depict the character reaching back his arm and then throwing the paper airplane. In the narrative grammar, these first two panels would be characterized as an Initial (reach back) and Peak (throw), which together would comprise an Initial constituent. They would be followed by a Prolongation (showing the airplane's path) and then another Peak (hitting the teacher). If this sequence were filmed, the first two panels may comprise a single shot, holding steady on the character as he carried out the action of reaching back and throwing. The hypothesis here is that these event states would not create individuated narrative categories (i.e., Initial-Peak), but rather would together become an Initial—which in drawn form would be at the constituent level. Thus, the continuous temporality of shots in filmic sequences may "gloss over" what would be a lower-level of narrative structure in a drawn sequence, and instead facilitate narrative structures at a higher level of structure.

Thus far I have argued that the temporality and motion of filmed narratives create a tension between units and sequences which would otherwise be more distinct in drawn visual narratives like comics. A theory with a strong view might claim that cuts between shots would be required for individuating narrative units, while the absence of cuts would just depict event structures with no mapping to narrative. A theory with a contrasting perspective might argue that cuts are not required for unitizing narrative elements at all, and that meaningful aspects of a film can map to narrative within the flow of a continuous, temporal, and moving shot. Such a stance would be consistent with theories of event cognition and discourse which posit similar segmental structures in the cognition of visual events and film cuts (Radvansky and Zacks 2014; Zacks 2014; Zacks and Magliano 2011), but which do not distinguish a parallel level of narrative representation.

A theory with a more nuanced perspective might acknowledge that film cuts may provide cues for narrative structure, but they are not deterministic. Narrative structures must exist without some form of cuts since live theatre clearly has narrative outside of hard scene breaks. This is similarly true of films with single sustained shots, such as *Birdman*, where the narrative progresses with no cuts at all. Indeed, durations of film shots have grown shorter over the past 100 years of cinema, while the number of shots has increased (Cutting, DeLong, and Nothelfer 2010)—surely older films had narrative structures more than that cued by their cuts. What is needed from this view then is a way to distinguish how event structures that cue narrative structures would be distinguished from that of everyday events, which are clearly different phenomena.

A converse issue is when film cuts themselves do not cue a narrative structure. Narrative structures should not necessarily be implied by the cuts between the filmed elements of live events, such as sports, concerts, news broadcasts, political rallies, and others. These contexts all use film cuts, varying camera angles, panning, zooming, etc., but may not imply any sort of storytelling with the progression of shots (Huff et al. 2017). Indeed, these contexts are often not narratives at all (despite the spin that might be given to events like politics or sports). Thus, cuts on their own are not always cues for narrative units.

One possibility is that filmic conventions like cuts, pans, and zooms have the potential for being cues to narrative segmentation, so long as they signal changes between "units" that may even exist within single shots. A single shot of event structures (such as if the first two panels of Figure 8.2 were filmed in one shot) would therefore not break down into separate narrative units, but they would create different portions of an event structure. Conventions like pans and zooms do not appear in general perception, and thus would be "marked" to provide more of a cue for narrative segmentation. A long gradual zoom may be too subtle to establish separate narrative units, but a crash zoom (a sudden rushing in from a longer to close-up framing) might provide a distinct enough cue to mark separate narrative units within a continuous shot.

8.2 Proficiency in Filmic Narratives

Altogether, the previous section argued that various aspects of the modalities of static, drawn visual narratives and dynamic, filmed narratives modulate differences in their structure and comprehension. The primary areas of differences arise because film uses naturalistic percepts, motion, and temporality that do not arise in static visual narratives. These differences overall are summarized in Table 8.1.

Given these affordances between static and dynamic visual narratives, and given our preceding discussion of fluency in drawn visual narratives, what might this mean for the comprehension of filmic narratives cross-culturally and across children's development? A first prediction would be that similar limitations in comprehension would appear for filmed narratives

TABLE 8.1 Differences in various dimensions of prototypical drawn and filmed narratives

Static, drawn narratives	Moving, filmic narratives
Production is a biologically natural human ability (drawing)	Production is technologically mediated (non-natural)
Modality uses a patterned graphic structure using a visual vocabulary	Modality uses general percepts (except in animation)
Units contain static content	Units contain moving content
Units are presented statically	Units can be presented dynamically with a moving camera (panning, zooming)
Temporality between units is ambiguous unless cues show event progression	Temporality between units is a feature of the modality, giving a pervasive sense of conceptual temporality
Spatially sequential layout of units requires a system of navigation to derive the sequence	Temporally sequential layout unfurls units without additional navigational structure, including when juxtaposing frames (e.g., split screen)
Comprehender can control the pace of processing	Comprehender has little control over pace of processing

as drawn visual narratives, except where mediated by affordances of the modalities.

8.2.1 Cross-cultural Film Comprehension

Several studies have examined cross-cultural research of film comprehension (Forsdale and Forsdale 1970; Hobbs et al. 1988; Worth and Adair 1972). For example, one study looked at the understanding of films by individuals from the seminomadic Pokot tribe in Kenya (Hobbs et al. 1988), who at the time had little experience with mass media like film—only 40 percent reported as having seen a single film, which was a government development film. The researchers showed the Pokot participants filmed stories about individuals from the tribe. Overall, the participants recalled roughly half of the critical events in the film, no matter whether it maintained a single continuous viewpoint or varied in the scale of the shots (long, medium, close up, etc.), and comprehension was not modulated by participants' exposure to mass media.

Recent work by cognitive film researcher Sermin Ildirar and colleagues has provided more nuanced insights (Ildirar and Schwan 2015; Ildirar et al. 2018; Schwan and Ildirar 2010). They studied the comprehension of filmic sequencing conventions by villagers from rural Turkey who had no experience with film. Unlike many of the cross-cultural studies reviewed in Chapter Four related to drawn visual narratives, these studies carefully compared different sequences to see which patterns may or may not be difficult to understand. Overall, these inexperienced film viewers were fairly proficient at recognizing filmic conventions when they maintained basic perception and continuing events (Ildirar and Schwan 2015; Schwan and Ildirar 2010). They interpreted cross-cutting between simultaneous events (i.e., back and forth shots between characters) fairly accurately, along with recognizing the meaning of a scene that jumped forward in time. However, other conventions proved more difficult to understand, such as using an exterior location as establishing shot with or without a zoom, panning across a scene, point-of-view shots depicting the viewpoint of characters in the scene, or a shot/reverse shot sequence that depicted two separate characters in shots.

These sequences where viewers deviated from a standard film interpretation often involved modification or inference, and were primarily situations that required combining disparate information into an integrated mental model (Schwan and Ildirar 2010). For example, shot/reverse shot patterns (Environmental-Conjunction in VNG) would require combining two different characters into a common environment. Similarly, locative establishing shots involve a shift from an outdoor location (exterior of a building) to inside that building, which requires a spatial inference of the first shot as the superordinate location of the second shot. Point-of-view shots require inferring that a shot depicts the viewpoint of a person in another shot. Some standard interpretations were aided by the presence of a concurrent audio track (Ildirar et al. 2018).

It should be pointed out that when these villagers deviated from a standard interpretation, they did not necessarily reject the continuity constraint across film shots—by and large the same identities were recognized as maintaining across successive shots. However, one clip did challenge the continuity constraint across shots. This clip showed a cow in different viewpoints, which was subsequently interpreted as successive shots of different cows (Ildirar and Schwan 2015). It is perhaps noteworthy that the continuity constraint here was strained only when attempting to show different views of the same object, a type of sequencing modifier. This is different from examples when referential continuity was not construed in the cross-cultural findings discussed in Chapter Four, where sequences of images depicting changes in time were not recognized as having the same characters, and/or were viewed as isolated scenes. Thus, film sequences mostly maintain referential continuity even for inexperienced viewers.

It is worth contrasting these results with older work that has studied film production. In an anthropological study, Worth and Adair (1972) taught individuals from a Navajo community how to create their own films and then studied the features of their creations. This study was undertaken at a time when most of the Navajo participants had never seen a movie and film creation still involved recording on actual film strips, with editing using the physical cutting of these films. Despite not having seen films, most of the participants in this study quickly and effectively learned how to carry out film editing without having been taught any concepts of film theory.

Worth and Adair compared these Navajo films to the structures that they found in other similar studies. While they found that films created by inner city American children largely reflected the properties of Hollywood movies, there were several features of the Navajo's films that differed. The most noteworthy difference in the Navajo films was that they did not maintain the expectations of continuity film editing (in this case for contiguous action, rather than referential continuity of characters' identities across shots). For example, in their editing of people walking, cuts in the film made the figure appear to jump across the screen in a discontinuous way, instead of fluidly moving from shot to shot in a manner that maintains the flow of the action. Not only did their Navajo participants create discontinuous sequences, but they do not seem to have any perception of it being awkward or infelicitous.

Altogether, these findings related to cross-cultural comprehension and production are important, just as for drawn visual narratives, for providing a contrast to the experiences that fluent comprehenders take for granted when being immersed in an expressive system. Such findings imply that traits that may seem "natural," and which may be interpreted as reflecting basic aspects of perceptual or event cognition, may also involve some degree of conventionality and habituation. Again, even if drawn or filmed narratives make use of basic cognitive functions, they may be activated or accompanied by culturally specific, learned patterns.

8.2.2 Development of Film Comprehension

As with our previous discussion about when children begin to understand a static sequence of images, we can also ask about the development of film comprehension (for additional review, see Jajdelska et al. 2019). The overall development of film understanding appears to align with that of static visual narratives discussed in Chapter Five. Children younger than 18 months have been observed to have difficulty comprehending the sequential qualities of edited film sequences (Pempek et al. 2010; Richards and Cronise 2000), and may perceive them as isolated, separate incidents (Noble 1975). This is especially notable because children acquire basic perceptual acuity much earlier than this. As discussed in Chapter Five, children within their first months after birth can perceive variance in visual features across objects

(Johnson 2013), and 15-month-old infants discriminate between subtle violations of object continuities in scenes presented in a temporal sequence (Duh and Wang 2014). Given that these basic perceptual discontinuities are recognized at very young ages, but edited film sequencing (and the continuity constraint in drawn sequences) appears to be recognized later, additional mediating factors must be involved in visual narrative comprehension beyond perception alone.

As with static visual narratives, children appear to increase in their understanding of film editing between ages 4 and 6, although this proficiency appears to differ across types of filmic patterns. For example, a study of 3- and 5-year-old children found that filmed sequences with shots broken up by cuts, pans, and zooms were comprehended to the same degree as unedited segments (Smith, Anderson, and Fischer 1985). However, in a second experiment, 4-year-olds had worse comprehension than 7-year-olds for more complicated film conventions like omission of scenes (ellipsis), cross-cutting alternation of simultaneous actions, and shots demanding spatial inference.

Another study of predominantly white middle-class American second graders (mean age: 7.7) to eighth graders (mean age: 13.5) examined children's memory for aspects of action-adventure television plots and showed that recall got better across age groups (Collins et al. 1978). This improvement was characterized by increased focus on the explicit important information in the film and ignoring the less important information. Yet, second-grade boys could not distinguish ordered versus scrambled film sequences, while second-grade girls and all other grade levels had proficient comprehension. Nevertheless, this study would now be considered fairly old and rates of exposure may have changed such results.

Such comprehension may also negotiate the balance between age and frequency of exposure to filmic conventions. A study of urban American children aged 4 to 11 found they had an easier time recalling the order of events in a TV show presented in its regular order, a reversed order, or with jumps in time (Abelman 1990). Yet, understanding of these latter sequences with complex time jumps was greater for children who watched television more often, suggesting a possible interaction between film comprehension and exposure. Such proficiency related to exposure has been shown even for 12-to-18-month-old infants (Barr et al. 2008).

More recent research has examined the eye-movements of children aged 4, 6, and 8 years old to the cuts between shots in films (Munk et al. 2012). Children of all ages were disturbed by discontinuities in the temporal order of the narrative sequence, but only children between 6 and 8 years had increased disturbances for shots that reversed the positions of the actors. These older ages were thus more sensitive to the "errors" than the younger 4-year-olds, suggesting that the older children had more efficient eye movements than the younger children. In addition, fewer eye-movements were found in response to film cuts for 6- or 8-year-old children compared to 4-year-olds. These results again point towards a crucial developmental shift between ages 4 and 6 in the comprehension of sequential images.

8.3 Fluency in Drawn versus Filmed Narratives

Altogether, these findings suggest that understanding film taps into similar aspects of fluency as static sequential images. However, because of its affordances, film may bypass certain levels of fluency that would be required by static drawn narratives. While these studies suggest age and exposure modulates fluency across development, such effects typically relate to broader aspects of comprehension or filmic conventions demanding inference. Unlike the studies of drawn narratives, studies of film do not seem to show deficits in the continuity constraint—only in rare cases do the viewers have difficulty recognizing that the characters in one shot are the same as those in other shots. These differences may be attributable to the two primary ways that drawn and filmed narratives differ in their modalities: the nature of the percepts and the juxtaposition of their units.

First, because films generally use basic percepts instead of drawings (besides animation), they require little decoding of the visual signal itself, unlike the fluency required to comprehend and produce drawn information. In contrast to the natural percepts in film, drawings require decoding of a graphic structure, and across sequences this requires recognizing that referential continuity persist despite depicted differences in line configurations that signal changes in postures, viewpoint, etc. Natural percepts captured by a camera require no such decoding process of the modality itself. Second, because events unfold temporally in film, instead of spatially across a layout, basic referential and event information can be comprehended with little decoding of juxtaposed units. The temporally sequential juxtaposition of film relieves most of the need for a continuity constraint, since repeating entities do not need to be linked across a spatial layout with differing visual characteristics, unless that temporal sequence is confounded with changes in viewpoint (Ildirar and Schwan 2015).

These differences in the affordances of the modalities may explain why basic film comprehension retains referential continuity with natural percepts by low-exposure and young film viewers (Ildirar and Schwan 2015), but might create challenges for inexperienced comprehenders of drawn visual narratives (e.g., Bishop 1977; Byram and Garforth 1980; Cook 1980; Gawne 2016; San Roque et al. 2012). Drawn visual narratives require basic decoding of the modality and this decoding process is contingent on exposure to visual narratives. Once comprehension extends above these basic aspects of the modality, film appears to demand similar fluency as static visual narratives. Patterns going beyond basic sequencing to involve inferencing—i.e., when they use a narrative structure—demand additional comprehension processes that may remain difficult for comprehenders with little experience or exposure.

The prior sections have argued that filmic and static visual narratives involve mostly the same underlying structures, differing primarily in the modality itself. The modalities thus create different affordances for how meaning may be structured or conveyed. In addition, certain characteristics of proficiency appear between filmic and static visual narratives in terms of their development and cross-cultural understanding, albeit modulated by the affordances of the modalities. This range of structural overlap and departure thus raises a question of whether fluency can be transferred across modalities. Specifically, can exposure and practice with film lead to fluency of drawn visual sequences?

While evidence is limited, results so far suggests that film does not provide the requisite exposure for proficiency in drawn visual narratives. First, developmentally, infants will imitate the actions from television more readily than those from picture books (Simcock, Garrity, and Barr 2011), suggesting a better comprehension of the filmic events. Several cross-cultural studies reviewed in Chapter Four found that respondents could not construe the continuity constraint in drawn visual narratives, despite being exposed to television (e.g., Byram and Garforth 1980; Fussell and Haaland 1978; Gawne 2016). This suggests that exposure to filmic narratives did not aid the comprehension of static spatially sequential drawn narratives. Furthermore, in Brent and Marjorie Wilson's studies of children drawing image sequences, village children in Egypt who were not exposed to picture books or comics had substantial difficulties in drawing their own coherent visual narrative sequences, despite having exposure to television and cartoons (Wilson 2016; Wilson and Wilson 1987).

These observations provide evidence that filmed narratives are not sufficient exposure to provide fluency in visual languages, even though both filmic and drawn visual narratives involve similar cognitive structures on the back-end. Fluency then must not only be considered as engaging the comprehension processes themselves, but also acquiring the structures and patterns that allow for activation of those comprehension processes in the first place. That is, familiarity with decoding of the modality and its grammar allows for access to the meaning.

CHAPTER NINE

Visual Language Fluency

This book has asked the question: *Who can understand sequences of images, like in comics?* Altogether, I have posited that a Sequential Image Transparency Assumption—a belief that sequential images are universally transparent to understand—underlines the typical conceptions of how visual sequences are comprehended. We then questioned this assumption by examining comprehension and production across developmental, cross-cultural, and neurodiverse contexts. In particular, this survey of this wide body of literature has emphasized that combining empirical research can characterize the ways visual narratives are comprehended. To summarize these findings:

1 Visual narratives are a fundamental and natural potential of human expression.

2 Visual narratives use systematic yet diverse patterns across culturally codified systems.

3 Visual narratives are understood via a *fluency* that is acquired through exposure and practice.

4 Visual narrative fluency applies both to visual narratives in general, and to the properties of particular cultural systems.

5 Visual narrative fluency matures across a developmental trajectory that is modulated by exposure.

6 Visual narrative fluency can be asymmetrical for comprehension and production.

7 Visual narratives are complex systems and deficits in their understanding can involve many interacting factors.

8 While visual narrative fluency may involve domain-general and cross-modal systems, the degree to which fluency is transferable across modalities remains unclear.

Given that this wealth of evidence suggests a fluency is required to understand sequences of images, there has to be something for people to be *fluent in*. Fluency requires proficiency with the patterns found in system(s) of representation. Such systems constitute *visual languages*.

Thus, the findings presented throughout this book support the claims made from Visual Language Theory that the structure and cognition of sequential images parallels language. While the capacity to comprehend and produce images is universally accessible to any neurotypical human brain, it relies on exposure and practice with an external system in order to develop. Without this exposure, the requisite structures (or interfaces between structures) may not develop. In addition, just as languages differ in systematic ways, visual languages also manifest in culturally diverse systems. This means that exposure may habituate a comprehender toward fluency of the structures in their "native visual language," and such structures may conflict with those from other systems (Cohn 2013b; Cohn and Kutas 2017; Nakazawa and Shwalb 2012; Wilkins 1997/2016).

These interpretations have consequences on the many areas using and advocating for sequential images on the basis of the assumption that they are transparent to understand. Overall, the use of visual narratives as a communication method, as educational materials, as a tool for measurement, and/or as experimental stimuli needs to bear in mind two key points. First, visual narratives need to be recognized as having a structure of their own which is not inherently transparent. Second, fluency is required to comprehend that structure.

9.1 Consequences of Fluency on Educational Advocacy

Recent years have seen a growing promotion for using multimodal visual narratives like comics in educational settings (Cary 2004; Sousanis 2015), and for communicating about health (Green and Myers 2010) and science (Bach et al. 2017; Farinella 2018). If such advocacy is motivated by the idea that the visual component of these multimodal documents is universally transparent, then that position is complicated by the fluency issues discussed throughout. In such contexts, if comprehenders do not have the requisite understanding, then they will not receive the benefit of the advantages that such a format is thought to confer. Indeed, it may not be that formats like in comics are advantageous for comprehension because the reader understands the images "for free" which can further aid comprehension of the text (i.e., the Visual Ease Assumption). It may be that characteristics of the multimodal meaning—with text and images combining to create broader message—may provide a benefit. Yet, this requires a comprehender to gain fluency in patterns that underlie the text, visuals, and/or their combination.

Another complication is that such recommendations often profess the benefits of "comics" in general, as if "comics" have a uniform generic structure that persists across different cultures and contexts. Rather, as was discussed in Chapter Three, visual languages used in comics have cross-culturally variable patterns that appear in systematic ways. Thus, if one is advocating to use "comics" in educational and communicative contexts, which visual language specifically is being advocated? This also runs the risk of perceiving or promoting a specific visual language (such as the American Visual Language used in superhero comics) as a "default generic system," rather than acknowledging that it too has a relative structure, the comprehension of which may conflict with other visual languages preferred by individuals in a culture or students in a class.

Nevertheless, even if they are not universal and transparent, such materials can still be useful, and such complications should not discourage the use of visual languages in these contexts. Although they might be culturally relative, visual languages *do* appear to be beneficial. Studies indeed support that conveying information in multimodal visual narratives is effective for science communication (Aleixo and Sumner 2017; Wang et al. 2019); education and training (Nalu and Bliss 2011; Short, Randolph-Seng, and McKenny 2013; Zhang-Kennedy, Baig, and Chiasson 2017); and learning and literacy for both first or second languages (Jennings, Rule, and Vander Zanden 2014; Wong et al. 2017), among various other benefits. In addition, despite the pitfalls discussed in their cross-cultural application, sequential images have been shown to be useful for communicating in some humanitarian contexts (Cooper et al. 2016; Stenchly et al. 2019).

Thus, in order to fully leverage their benefits, such advocacy has to progress with the right mindset, rather than presuming that visual languages like in comics are a "magic bullet" for effective, universal communication. This comes with a need for sensitivity to 1) the audience and 2) their relationship with the materials being used. Regarding basic fluency, can the audience be presumed to already be proficient in visual language in general and/or the specific visual language being used? Will those materials be comprehended up front or are they intended to simultaneously teach the visual language? Regarding cross-cultural patterns, which visual language is being proposed for use and which structures might the audience be familiar with already?

Thus, advocacy of using visual languages in comics in educational and communicative contexts should integrate considerations for assessing or teaching fluency. If an intended audience already has some basis for fluency in visual language(s), their use in comics should be able to provide a benefit. Yet, advocacy for using visual languages with audiences who may have lower fluency might also be warranted. It is certainly possible that visual languages in these contexts might also provide the necessary exposure and practice for developing fluency. This allows such usage to be a tool for fluency in the first place, rather than hoping for benefits of a presumed transparent comprehension. Advocacy in these contexts should thus come with recommendations for how to implement methods of simultaneously teaching fluency in these materials and also incorporating lessons in the visual languages themselves (along with specifying *which* visual language(s) that might be).

9.2 Consequences of Fluency on General Research

Because many studies of cognition use sequential images as experimental stimuli to test cognition not expressly about sequential images, visual narrative fluency can influence performance on those tasks and interpretations about what they mean. This can be particularly problematic for domains that employ visual narratives as diagnostics (e.g., clinical contexts, IQ), or that base developmental trajectories of different cognitive domains on children's performance of visual narrative tasks. As with advocacy for using these materials to educate, the two primary areas here are, 1) recognition of the internal structure of visual narratives themselves and 2) recognition of the fluency required to understand this structure.

Particularly illustrative examples come from the use of visual narratives in developmental research, which often use image sequences assuming they are simple, easily controllable, transparent to understand, and circumvent spoken/written language. However, whatever developmental trajectory of a cognitive ability researchers may attempt to study with visual narratives may be confounded by the *concurrent development* of visual narrative fluency. As demonstrated in Chapter Five, children have an incremental growth for proficiency through the age of 6, with sequential construal only manifesting between 4 and 6 years old. This is problematic for using visual narratives to study the development of cognitive mechanisms like Theory of Mind (Baron-Cohen, Leslie, and Frith 1986; Sivaratnam et al. 2012), where sequential image comprehension would occur within or *after* the window of development for ToM which is said to emerge between 3 and 4 years old (Wellman, Cross, and Watson 2001). Without a way to report on children's visual narrative exposure and fluency, it is hard to disentangle where children's performance on such tasks reflects ToM or visual narrative fluency. Comparable issues are faced by developmental research using visual narratives to study temporal cognition (Ingber and Eden 2011; Weist 2009) and sequential reasoning (Zampini et al. 2017).

The use of visual narratives in studies of verbal narrative are particularly challenging, given their potential to share cognitive machinery (as discussed in Chapter Two). Many studies use visual narratives like "picture stories" to elicit verbal narration, such as the various "Frog Stories" by Mercer Mayer (Berman and Slobin 1994). In fact, visual narrative elicitation tasks make up most of the research on how verbal narrative abilities develop in children (Burris and Brown 2014). Yet again, with prior assessment of visual narrative fluency, it is hard to know whether these tasks are telling us about proficiency in creating verbal narratives, comprehending visual narratives, or some general narrative abilities that transfer across modalities. This can help explain why questioning children about the narrative content in picture stories improves their narrative abilities, because such questioning may actually bootstrap their comprehension of the visual sequences through the verbal cues (Silva and Cain 2019; Silva, Strasser, and Cain 2014).

In addition, these narrative elicitation tasks also may mischaracterize what such narration indexes in the first place. In these tasks, participants read through a wordless visual narrative and narrate what they see, and the produced verbal language is then analyzed for its narrative qualities. However, *the visual materials themselves also have a narrative structure*, meaning that this task is not one of verbal narrative production, but of *cross-modal translation* of the narrative structure from the visual to the verbal modality. This would account for why children have more coherent narratives in these tasks with visual narratives than when they tell original stories (Nurss and Hough 1985; Shapiro and Hudson 1991), because the visual narratives provide a coherent structure to translate rather than derive from scratch.

As with advocacy of comics in educational and communicative contexts, researchers do not need to entirely stop using visual narratives in experimental tasks. However, they do need to adequately understand what issues are involved with their use and need to be sensitive of potential confounds which include limitations of the task itself, an accounting for the structure of the visual narratives, and participants' fluency in those visual languages. Using visual narratives in experimental tasks should follow similar considerations of verbal language-based stimuli, where researchers analyze the linguistic properties of their stimuli and assess participants' fluency. Studies using visual languages should thus uphold similar standards.

9.3 Consequences of Fluency on Visual Narrative Research

Finally, recognition of visual narrative fluency opens the door to address various questions about basic aspects of visual narratives themselves and their interactions in multimodal expressions. The Sequential Image Transparency Assumption has potentially held back research, because it also presumes a lack of complex structure, a lack of organizational patterns, and/or an ease of comprehension. Together, these presumptions stymie the idea that visual languages have a need to be studied in the first place, because why would one need to investigate something so simple? Without the shackles of an assumption of universal transparency, scholarship can progress to ask more detailed questions about how visual languages may be structured, processed, and developed. Some potential queries might include, but are not limited to:

- *Cross-linguistic variability:* How variable are the cultural patterns across visual languages? Are there visual language families? Are there typological universals? Do visual languages change in time in systematic ways?

- *Cross-modal cross-linguistic relationships:* To what degree do potential typological properties of visual languages overlap with those of verbal languages? Are the structure of visual languages influenced by the structure of verbal languages (or vice versa?) To what degree does the language one speaks affect the language one draws (or vice versa)?

- *General and specific fluency:* To what degree is fluency specific for particular visual languages? Does access to any visual language structure increase the likelihood of proficiency in understanding any visual language? Can we characterize recognizable levels of fluency? Can we develop further metrics to assess this fluency?

- *Visual language development:* To what degree does age and experience factor into the comprehension of visual languages? How much exposure and practice are necessary to achieve fluency? What is the developmental trajectory involved with learning to understand and produce visual languages? Are there stages? Are there critical learning periods? How does visual language comprehension change throughout the lifespan?

- *Cross-modal development:* To what degree is the development of visual language similar to or different from that of spoken or signed languages? How does the development of sequential image comprehension and production interact with that of creating individual images? How does visual language development interact with that of spoken or sign language acquisition and/or other general cognitive processes?

- *Cognitive neuroscience:* To what degree do the neural mechanisms involved with processing visual language overlap with those of other expressive modalities? To what degree are the neurocognitive systems for visual and verbal languages separate?

- *Cognition and health:* To what degree are general cognitive processes affected by visual language fluency? How does fluency in visual languages interact with other cognitive processes, such as spatial reasoning, attention, working memory, or Theory of Mind? Can visual language fluency benefit other cognitive processes, like perception, spatial cognition, or verbal reading comprehension?

- *Neurodiversity:* What can the comprehension of visual languages by neurodiverse populations tell us about the structure and processing of visual language more broadly? To what degree does visual language fluency influence comprehension processes for neurodiverse populations? Can visual languages provide benefits for comprehension, cognition, or behavior for neurodiverse populations, and how might it change depending on the type of neurodiversity?

While this book has discussed most of these broader topics, the body of literature surveyed here only provides a start toward answering these questions. Indeed, many of the works contributing to this review are decades old, yet they have been scattered across diverse disciplines without recognition of common findings or shared questions. Future scholarship can use the integration of this literature to provide a foundation on which research can grow with more nuance and seriousness. Such research questions can only be addressed with clarity of the issues at hand across a consolidated research effort, rather than disparate studies scattered across researchers and fields, lacking cohesion.

9.4 Conclusion

Throughout this book, we have explored the evidence for the ways in which visual narratives like comics and picture stories are comprehended. This cognitive approach puts *people* at the forefront. Although we have explored the question of "How are sequences of images comprehended?" answering it reframes the question to "Who comprehends sequences of images, and how do they do it?" This view contrasts theories that treat the properties of visual narratives as divorced from the people who create and comprehend them, as if the structure of graphic expression somehow exists independently of the mechanisms of comprehension themselves. Rather, this cognitive perspective places visual narrative understanding in the minds of people, and *people can differ from each other.* This variation may be "external" to the mind in how much exposure to visual narratives people receive and the varying types of patterns used by those visual narratives. Or, variation may be "internal," differing in people's neurodiversities of cognition itself. Throughout, these differences across people will affect the comprehension of a sequence of images. While emphasizing the universal traits of visual languages can provide a unifying focus, recognizing this diversity is also important so as not to forget the "who" involved in that presumed universality.

So, is the understanding of the sequential images in visual narratives universal? This review of the extant literature suggests that they are not "universally transparent." Rather, as with spoken and signed language, the visual languages that constitute visual narratives are "universal" in that typically developing human brains have an innate capacity for the cognitive structures required to gain fluency in their understanding. This fluency is conditioned on receiving the requisite exposure to and practice with an external cultural system, acquired across a developmental trajectory. This potentiality is a testament to the fundamental role of creating sequential images in human expression, spanning across history and cultures, and it places visual languages on par with our other basic aspects of human communication and expression.

APPENDIX 1

Corpus Analyses

The table below lists the comics coded within the Visual Language Resource Corpus (VLRC: http://www.visuallanguagelab.com/vlrc), along with their country of origin, year, sub-classification (genre, demographics), total pages analyzed, and total panels analyzed.

Country	Year	Book. Author(s). Publisher	Subtype	Total pages	Total panels
USA	2002	*100%*. Paul Pope. DC Comics	Indy	25	139
USA	2003	*Same Difference*. Derek Kirk Kim. Xeric Foundation	Indy	25	173
USA	2003	*Blankets*. Craig Thompson. Top Shelf Productions	Indy	28	128
USA	2005	*NorthWest Passage 1*. Scott Chantler. Oni Press	Indy	25	91
USA	2009	*Far Arden*. Kevin Cannon. Top Shelf Productions	Indy	24	118
USA	2010	*Set to Sea*. Drew Weing. Fantagraphics Books	Indy	134	134
USA	2011	*The Story of Roberto Clemente*. Wilfred Santiago. Fantagraphics Books	Indy	25	141
USA	2012	*Sumo*. Thien Pham. First Second	Indy	25	119

Country	Year	Book. Author(s). Publisher	Subtype	Total pages	Total panels
USA	2013	*Heck*. Zander Cannon. Top Shelf Productions	Indy	25	159
USA	2013	*Boxers*. Gene Luen Yang. First Second	Indy	25	136
USA	2014	*Shackleton Antarctic Odyssey*. Nick Bertozzi. First Second	Indy	23	142
USA	2014	*Andre the Giant: Life and Legend*. Box Brown. First Second	Indy	25	131
USA	1940	*The Flame* #3. Basil Berold and Will Eisner. Fox Comics	Mainstream	20	146
USA	1941	*Captain Marvel Adventures* #1. Manly Wade Wellman and Jack Kirby. Fawcett Comics	Mainstream	47	278
USA	1942	*Captain Midnight* #1. Jack Binder. Fawcett Comics	Mainstream	50	242
USA	1943	*Black Hood* #9. Clem Weisbecker and B. Vagoda. MLJ Magazine	Mainstream	23	146
USA	1949	*Lady Luck* #86. Klaus Nordling. Quality Comics	Mainstream	32	221
USA	1950	*Doll Man* #30. Bill Quackenbush and Will Eisner. Comic Favorites	Mainstream	30	208
USA	1951	*Lars of Mars* #11. Jerry Siegel and Murphy Anderson. Approved Comics	Mainstream	31	116
USA	1955	*Blue Beetle* #18. Louis Ferstadt, A. Fago, and V. Fox. Charlton Comics	Mainstream	28	112
USA	1956	*Plastic Man* #64. Jack Cole and B. Woolfolk. Comic Magazines	Mainstream	29	152
USA	1959	*Action Comics* #252. Robert Bernstein and Al Plastino. DC Comics	Mainstream	27	115
USA	1962	*Brain Boy* #2. Herb Kastle and Frank Springer. Dell Comics	Mainstream	27	159.5

Country	Year	Book. Author(s). Publisher	Subtype	Total pages	Total panels
USA	1964	*Daredevil* #5. Stan Lee and Wallace Wood. Marvel Comics	Mainstream	20	130
USA	1965	*Captain Atom* #78. Joe Gill and Steve Ditko. Charlton Comics	Mainstream	20	103
USA	1967	*The Blue Beetle* #3. D.C. Glanzman and Steve Ditko. Charlton Comics	Mainstream	17	124
USA	1968	*Nick Fury Agent of S.H.I.E.L.D.* #1. Jim Steranko. Marvel Comics	Mainstream	20	97.5
USA	1970	*Green Lantern* #76. Dennis O'Neil and Neil Adams. DC Comics	Mainstream	23	104
USA	1973	*The Flash* #211. Cary Bates and Irv Novick. DC Comics	Mainstream	26	95.5
USA	1975	*Justice League of America* #122. Martin Pasko and Dick Dillion. DC Comics	Mainstream	18	109
USA	1977	*The Invincible Iron Man* #100. Bill Mantlo and George Tuska. Marvel Comics	Mainstream	18	87
USA	1978	*Detective Comics* #475. Steve Englehart and Marshall Rogers. DC Comics	Mainstream	17	114
USA	1981	*The Avengers* #210. Bill Mantlo and Gene Colan. Marvel Comics	Mainstream	19	99.5
USA	1982	*Wonder Woman* #289. Roy Thomas and Gene Colan. DC Comics	Mainstream	26	121
USA	1984	*Fantastic Four* #269. John Byrne. Marvel Comics	Mainstream	22	91.5
USA	1988	*Batman: The Killing Joke.* Alan Moore and Brian Bolland. DC Comics	Mainstream	20	133
USA	1989	*Captain America* #358. Mark Gruenwald and Kieron Dwyer. Marvel Comics	Mainstream	22	114

Country	Year	Book. Author(s). Publisher	Subtype	Total pages	Total panels
USA	1990	*The Amazing Spider-Man* #328. David Michelinie and Todd McFarlane. Marvel Comics	Mainstream	23	106
USA	1993	*Venom: Funeral Pyre* #2. Carl Potts and Tom Lyle. Marvel Comics	Mainstream	22	95.5
USA	1997	*The Incredible Hulk* #454. Peter David and Adam Kubert. Marvel Comics	Mainstream	25	110.5
USA	1998	*Wolverine* #121. Warren Ellis and Leinil Francis Yu. Marvel Comics	Mainstream	21	78
USA	1999	*Daredevil* #8. Kevin Smith and Joe Quesada. Marvel Comics	Mainstream	20	133
USA	2001	*The Punisher* #6. Garth Ennis and Steve Dillon. Marvel Comics	Mainstream	22	80
USA	2004	*Darkness Resurrection* 4. Paul Jenkins, Dale Keown, and Matt Milla. Top Cow Productions	Mainstream	23	102
USA	2004	*Fierce* #1. Jeremy Love and Robert Love. Dark Horse Books	Mainstream	21	113
USA	2005	*BPRD: The Black Flame*. Mike Mignola, John Arcudi, and Guy Davis. Dark Horse Books	Mainstream	24	102
USA	2005	*Superman-Batman Absolute Power*. Jeph Loeb and Carlos Pacheco. DC Comics	Mainstream	23	71
USA	2005	*Green Lantern: Rebirth* #5. Geoff Johns and Ethan Van Sciver. DC Comics	Mainstream	21	86
USA	2006	*Blessed Thistle*. Steve Morris. Dark Horse Books	Mainstream	19	109
USA	2006	*Rising Stars 4: Voices of the Dead/ Bright*. Fiona Avery, Dan Jurgens, Staz Johnson, and Al Rio. Image Comics	Mainstream	19	93

Country	Year	Book. Author(s). Publisher	Subtype	Total pages	Total panels
USA	2006	*Star Wars: Empire* 6. Thomas Andrews, Scott Allie, Adriana Melo, Joe Corroney, and Michel LaCombe. Dark Horse Books	Mainstream	22	96
USA	2007	*Arch Enemies* 1. Drew MelBourne, Yvel Guichet, and Joe Rubinstein. Dark Horse Books	Mainstream	20	92
USA	2007	*DMZ Body of a Journalist* #2. Brian Wood and Riccardo Burchielli. DC Comics	Mainstream	20	90
USA	2007	*Amazing Spider-Man* #539. J. Michael Straczynski and Ron Garney. Marvel Comics	Mainstream	23	88.5
USA	2008	*Black Panther* #35. Reginald Hudlin and Cafu. Marvel Comics	Mainstream	22	104
USA	2009	*Deadpool* #11. Daniel Way and Paco Medina. Marvel Comics	Mainstream	22	94
USA	2010	*Green Lantern Corps* #42. Peter Tomasi and Patrick Gleason. DC Comics	Mainstream	23	90
USA	2011	*Batman The Dark Knight* #2. Paul Jenkins and David Finch. DC Comics	Mainstream	20	79.5
USA	2012	*Uncanny X-Men* #10. Kieron Gillen and Carlos Pacheco & Paco Diaz. Marvel Comics	Mainstream	21	100.5
USA	2013	*Savage Dragon: The End.* Erik Larsen. Image Comics	Mainstream	19	114
USA	2013	*Constantine* #1. Ray Fawkes, Jeff Lemire and Renato Guedes. DC Comics	Mainstream	21	74
USA	2014	*The Punisher* #5. Nathan Edmondson and Mitch Gerads. Marvel Comics	Mainstream	21	99

Country	Year	Book. Author(s). Publisher	Subtype	Total pages	Total panels
USA	1991	*Twilight X* 1. Joseph Wight. Antarctic Press	OEL Manga	17	80
USA	1997	*Luftmatte 1946* #1. Ted Nomura. Antarctic Press	OEL Manga	20	81
USA	2001	*Chronicles of the Universe* 1. Rod Espinosa. Antarctic Press	OEL Manga	34	134
USA	2003	*Gigantor* 1. Ben Dun, David Hutchinson, and Ted Nomura. Sentai Studios	OEL Manga	15	87.5
USA	2003	*Legends From Darkwood* 1. Christopher Reid and John Kantz. Antarctic Press	OEL Manga	31	230.5
USA	2003	*The Agents* #3. Kevin Gunstone and Ben Dunn. Antarctic Press	OEL Manga	24	127
USA	2004	*Assemby* 1. Sherard Jackson. Antarctic Press	OEL Manga	27	84
USA	2004	*Myth Warriors* 1. Robert Place Napton and PH. Image Comics	OEL Manga	20	74
USA	2004	*Once in a Blue Moon* 1. Nunzio Defilippis, Christina Weir, and Jennifer Quick. Oni Press Inc	OEL Manga	20	93
USA	2004	*Tokyo Knights* 1. Michael Renegar. Image Comics	OEL Manga	20	76
USA	2005	*Blue Monday* 4. Chynna Clugston. Oni Press	OEL Manga	26	162
USA	2005	*Scott Pilgrim vs. The World* 2. Bryan Lee O'Malley, Keith Wood. Oni Press	OEL Manga	21	88
USA	2006	*Gold Digger* 1. Fred Perry and Craig Babiar. Antarctic Press	OEL Manga	20	69
USA	2006	*Ninja High School Hawaii* 1. Katie Bair and Robby Bevard. Antarctic Press	OEL Manga	22	114.5

Country	Year	Book. Author(s). Publisher	Subtype	Total pages	Total panels
USA	2006	*OZ The Manga* 1. David Hutchison. Antarctic Press	OEL Manga	30	98
USA	2014	*Pride and Prejudice*. Jane Austen (adaptation by Stacy King) and Po Tse. Manga Classics	OEL Manga	25	88
Chinese	2002	*Mega Dragon & Tiger Future Kung Fu Action* 5. Tony Wong. Comics One		26	153
Chinese	2002	*Saint Legend Prelude*. Andy Seto and Ying-Hsiang Lin. Comics One		26	152
Chinese	2002	*Heaven Sword and Dragon Sabre* 1. Louis Cha and Wing Shing Ma. Comics One		26	161
Chinese	2002	*Storm Riders* 1. Wing Shing Ma. Comics One		27	147.5
Chinese	2003	*Divine Melody* 1. I-Huan. DGN Publications		25	95
Chinese	2003	*SVC Chaos: SNK vs Capcom* 1. Chi Wen Shum. DGN Publications		26	88
Chinese	2004	*1/2 Prince*. Yu Wo and Choi Hong Chong. Dragon Youth Comic		25	101
Chinese	2004	*The King of Fighters* 3. Wing Yan, King Tung, Bryce Gunkel, and Calvin Chai. DGN Publications		24	156
Chinese	2005	*Xiewang Lin Jie* #445. Rongcheng M. Tian xia chu ban		25	187
Chinese	2010	*Tiger x Crane Record of the Demon Master*. Huang Xiao Da. U17		25	121
Chinese	2015	*Yin Zhi Shoumuren (Silver Gravekeeper)* C1. Zero League and Moon Cake. Tencent Manhua		23	72
Japanese	2014	*Ashi-girl* 28. Kozueko Morimoto. Shueisha: Cocohana	Josei	21	96

Country	Year	Book. Author(s). Publisher	Subtype	Total pages	Total panels
Japanese	2014	*Blue Something.* Fumiko and Tanikawa. Shueisha: Cocohana	Josei	23	127
Japanese	2014	*Bread & Butter* #3. Ashihara Hinako. Shueisha: Cocohana	Josei	28	148
Japanese	2014	*Clover: Trèfle.* Toriko Chiya. Shueisha: Cocohana	Josei	28	100
Japanese	2014	*Iromen ~Juunintoiro~* #21. Yumi Tamura. Shueisha: Cocohana	Josei	12	83
Japanese	2014	*Kakukaku Shikajika.* Akiko Higashimura. Shueisha: Cocohana	Josei	17	99
Japanese	2014	*Kyo wa Kaisha Yasumimasu* #24. Mari Fujimura. Shueisha: Cocohana	Josei	16	97
Japanese	2014	*Marmalade Boy Little* #12. Wataru Yoshimizu. Shueisha: Cocohana	Josei	28	124
Japanese	2014	*Moment-Eien no Isshun* #3. Satoru Makimura. Shueisha: Cocohana	Josei	31	148
Japanese	2014	*Poison Berry in My Brain* #20. Setona Mizushiro. Shueisha: Cocohana	Josei	22	69
Japanese	2009	*One Punch-Man* 25. Yūsuke Murata. Viz Media	Seinen	19	64
Japanese	2014	*Billy Bat* #113. Naoki Urasawa and Takashi Nagasaki. Kodansha: Morning	Seinen	16	99
Japanese	2014	*Chairman Shima Kosaku* #11. Kenshi Hirokane. Kodansha: Morning	Seinen	15	63
Japanese	2014	*Gangoose* #12. Keisuke Koetani. Kodansha: Morning	Seinen	17	102
Japanese	2014	*Giant Killing* #316. Masaya Tsunamoto and Tsujimoto. Kodansha: Morning	Seinen	18	97

Country	Year	Book. Author(s). Publisher	Subtype	Total pages	Total panels
Japanese	2014	*Gurazeni* #66. Yuji Moritaka and Keiji Adachi. Kodansha: Morning	Seinen	23	119
Japanese	2014	*Ihoujin* #19. Matsuki Yamamoto. Kodansha: Morning	Seinen	26	125
Japanese	2014	*Kou no Dori* #44. Yuu Suzunoki. Kodansha: Morning	Seinen	18	99
Japanese	2014	*Regalo*. Hoshino Yukinobo. Kodansha: Morning	Seinen	28	120
Japanese	2014	*Saireen* #31. Sayaka Yamazaki. Kodansha: Morning	Seinen	18	100
Japanese	2014	*Vagabond* #322. Takehiko Inoue. Kodansha: Morning	Seinen	24	95
Japanese	2007	*Absolute Boyfriend* #24. Yuu Watase. Viz Media: Shojo Beat	Shojo	25	100
Japanese	2007	*Baby and Me* #24. Marimo Ragawa. Viz Media: Shojo Beat	Shojo	19	99
Japanese	2007	*Crimson Hero* #24. Mitsuba Takanashi. Viz Media: Shojo Beat	Shojo	22	101.5
Japanese	2007	*love☆com Preview*. Aya Nakahara. Viz Media: Shojo Beat	Shojo	27	158
Japanese	2007	*Nana*. Ai Yazawa. Viz Media: Shojo Beat	Shojo	19	100
Japanese	2013	*12 sai. ~Kokoro~*. Maita Nao. Shogakukan: Ciào	Shojo	30	142
Japanese	2013	*Dolly Kanon* #19. Yuu Yabuuchi. Shogakukan: Ciào	Shojo	30	146.5
Japanese	2013	*Kimi wa Sora no Subete*. Keiko Notoyama. Shogakukan: Ciào	Shojo	37	152.5
Japanese	2013	*Kocchi Muite! Miiko* #221. Eriko Ono. Shogakukan: Ciào	Shojo	16	76
Japanese	2013	*Oyasumi Memories* #32. Hihumi Sasaki. Shogakukan: Ciào	Shojo	31	141
Japanese	2003	*Air Gear* 4. Oh! Great. Del Ray	Shonen	21	109

Country	Year	Book. Author(s). Publisher	Subtype	Total pages	Total panels
Japanese	2003	*History's Strongest Disciple Keichi* 3. Matsuene Syun. Shogakukan	Shonen	14	66
Japanese	2007	*Fairy Tail* 4. Hiro Mashima. Del Rey	Shonen	19	115
Japanese	2008	*The World God Only Knows* 4. Wakaki Tamiki. Viz Media: Shonen Sunday	Shonen	17	97
Japanese	2009	*Cage of Eden* 4. Yamada Keiyou. Kodansha	Shonen	17	97
Japanese	2009	*Kimi No Iru Machi* 4. Seo Kouji. Kodansha	Shonen	18	91
Japanese	2010	*Ao no Exorcist* 4. Katou Kazue. Kazé	Shonen	21	112
Japanese	2010	*Beelzebub* 4. Tamura Ryūhei. Viz Media: Shonen Jump	Shonen	17	80
Japanese	2011	*Claymore* 18. Yagi Norihiro. Viz Media	Shonen	19	95
Japanese	2011	*Bleach* 106. Tite Kubo. Viz Media: Shonen Jump	Shonen	24	105
Japanese	2011	*Naruto* 508. Masashi Kishimoto. Viz Media: Shonen Jump	Shonen	18	99
Japanese	2011	*One Piece* 591. Eiichiro Oda. Viz Media: Shonen Jump	Shonen	17	109.5
Japanese	2011	*Psyren* 16. Toshiaki Iwashiro. Viz Media: Shonen Jump	Shonen	19	100
Japanese	2011	*Yu-Gi-Oh! 5D's* 7. Masahiro Hikokubo and Masashi Sato. Viz Media: Shonen Jump	Shonen	21	104
Japanese	2012	*Magi: The Labyrinth of Magic* 4. Shinobu Ohtaka. Viz Media: Shonen Sunday	Shonen	18	117.5
Japanese	2012	*Nisekoi* 4. Komi Naoshi. Jump Comics	Shonen	16	107.5
Japanese	2013	*Shokugeki No Soma* 4. Tsukuda Yuuko and Saeki Shun. Shūeisha	Shonen	17	92

Country	Year	Book. Author(s). Publisher	Subtype	Total pages	Total panels
Japanese	2013	*Trinity Seven* 7. Saitou Kenji and Nao Akinari. Dragon Comic Age	Shonen	32	111
Japanese	2013	*Assassination Classroom* 68. Yuusei Matsui. Shueisha: Weekly Shonen Jump	Shonen	19	94.5
Japanese	2013	*Gintama*. Hideaki Sorachi. Shueisha: Weekly Shonen Jump	Shonen	17	106
Japanese	2013	*Haikyuu!!* 86. Haruichi Furudate. Shueisha: Weekly Shonen Jump	Shonen	17	101.5
Japanese	2013	*Kuroko's Basketball* 238. Tadatoshi Fujimaki. Shueisha: Weekly Shonen Jump	Shonen	18	96.5
Japanese	2013	*Shokugeki no Soma* 48. Yuto Tsukuda and Shun Saeki. Shueisha: Weekly Shonen Jump	Shonen	17	99
Japanese	2014	*Ansatsu Kyoushitsu* 75. Matsui Yuusei. TBA Online	Shonen	19	95
Korean	1987	*In The Starlight* 3. Kyungok Kang. First Second		20	82
Korean	1992	*Kingdom of the Winds* 1. Kimjin. Net Comics		21	68
Korean	1998	*Zero/Six* 3. Youjung Lee. Net Comics		20	71
Korean	2000	*Emperor's Castle* 1. Sungmo Kim. Netcomics		20	64
Korean	2001	*Aegis* 1. Jinha Yoo. Netcomics		20	85
Korean	2001	*Kwaidan*. Jung, Jee-Yun. Dark Horse Books		18	138
Korean	2003	*Invincible Yeonbyeongeol* 1. Hwang Mi Ri. Samyang Publisher		18	73
Korean	2003	*The Color of Earth* 1. Kim Dong Hwa. First Second		29	114

Country	Year	Book. Author(s). Publisher	Subtype	Total pages	Total panels
Korean	2004	*Zippy Ziggy* 8. Kim Un-jung and Hwang Seung-man. Haksan Publishing		20	78
Korean	2005	*The Great Catsby* 2. Doha. Netcomics		32	70
Korean	2006	*9 Faces of Love* 1. Wann. Netcomics		23	123
Korean	2006	*He was Cool* 1. Gui Yeoni and Kim Jea-eun. Bandi Publishing Co.		19	71
Korean	2006	*Lie to Me* 1. Lee Youngran. Netcomics		18	83
Korean	2007	*Boy of the Female Wolf* 11. Han Yu-rang. Samyang Publisher		30	103
Korean	2010	*The Breaker New Waves* 36. Geuk-Jin Jeon and Jin-Hwan Park. Daum Communications		18	101
Dutch	1940	*Dick Bos* 1. Maz. De Arbeiderspers		25	100
Dutch	1940	*Sjors, voorzitter van de Rebellenclub* 4. Frans Piët. Big Balloon		13	154
Dutch	1943	*Tom Poes Weekblad* 3. Marten Toonder. Boumaar		15	142
Dutch	1946	*Kapitein Rob*. Pieter Kuhn and Evert Werkman. De Nieuwe Pers		51	152
Dutch	1948	*Eric de Noorman*. Hans G. Kresse. t Kasteel van Aemstel		48	152
Dutch	1952	*Sjors en Sjimmie*. V-t and Frans Piët. De Spaarnestad		25	137
Dutch	1956	*De avonturen van Pinkie Pienter*. J.H. Koeleman. Mulder & Zonen		12	152
Dutch	1957	*Alle verhalen van Olie B*. Bommel en Tom Poes. Marten Toonder. De Bezige Bij		25	75
Dutch	1958	*De avonturen van Pinkie Pienter*. Johan Hendrik Koeleman. Mulder		12	151

Country	Year	Book. Author(s). Publisher	Subtype	Total pages	Total panels
Dutch	1958	*Panda*. Marten Toonder. Uitgeverij Skarabee		25	70
Dutch	1961	*Alleen op de wereld*. Hector Malot and Piet Wijn. Big Balloon		22	155
Dutch	1964	*Tom Poes*. Marten Toonder. De Bezige Bij		25	74
Dutch	1964	*Mario en de toverpluisbloem*. Lea Smulders and Carol Voges. Drukkerij de Spaarnestad		19	152
Dutch	1966	*Sjors en Sjimmie*. Frans Piët. Uitgeverij de Spaarnestad		28	155
Dutch	1968	*De Argonautjes*. Dick Matena and Lo Hartog van Banda. De Paul Rijperman Uitgaven		18	154
Dutch	1970	*Blook*. Johnn Bakker and L. Hartog van Banda. De geïllustreerde pers nv		15	159
Dutch	1970	*Jan, Jans en de kinderen*. Jan Kruis. Joop Wiggers Produkties BV		18	153
Dutch	1972	*Ambrosius*. Gideon Brugman, L. Hartog van Banda, and R. Ringers. De Geïllustreerde Pers nv		19	156
Dutch	1978	*Agent 327 #7*. Martin Lodewijk. Uitgeverij M		16	152
Dutch	1978	*Baron van Tast tot Zeveren #22*. Frits van der Heide and Jan van Haasteren. Oberon		18	150
Dutch	1980	*Jan, Jans en de kinderen*. Jan Kruis. Joop Wiggers Produkties BV		18	152
Dutch	1981	*Een avontuur van Roel Dijkstra*. Andries Brandt and Jan Steeman. Oberon		16	152

Country	Year	Book. Author(s). Publisher	Subtype	Total pages	Total panels
Dutch	1982	*De avonturen van Douwe Dabbert.* Thom Roep and Piet Wijn. Big Balloon		24	156
Dutch	1986	*De Familie Doorzon* #3. Gerrit de Jager and Wim Stevenhagen. Big Balloon		12	153
Dutch	1988	*Een avontuur van Elno.* Jan Vervoort. Oberon b.v.		11	150
Dutch	1990	*Claudia Brucken.* Willem Ritsier and Minck Oosterveer. Boumaar		19	154
Dutch	1992	*Franka* #10. Henk Kuijpers. Franka		15	159
Dutch	1993	*Joop Klepzeiker* #6. Eric Schreurs. Uitgeverij C.I.C.		17	154
Dutch	1994	*De Nakomertjes.* Toon van Driel. Land Productions		19	154
Dutch	1995	*Don't panic!* Martin Leijen and Fred de Heij. Drukkerij Zuidam & Zonen		16	152
Dutch	2000	*Sjors & Sjimmie* #1. Unknown. Big Balloon B.V.		13	151
Dutch	2001	*Noortje* #14. Patty Klein and Jan Steeman. VNU Tijdschriften		21	151
Dutch	2003	*De ontdekking.* Eric Heuvel, Menno Metselaar, Ruud van der Rol, and Hans Groeneweg. Anne Frank Stichting		18	151
Dutch	2003	*Dik van Dieren en zo.* Gerard Leever. Strip 2000		15	150
Dutch	2003	*Je geld of je leven.* Barbara Stok. Nijgh & Van Ditmar		25	114
Dutch	2012	*De Ruyter.* Herman Roozen and Pieter Hogenbirk. Strip 2000		18	151

Country	Year	Book. Author(s). Publisher	Subtype	Total pages	Total panels
Dutch	2014	*Rood.* Rob van Barneveld. Het Syndikaat		14	161
Dutch	2014	*Zonder Filter.* Robert van Raffe. Oog & Blik		25	127
Dutch	2015	*Quaco.* Eric Heuvel and Ineke Mok. Walburg Pers		17	151
Dutch	2016	*In The Pines: 5 murder ballads.* Erik Kriek. Scratch		25	139
Flemish	1946	*Suske en Wiske.* Willy Vandersteen. Standaard Uitgeverij		13	156
Flemish	1946	*Suske en Wiske.* Willy Vandersteen. Standaard Uitgeverij		11	152
Flemish	1947	*De Vrolijke Bengels* V1. Willy Vandersteen. Uitgeversmij		19	152
Flemish	1948	*Detective Van Zwam.* Marc Sleen. Standaard		11	156
Flemish	1949	*Suske en Wiske.* Willy Vandersteen. Standaard Uitgeverij		13	152
Flemish	1954	*De avonturen van Nero en Co* #19. Marc Sleen. Drukkerij Het Volk		14	161
Flemish	1954	*Jan Zonder Vrees.* Jan Waterschoot. De Dageraad		25	151
Flemish	1955	*Meesterwerken in Beeld.* Daniël Defoe and Jan Waterschoot. L. Opdebeek		25	91
Flemish	1957	*Suske en Wiske.* Willy Vandersteen. Standaard Uitgeverij		13	158
Flemish	1959	*De Rode Ridder.* Willy Vandersteen. Standaard Uitgeverij		20	157

Country	Year	Book. Author(s). Publisher	Subtype	Total pages	Total panels
Flemish	1963	*De avonturen van Nero en Co.* Marc Sleen. Drukkerij Het Volk		13	158
Flemish	1964	*De rode ridder* #20. Willy Vandersteen. Standaard Uitgeverij		16	155
Flemish	1964	*Jerom* #5. Willy Vandersteen. Standaard Uitgeverij		15	150
Flemish	1965	*Piet Pienter en Bert Bibber* #24. Jozef van Hove (Pom). Standaard Uitgeverij		13	160
Flemish	1966	*De avonturen van Jommeke* #5. Jef Nys. Het Volk N.V.		12	155
Flemish	1972	*Suske en Wiske* 67. Willy Vandersteen. Standaard Uitgeverij		14	161
Flemish	1973	*Willeke* 4. Edgard Gastmans. Studio Rigida		13	152
Flemish	1976	*Kari Lente & Co* 4. Bob Mau. Born		15	150
Flemish	1976	*Sloeber* 4. Jeff Broeckx. Standaard		20	157
Flemish	1978	*Bessy* 127. Willy Vandersteen. Standaard Uitgeverij		21	156
Flemish	1981	*Suske en Wiske.* Willy Vandersteen. Standaard Uitgeverij		14	156
Flemish	1981	*Jommeke.* Jef Nys. Ballon		15	154
Flemish	1984	*De Avonturen van Urbanus* 7. Urbanus and W. Linthout. Loempia		16	161
Flemish	1986	*Bessy Natuurkommando* 3. Marck Meul and Jeff Broeckx. Standaard Uitgeverij		20	153
Flemish	1988	*De Spookjes* 67. Mahy Michel. Reprint Books		19	151

Country	Year	Book. Author(s). Publisher	Subtype	Total pages	Total panels
Flemish	1990	*Kiekeboe* 55. Merho. Standaard Uitgeverij		14	151
Flemish	1990	*De avonturen van Johan en Stefan.* Bob de Moor. Boumaar		11	148
Flemish	1996	*Baxter* 2. Eric D'Hondt and Raf Ravijts. Standaard Uitgeverij		19	153
Flemish	1998	*Thomas Pips*. Leo de Budt. 9de kunst		14	154
Flemish	1999	*Waterland* 55. Marc Legendre and Jeff Broeckx. Standaard Uitgeverij		18	137
Flemish	2001	*Biebel*. Marc Legendre. Standaard Uitgeverij		20	151
Flemish	2003	*Samson & Gert* 30. Danny Verbiest, Gert Verhulst, Hans Bourlon, Jean-Pol, and Wim Swerts. Studio 100		15	153
Flemish	2004	*W817* #3. Hec Leemans and Swerts & Vanas. Standaard Uitgeverij		15	152
Flemish	2006	*K3*. Patrick Roelens and Jan Ruysbergh. Studio 100		18	154
Flemish	2009	*Weer over naar jou*. Adriaan van Aken and Philip Paquet. Bries		21	154
Flemish	2010	*Het Grote Kabouter Wesley Boek.* Jonas Geirnaert and Jonas Geirnaert. De Harmonie		7	168
Flemish	2013	*Otto* V2. Frodo De Decker. Het Syndikaat		10	150
Flemish	2014	*De Kiekeboes* 123. Merho. Standaard Uitgeverij		13	151
Flemish	2016	*F.C. De Kampioenen* 56. Hec Leemans. Standaard Uitgeverij		14	155
Flemish	2016	*FC Schwalbe*. D'Auwe. Strip2000		18	151

Country	Year	Book. Author(s). Publisher	Subtype	Total pages	Total panels
French	1985	*La Voyageuse: De petite Ceinture.* Pierre Christin and Anne Goetinger. Dargaud		23	153
French	1992	*Catman: Une aventure de Cliff Burton.* Rodolphe and Michel Durand. Dargaud		20	155
French	2000	*Loranne* #3. Dieter and Nicaise. Glénat		20	159
French	2002	*Screaming Planet.* Alexandro Jodorowsky and Marc Riou & Mark Vigouroux. Humanoids		30	171
French	2003	*Une Folie Très Ordinaire.* Christian Godard, Phillipe Jarbinet, Franck Bonnet, Alain Mounier, and Marc Malès. Glénat		20	152
French	2004	*La Vie En Rose* V3. Dieter, Viviane Nicaise, and Dina Kathelyn. Glénat		19	151
French	2010	*Le Cahier à Fleurs.* Laurent Galandon and Viviane Nicaise. Grand Angle		19	153
French	2011	*Abelard* 2. Hautiere and Dillies. Dargaud		30	175
French	2011	*Alter Ego.* Denis Lapière, Pierre-Paul Renders, and Mathieu Reynès. Dupuis		19	156
French	2011	*Skipper* 1. Callède, Gihef, and Lenaerts. Dupuis		19	151
French	2012	*Percy Shelley* 1. David Vandermeulen and Daniel Casanave. Le Lombard		17	146
French	2012	*Notre Dame* 1. Robin Recht and Jean Bastide. Glénat		23	157

Country	Year	Book. Author(s). Publisher	Subtype	Total pages	Total panels
French	2013	*Tsunami*. Stéphane Piatzszek and Jean-Denis Pendanx. Futuropolis		25	93
French	2013	*Le Muret*. Fraipont and Bailly. Casterman		25	146
French	2013	*Pietrolino*. Alexandro Jodorowsky and O.G. Boiscommun. Humanoids		25	147
French	2013	*Trans-Amazonie*. Yves Rodier and Frédéric Antoine. Lombard		22	149
French	2014	*Child of the Storm*. Manuel Bichebois and Didier Poli. Humanoids		28	202
French	2014	*Final Incal*. Alexandro Jodorowsky and Ladrönn. Humanoids		28	205
French	2014	*Le Soldat*. Olivier Jouvray and Efa. Le Lombard		30	184
French	2014	*Metabarons Genesis: Castaka*. Alexandro Jodorowsky and Das Pastoras. Humanoids		30	148
French	2014	*Donjon*. Joann Sfar, Lewis Trondheim, and Mazan. Delcourt		25	206
German	1987	*Mulle*. Werner Geismar and Claus Pollmer. Bastei		31	157
German	1990	*Fix und Foxi* 36. Rolf Kauka. Kauka Publishing		18	151
German	1991	*Operation Odin*. Mike Maurus and Wolfgang Schneider. Comic Art		35	161
German	1992	*Werner*. Brösel. Achterbahn-Versand		31	153
German	2004	*Die Band*. Markus Mawil Witzel. Reprodukt		25	155

Country	Year	Book. Author(s). Publisher	Subtype	Total pages	Total panels
German	2009	*König Kobra* #1. Bela Sobottke. Gringo Comics		40	155
German	2010	*Larry Potter: Zaubern ist nicht alles.* FIL. Leichenpflasternseinen-wegverlag		24	152
German	2010	*Moga Mobo* #11.2. Jonas Greulich. Moga Mobo		23	156
German	2010	*Moga Mobo* #11.3. Thomas Gronle. Moga Mobo		24	154
German	2010	*Moga Mobo* #11.1. Titus Ackermann. Moga Mobo		30	131
Swedish	1980	*Bamse: världens starkaste björn* #17. Rune Andréasson and Francisco Tora. Egmont Kärnan		3	18
Swedish	1994	*Bamse: världens starkaste björn 7: Om Fotboll.* Various. Egmont Kärnan		14	88
Swedish	1994	*Bamse: världens starkaste björn 7: Krosus Gladland II.* Various. Egmont Kärnan		13	74
Swedish	1994	*Bamse: världens starkaste björn 7: Om Sandslott.* Various. Egmont Kärnan		16	91
Swedish	1995	*Bamse: världens starkaste björn 9: Sorktyg i Skogen II.* Various. Egmont Kärnan		7	43
Swedish	1995	*Bamse: världens starkaste björn 9: Den Mystiska Bilen.* Various. Egmont Kärnan		12	84
Swedish	1995	*Bamse: världens starkaste björn 9: Bamse och Farmors Kista.* Various. Egmont Kärnan		12	56
Swedish	1996	*Bamse: världens starkaste björn 1: Teddy Blir Detektiv.* Various. Egmont Kärnan		17	107

Country	Year	Book. Author(s). Publisher	Subtype	Total pages	Total panels
Swedish	1996	*Bamse: världens starkaste björn 1: Drullevarg Matar Fåglarna (fastän han inte vill).* Various. Egmont Kärnan		11	68
Swedish	2000	*Bamse: världens starkaste björn 12: Tidsresan: Bamse och de Mystiska Strålarna.* Kenneth Hamberg, Jan Magnusson, and Kerstin Hamberg. Egmont Kärnan		15	84
Swedish	2000	*Bamse: världens starkaste björn 12: Bamse och Årstidsnyckeln.* Sören Axén and Francisco Tora. Egmont Kärnan		22	125
Swedish	2002	*Bamse: världens starkaste björn 17: Skalman och Mullvalen.* Kenneth Hamberg and Kerstin Hamberg. Egmont Kärnan		20	98
Swedish	2002	*Bamse: världens starkaste björn 17: Pellefant: Snöballskriget.* Joakim Gunnarsson and Ann Härdfeldt. Egmont Kärnan		6	32
Swedish	2002	*Bamse: världens starkaste björn 17: Vargen och Klockkuppen.* Sören Axén and Bernt Hanson. Egmont Kärnan		15	94
Swedish	2003	*Bamse: världens starkaste björn Bamse och Jätten Gorm.* Sören Axén and Juan Aparici. Egmont Kärnan		13	72
Swedish	2003	*Bamse: världens starkaste björn Mini-Hop och Barnvakten.* David Liljemark, Jan Magnusson, Bo Michanek, Dan Andréasson, and Bert Hanson. Egmont Kärnan		7	42

Country	Year	Book. Author(s). Publisher	Subtype	Total pages	Total panels
Swedish	2003	*Bamse: världens starkaste björn Fixare-sorkarna på Stallstigen.* Sören Axén and Bernt Hanson. Egmont Kärnan		4	26
Swedish	2003	*Bamse: världens starkaste björn Professor Murmeldjur har Bråttom.* Olof Silverbo and Juan Aparici. Egmont Kärnan		6	30
Swedish	2004	*Herman Hedning* #2. Jonas Darnell. Egmont Kärnan		10	77
Swedish	2011	*Hälge: Varning för älgskador!* #20. Lars Mortimer. Egmont Kärnan		9	127

APPENDIX 2

Analysis of Neurodiversities

In Chapter Seven, I reported an analysis of results in various studies of participants who were typically developing (TD) or were individuals with Autism Spectrum Disorder (ASD), Developmental Language Disorder (DLD), or Schizophrenia Spectrum Disorder (SSD). The table below provides the raw data for this analysis. Numerical values are the proportion of "correct" responses in the tasks, calculated from the total number of correct responses out of the total number possible, as provided in the Results sections of these papers.

Some papers differentiate the sequence types used in picture arrangement tasks (PAT) or sequence completion tasks (SCT). This is often done to distinguish between visual narratives where some aspect of Theory of Mind (ToM) is necessary to understand the story compared with narratives which do not necessarily require knowledge of characters' intentions. Where relevant, a paper's results are split across these different sequence types, however the averages reported in Chapter Seven collapse across these types.

Reference	Task	Sequence type	TD	ASD	DLD	SSD
Allen et al. 1991	PAT			0.27	0.58	
Baker 2013	PAT		0.96		0.66	
Baron-Cohen et al. 1986	PAT	Mechanical	0.56	0.96		
Baron-Cohen et al. 1986	PAT	Behavioral	0.73	0.74		
Baron-Cohen et al. 1986	PAT	Intentional (ToM)	0.87	0.29		

Reference	Task	Sequence type	TD	ASD	DLD	SSD
Brizzolara et al. 2011	PAT		0.70		0.73	
Brüne 2005	PAT		0.82			0.40
Brüne et al. 2007	PAT		0.80			0.68
Brüne et al. 2005	PAT		0.98			0.70
Brüne et al. 2011	PAT	Mechanical	0.65			0.59
Brüne et al. 2011	PAT	Social script	0.64			0.60
Brüne et al. 2011	PAT	Capture control	0.46			0.47
Brüne et al. 2011	PAT	False belief (ToM)	0.60			0.47
Brunet et al. 2003	SCT	Intentional (ToM)	0.93			0.79
Brunet et al. 2003	SCT	Physical causality (characters)	0.98			0.93
Brunet et al. 2003	SCT	Physical causality (objects)	0.99			0.96
Ciaramidaro et al. 2015	SCT	Physical causality (characters)	0.94	0.78		0.90
Ciaramidaro et al. 2015	SCT	Private intention (ToM)	0.89	0.68		0.79
Ciaramidaro et al. 2015	SCT	Communicated intention	0.87	0.69		0.84
Langdon et al. 2001	PAT	Mechanical	0.96			0.89

Reference	Task	Sequence type	TD	ASD	DLD	SSD
Langdon et al. 2001	PAT	Social script	0.97			0.94
Langdon et al. 2001	PAT	Capture control	0.72			0.58
Langdon et al. 2001	PAT	False belief (ToM)	0.92			0.68
Langdon et al. 2008	PAT	Mechanical	0.93			0.84
Langdon et al. 2008	PAT	Social script	0.99			0.91
Langdon et al. 2008	PAT	Capture control	0.75			0.57
Langdon et al. 2008	PAT	False belief (ToM)	1.00			0.59
Loucas et al. 2013	PAT		0.85	0.84	0.88	
Nenadović et al. 2014	PAT		0.85		0.63	
Roux et al. 2016	SCT	Intentional (ToM)	0.67			0.58
Roux et al. 2016	SCT	Physical causality (characters)	0.83			0.70
Sarfati, Hardy-Baylé, Besche et al. 1997	SCT		0.89			0.66
Sarfati et al. 1999	SCT		0.87			0.58
Sarfati, Hardy-Baylé, Nadel, et al. 1997	SCT	Intentional (ToM)	0.93			0.79

Reference	Task	Sequence type	TD	ASD	DLD	SSD
Sarfati, Hardy-Baylé, Nadel, et al. 1997	SCT	False belief (ToM)	0.85			0.49
Sarfati et al. 2000	SCT		0.91			0.71
Sivaratnam et al. 2012	SCT	Intentional (ToM)	0.85	0.58		
Sivaratnam et al. 2012	SCT	Emotions	0.85	0.83		
Sivaratnam et al. 2012	SCT	Controls	0.83	0.78		
Watkins et al. 2002	PAT		0.54		0.40	
Zalla et al. 2010	SCT	Familiar	1.00	0.70		
Zalla et al. 2010	SCT	Unfamiliar	0.90	0.70		

NOTES

Chapter One

1   It is worth differentiating "fluency" here from "literacy," which imply different types of development. Literacy is a process associating one modality (speech sounds) to another modality (graphics), which thereby gives another pathway to access meanings. This is entirely unnatural, and thus requires active learning and instruction. In contrast, drawing development is learning systematic configurations of graphics mapped directly to meaning, just like the direct mapping of sounds to meaning in speech. This is a natural process that children do with exposure and practice (Willats 2005; Wilson and Wilson 1982; Wilson 2016) across a developmental "critical period" that apexes around puberty, similarly to language (Cohn 2012a). Literacy has no comparable critical period, and people can learn to read and write well into adulthood. As we will explore throughout this book, development of understanding sequential images similarly begins at young ages and gradually improves with exposure and practice, although further research is needed to understand the details.

Chapter Two

1   This chapter draws from and expands on ideas presented previously in Cohn (2019c, 2020b), including the original analysis of the example from *Pang: The Wandering Shaolin Monk*.

2   Given the similarities in processing between verbal and visual information, the question is often posed whether it's possible that people are "translating" the visual information into verbal representations in processing. That is, do comprehenders use some form of subvocalization (i.e., latent inner speech) or conversion where the verbal modality is the base representation used by the visual representation? There are several reasons that this is unlikely. First, both visual and verbal information elicit N400s in semantic processing between 250 and 500 milliseconds after seeing a word or image appear. The time-course of this brain response is relatively consistent across modalities (Kutas and Federmeier 2011), implying that there is no delay indicating a "translation" process. In addition, the scalp distribution of the N400 is slightly different for visual (centro-anterior) and spoken or written (parietal) information (Kutas and Federmeier 2011), suggesting inexact neural generators despite the similar mechanisms. Finally, the N400 in response to visual information is preceded by an N300, a waveform typically associated with object identification or

categorization (Hamm, Johnson, and Kirk 2002; McPherson and Holcomb 1999), and which does not appear as a reaction to spoken or written information. Thus, neural evidence does not suggest a subvocalization or translation process from visual into verbal information.

Chapter Three

1   Coders of the VLRC include: Jessika Axnér, Michaela Diercks, Mark Dierick, Ryan Huffman, Lincy van Middelaar, Kaitlin Pederson, Ryan Taylor, Rebecca Yeh, and Vivian Wong.

2   It is worth noting that additional analyses are possible other than deriving means per book. For example, we can search the raw panel-by-panel data for structural patterns that may appear "bottom-up" from the combination of various coded dimensions. Such computational analyses are already underway with the data in the VLRC.

3   An additional possibility might be that framing of panels is affected by structures in the spoken languages of these cultures. Specifically, if panels depict only parts of a scene, it requires that readers must infer the undepicted information. This is similar to what occurs in sentence structures using *zero anaphora* (or *pro-drop*), where grammatical subjects or objects are dropped from syntax and such content is left inferred (Haspelmath et al. 2001; Huang 1984). Zero anaphora indeed appears more prevalently in Asian languages than European languages (Haspelmath et al. 2001; Huang 1984), consistent with our findings that Asian comics depict more single characters (monos), while European comics use more full scenes (macros). Annotation of Spanish and Italian comics could test this, since they use zero anaphora but belong to European cultures. It's worth noting that the full VLRC does include coding of two Spanish comics, which indeed trend more like Asian comics in their framing. However, coding of only two comics makes these data less reliable. Further analyses are needed to make any substantive claims, and this low proportion is why they were left out of analyses in this chapter. Upcoming research will further test this hypothesis about linguistic influence on framing.

4   If we are to seriously entertain the explanation of cross-cultural differences based on patterns of psychological attention (Masuda and Nisbett 2001; Nisbett and Masuda 2003), then paneling in OEL manga might reflect an attempt to reconcile the conventionalized panel framing of Japanese manga with the psychological attentional preferences displayed by Americans. Creators and readers of manga in the United States would thus provide an interesting test of this "attentional theory", particularly if there could be a reverse effect. That is, would manga readership habituate their readers to have a more dispersed focus of attention? If so, might we expect that US readers/ creators of manga would focus on the broader environment of a scene along with its primary objects? Eye tracking experiments could explore this potential.

5   Although Dutch and Flemish comics do not seem to change across publication dates in terms of semantics and attentional framing, they alter in other dimensions. Various elements of visual morphology like speech balloons,

thought bubbles, and various upfixes have changed in their proportions over time (van Middelaar 2017). This suggests that the visual language is not static over time across all structures, again supporting that they are built from structures organized in a parallel architecture as proposed in Chapter One.

Chapter Four

1   Similar intentions persist in contemporary beliefs that comics can serve as a "universal" communicative tool. For example: www.comicsunitingnations.org

Chapter Six

1   I also attempted additional analyses which included the rates of reading books, or watching movies or cartoons, also both currently and when growing up. Each of these variables primarily clustered only with their own other type. That is, book reading at both ages formed a component, as did movie watching. Cartoon watching weakly associated with the "manga reading" component. As these variables mostly did not associate with other elements, I leave them out of the primary analysis reported here. However, the independence of book reading and movie watching from the other variables is informative in its own right.

Chapter Seven

1   Note again that this reliance on structural patterning would not be modality-specific. If this hypothesis holds true, it is also possible that acquisition of structural patterning in the verbal modality could provide an equal benefit.

2   Given the growing sophistication of methods of studying specific aspects of visual narrative processing using behavioral (reaction times, self-paced viewing times) and/or neurocognitive methods (ERPs), it is worth asking whether other methods could better inform detection and/or assessment of various cognitive disorders beyond PATs, SCTs, or NETs.

Chapter Eight

1   Note that the parallel architecture approach of Visual Language Theory can also account for the multimodal characteristics of film quite easily. As in the parallel architectures shown for unimodal visual narratives, this model allows different structures to operate independently, yet to coalesce to create a larger whole. Such an organization is ideal for accounting for emergent structures and meaning not present in one modality alone. For a multimodal extension of the parallel architecture, see Cohn (2016b).

REFERENCES

Abel, Jessica, and Matt Madden. 2008. *Drawing Words and Writing Pictures*. New York, NY: First Second Books.

Abelman, Robert. 1990. "You can't get there from here: Children's understanding of time-leaps on television." *Journal of Broadcasting & Electronic Media* 34 (4): 469–476. doi: 10.1080/08838159009386755.

Aleixo, Paul A., and Krystina Sumner. 2017. "Memory for biopsychology material presented in comic book format." *Journal of Graphic Novels and Comics* 8 (1): 79–88. doi: 10.1080/21504857.2016.1219957.

Allen, Kate, and John E. Ingulsrud. 2005. "Reading Manga: Patterns of Personal Literacies Among Adolescents." *Language and Education* 19 (4): 265–280. doi: 10.1080/09500780508668681.

Allen, Mark H., Alan J. Lincoln, and Alan S. Kaufman. 1991. "Sequential and simultaneous processing abilities of high-functioning autistic and language-impaired children." *Journal of Autism and Developmental Disorders* 21 (4): 483–502. doi: 10.1007/bf02206872.

Arbuckle, Katherine. 2004. "The language of pictures: Visual literacy and print materials for Adult Basic Education and Training (ABET)." *Language Matters* 35 (2): 445–458. doi: 10.1080/10228190408566228.

Arnheim, Rudolf. 1978. "Expressions." *Art Education* 31 (3): 37–38.

Bach, Benjamin, Nathalie Henry Richie, Sheelagh Carpendale, and Hanspeter Pfister. 2017. "The Emerging Genre of Data Comics." *IEEE Computer Graphics and Applications* 37 (3): 6–13. doi: 10.1109/MCG.2017.33.

Bach, Benjamin, Zezhong Wang, Matteo Farinella, Dave Murray-Rust, Nathalie Henry Riche, and WA Redmond. 2018. "Design Patterns for Data Comics." In *Proceedings of the Conference on Human Factors in Information Systems (CHI) 2018*. Montréal, QC, Canada.

Baggio, Giosuè. 2018. *Meaning in the Brain*. Cambridge, MA: MIT Press.

Baggio, Giosuè, Michiel van Lambalgen, and Peter Hagoort. 2008. "Computing and recomputing discourse models: An ERP study." *Journal of Memory and Language* 59 (1): 36–53. doi: http://dx.doi.org/10.1016/j.jml.2008.02.005.

Baker, Johanna M. 2013. "Verbal and nonverbal sequencing in children with specific language impairment." Masters Thesis, Psychology, San Diego State University.

Baldo, Juliana V., Selvi R. Paulraj, Brian C. Curran, and Nina F. Dronkers. 2015. "Impaired reasoning and problem-solving in individuals with language impairment due to aphasia or language delay." *Frontiers in Psychology* 6 (1523). doi: 10.3389/fpsyg.2015.01523.

Baron-Cohen, Simon, Sally Wheelwright, Richard Skinner, Joanne Martin, and Emma Clubley. 2001. "The Autism-Spectrum Quotient (AQ): Evidence from Asperger Syndrome/High-Functioning Autism, Males and Females, Scientists and Mathematicians." *Journal of Autism and Developmental Disorders* 31 (1): 5–17. doi: 10.1023/a:1005653411471.

Baron-Cohen, Simon, Alan M Leslie, and Uta Frith. 1986. "Mechanical, behavioural and intentional understanding of picture stories in autistic children." *British Journal of Developmental Psychology* 4 (2): 113–125.

Barr, Rachel, Elizabeth Zack, Amaya Garcia, and Paul Muentener. 2008. "Infants' Attention and Responsiveness to Television Increases With Prior Exposure and Parental Interaction." *Infancy* 13 (1): 30–56. doi:10.1080/15250000701779378.

Bateman, John A. 2007. "Towards a grande paradigmatique of film: Christian Metz reloaded." *Semiotica* 2007 (167): 13–64.

Bateman, John A., Annika Beckmann, and Rocío Inés Varela. 2018. "From Empirical Studies to Visual Narrative Organization: Exploring Page Composition." In *Empirical Comics Research: Digital, Multimodal, and Cognitive Methods*, edited by Alexander Dunst, Jochen Laubrock, and Janina Wildfeuer, 127–153. New York: Routledge.

Bateman, John A., and Karl-Heinrich Schmidt. 2012. *Multimodal Film Analysis: How Films Mean*. New York: Routledge.

Bateman, John A., and Francisco O. D. Veloso. 2013. "The semiotic resources of comics in movie adaptation: Ang Lee's Hulk (2003) as a case study." *Studies in Comics* 4 (1): 135–157. doi: 10.1386/stic.4.1.135_1.

Bateman, John A., Francisco O. D. Veloso, and Yan Ling Lau. 2019. "On the track of visual style: a diachronic study of page composition in comics and its functional motivation." *Visual Communication* 0 (0): 39. doi: 10.1177/1470357219839101.

Bateman, John A., Francisco O. D. Veloso, Janina Wildfeuer, Felix HiuLaam Cheung, and Nancy Songdan Guo. 2016. "An Open Multilevel Classification Scheme for the Visual Layout of Comics and Graphic Novels: Motivation and Design." *Digital Scholarship in the Humanities* 32 (3): 476–510. doi: 10.1093/llc/fqw024.

Bateman, John A., and Janina Wildfeuer. 2014. "A multimodal discourse theory of visual narrative." *Journal of Pragmatics* 74: 180–208. doi: 10.1016/j.pragma.2014.10.001.

Beatty, William W., Zeljko Jocic, and Nancy Monson. 1993. "Picture sequencing by schizophrenic patients." *Bulletin of the Psychonomic Society* 31 (4): 265–267.

Beatty, William W., and Nancy Monson. 1990. "Picture and Motor Sequencing in Parkinson's Disease." *Journal of Geriatric Psychiatry and Neurology* 3 (4): 192–197. doi: 10.1177/089198879000300403.

Beatty, William W., and Nancy Monson. 1994. "Picture and motor sequencing in multiple sclerosis." *Journal of Clinical and Experimental Neuropsychology* 16 (2): 165–172. doi: 10.1080/01688639408402627.

Berliner, Todd, and Dale J. Cohen. 2011. "The illusion of continuity: Active perception and the classical editing system." *Journal of Film and Video* 63 (1): 44–63.

Berman, Ruth A. 1988. "On the ability to relate events in narrative." *Discourse Processes* 11 (4): 469–497. doi: 10.1080/01638538809544714.

Berman, Ruth A., and Dan I. Slobin. 1994. *Relating Events in Narrative: A Crosslinguistic Developmental Study*. New Jersey: Lawrence Erlbaum Associates.

Bihrle, Amy M., Hiram H. Brownell, John A. Powelson, and Howard Gardner. 1986. "Comprehension of humorous and nonhumorous materials by left and right brain-damaged patients." *Brain and Cognition* 5: 399–411.

Bingham, Adelaide Bates, Karen L. Rembold, and Steven R. Yussen. 1986. "Developmental change in identifying main ideas in picture stories." *Journal of*

Applied Developmental Psychology 7 (4): 325–340. doi: https://doi. org/10.1016/0193-3973(86)90003-1.

Bishop, Alan. 1977. "Is a Picture Worth a Thousand Words?" *Mathematics Teaching* 81: 32–35.

Bishop, Dorothy V. M., and C. Adams. 1992. "Comprehension Problems in Children With Specific Language Impairment: Literal and Inferential Meaning." *Journal of Speech, Language, and Hearing Research* 35 (1): 119–129. doi: 10.1044/jshr.3501.119.

Bishop, Dorothy V. M., and Chris Donlan. 2005. "The role of syntax in encoding and recall of pictorial narratives: Evidence from specific language impairment." *British Journal of Developmental Psychology* 23 (1): 25–46. doi: 10.1348/026151004X20685.

Bitz, Michael. 2004a. "The comic book project: Forging alternative pathways to literacy." *Journal of Adolescent & Adult Literacy* 47 (7): 574–586.

Bitz, Michael. 2004b. "The Comic Book Project: The Lives of Urban Youth." *Art Education* 57 (2): 33–39. doi: 10.1080/00043125.2004.11653541.

Black, John B., and Robert Wilensky. 1979. "An evaluation of story grammars." *Cognitive Science* 3: 213–230.

Blum, Alexander. 2019. "Deficit or Difference? Assessing Narrative Comprehension in Autistic and Typically Developing Individuals: Comic vs. Text" Doctoral Dissertation, Education, University of California, Berkeley.

Bornens, Marie-Thérèse. 1990. "Problems brought about by "reading" a sequence of pictures." *Journal of Experimental Child Psychology* 49 (2): 189–226. doi: http://dx.doi.org/10.1016/0022-0965(90)90055-D.

Boroditsky, Lera, Alice Gaby, and Stephen C. Levinson. 2008. "Time in space." In *Field Manual Volume 11*, edited by Asifa Majid, 52–76. Nijmegen: Max Planck Institute for Psycholinguistics.

Bott, Oliver. 2010. *The Processing of Events*. Vol. 162. Amsterdam: John Benjamins Publishing Company.

Botting, Nicola. 2002. "Narrative as a tool for the assessment of linguistic and pragmatic impairments." *Child Language Teaching and Therapy* 18 (1): 1–21. doi: 10.1191/0265659002ct224oa.

Branigan, Edward. 1992. *Narrative Comprehension and Film*. London, UK: Routledge.

Breiger, Boris. 1956. "The use of the W-B picture arrangement subtest as a projective technique." *Journal of Consulting Psychology* 20 (2): 132.

Brewer, William F. 1985. "The story schema: Universal and culture-specific properties." In *Literacy, Language, and Learning*, edited by David R. Olson, Nancy Torrance and Angela Hildyard, 167–194. Cambridge: Cambridge University Press.

Brewer, William F., and Edward H. Lichtenstein. 1981. "Event schemas, story schemas, and story grammars." In *Attention and Performance IX*, edited by J. Long and A. D. Baddeley, 363–379. Hillsdale: Erlbaum.

Brienza, Casey. 2015. *Global Manga: "Japanese" Comics without Japan?* Surrey, UK: Ashgate Publishing, Ltd.

Brienza, Casey. 2016. *Manga in America: Transnational Book Publishing and the Domestication of Japanese Comics*. London: Bloomsbury Academic.

Brizzolara, Daniela, Filippo Gasperini, Lucia Pfanner, Paola Cristofani, Claudia Casalini, and Anna M. Chilosi. 2011. "Long-term reading and spelling outcome in Italian adolescents with a history of specific language impairment." *Cortex* 47 (8): 955–973. doi: https://doi.org/10.1016/j.cortex.2011.02.009.

Brouwer, Harm, Matthew W. Crocker, Noortje J. Venhuizen, and John C. J. Hoeks. 2016. "A Neurocomputational Model of the N400 and the P600 in Language Processing." *Cognitive Science* 41 (S6): 1318–1352. doi: 10.1111/cogs.12461.

Brouwer, Harm, Hartmut Fitz, and John Hoeks. 2012. "Getting real about Semantic Illusions: Rethinking the functional role of the P600 in language comprehension." *Brain Research* 1446: 127–143. doi: 10.1016/j.brainres.2012.01.055.

Brouwer, Herman. 1995. "Communicating with pictures: The role of pictures in health education in outpatient clinics of rural African hospitals." *Visual Sociology* 10 (1–2): 15–27. doi: 10.1080/14725869508583746.

Brown, Ann L. 1975. "Recognition, Reconstruction, and Recall of Narrative Sequences by Preoperational Children." *Child Development* 46 (1): 156–166. doi: 10.2307/1128844.

Brown, Ann L., and Lucia A. French. 1976. "Construction and Regeneration of Logical Sequences Using Causes or Consequences as the Point of Departure." *Child Development* 47 (4): 930–940. doi: 10.2307/1128428.

Brown, Ann L., and Martin D. Murphy. 1975. "Reconstruction of arbitrary versus logical sequences by preschool children." *Journal of Experimental Child Psychology* 20 (2): 307–326. doi: https://doi.org/10.1016/0022-0965(75)90106-X.

Brown, Penelope. 2012. "Time and Space in Tzeltal: Is the Future Uphill?" *Frontiers in Psychology* 3 (212). doi: 10.3389/fpsyg.2012.00212.

Brüne, Martin. 2005. "Emotion recognition, 'theory of mind,' and social behavior in schizophrenia." *Psychiatry Research* 133 (2): 135–147. doi: https://doi.org/10.1016/j.psychres.2004.10.007.

Brüne, Martin, Mona Abdel-Hamid, Caroline Lehmkämper, and Claudia Sonntag. 2007. "Mental state attribution, neurocognitive functioning, and psychopathology: What predicts poor social competence in schizophrenia best?" *Schizophrenia Research* 92 (1): 151–159. doi: 10.1016/j.schres.2007.01.006.

Brüne, Martin, and Luise Bodenstein. 2005. "Proverb comprehension reconsidered— 'theory of mind' and the pragmatic use of language in schizophrenia." *Schizophrenia Research* 75 (2): 233–239. doi: https://doi.org/10.1016/j.schres.2004.11.006.

Brüne, Martin, Daniela Schaub, Georg Juckel, and Robyn Langdon. 2011. "Social skills and behavioral problems in schizophrenia: The role of mental state attribution, neurocognition and clinical symptomatology." *Psychiatry Research* 190 (1): 9–17. doi: https://doi.org/10.1016/j.psychres.2010.03.015.

Brunet, Eric, Yves Sarfati, Marie-Christine Hardy-Baylé, and Jean Decety. 2003. "Abnormalities of brain function during a nonverbal theory of mind task in schizophrenia." *Neuropsychologia* 41 (12): 1574–1582. doi: https://doi.org/10.1016/S0028-3932(03)00119-2.

Burkhardt, Petra. 2007. "The P600 Reflects Cost of New Information in Discourse Memory." *NeuroReport* 18 (17): 1851–1854.

Burris, Silas, and Danielle Brown. 2014. "When all children comprehend: increasing the external validity of narrative comprehension development research." *Frontiers in Psychology* 5 (168): 1–16. doi: 10.3389/fpsyg.2014.00168.

Butcher, S.H. 1902. The Poetics of Aristotle. London: Macmillian and Co. Ltd.

Byram, Martin L., and Chris Garforth. 1980. "Research and testing non-formal education materials: a multi-media extension project in Botswana." *Educational Broadcasting International* 13 (4): 190–194.

Caldwell, Joshua. 2012. "Comic panel layout: A Peircean analysis." *Studies in Comics* 2 (2): 317–338. doi: 10.1386/stic.2.2.317_1.

Campbell, Jonathan M, and David M McCord. 1996. "The WAIS-R Comprehension and Picture Arrangement subtests as measures of social intelligence: Testing traditional interpretations." *Journal of Psychoeducational Assessment* 14: 240–249.

Carello, Claudia, Lawrence D. Rosenblum, and A. Grosofsky. 1986. "Static depiction of movement." *Perception* 15 (1): 41–58.

Carroll, Alice, Nicholas Evans, Darja Hoenigman, and Lila San Roque. 2009. "The family problems picture task." *Designed for use by the Social Cognition and Language Project. A collaboration of The Australian National University, Griffith University, University of Melbourne and the Max Planck Institute for Psycholinguistics.*

Carroll, Alice, Barbara Kelly, and Lauren Gawne. 2011. "The jackal and crow picture task." *Designed for use by the Social Cognition and Language Project. A collaboration of The Australian National University, Griffith University, University of Melbourne and the Max Planck Institute for Psycholinguistics.*

Carroll, John M. 1980. *Toward a Structural Psychology of Cinema.* The Hague: Mouton.

Cary, Stephen. 2004. *Going Graphic: Comics at Work in the Multilingual Classroom:* Greenwood Publishing Group, Incorporated.

Champagne-Lavau, Maud, Marion Fossard, Guillaume Martel, Cimon Chapdelaine, Guy Blouin, Jean-Pierre Rodriguez, and Emmanuel Stip. 2009. "Do patients with schizophrenia attribute mental states in a referential communication task?" *Cognitive Neuropsychiatry* 14 (3): 217–239. doi: 10.1080/13546800903004114.

Chan, Ting Ting, and Benjamin Bergen. 2005. "Writing Direction Influences Spatial Cognition." In *Proceedings of the Twenty-Seventh Annual Conference of Cognitive Science Society*, 412–417. Stresa, Italy, July 21–23, 2005.

Chavanne, Renaud. 2015. "The Composition of Comics." *European Comic Art* 8 (1): 111–144.

Cherry, David, and David Brickler. 2016. "Analysis of Gaze on Comic Book Panel Structure." accessed 2/1/2016. https://pdfs.semanticscholar.org/5dd3/8f29c4df1a 2ec9fd3bd068d15ee954c10f77.pdf.

Chiba, Shinichi, Takamasa Tanaka, Kenji Shoji, and Fubito Toyama. 2007. "Eye Movement in Reading Comics." In *Proceedings of the 14th Annual International Display Workshops*, 1255–1258.

Chomsky, Noam. 1965. *Aspects of the Theory of Syntax.* Cambridge, MA: MIT Press.

Cicci, Matthew. 2015. "Turning the page: Fandoms, multimodality, the transformation of the "comic book" superhero." Doctoral Dissertation, English, Wayne State University.

Coderre, Emily L. 2019. "Dismantling the "Visual Ease Assumption": A Review of Visual Narrative Processing in Clinical Populations." *Topics in Cognitive Science.* 12 (1): 224–255. doi: 10.1111/tops.12446.

Coderre, Emily L., Neil Cohn, Sally K. Slipher, Mariya Chernenok, Kerry Ledoux, and Barry Gordon. 2018. "Visual and linguistic narrative comprehension in autism spectrum disorders: Neural evidence for modality-independent impairments." *Brain and Language* 186: 44–59.

Coderre, Emily L., Elizabeth O'Donnell, Emme O'Rourke, and Neil Cohn. forthcoming. "Predictability modulates the N400 in non-verbal narrative processing."

Cohen, Jonathan D, and David Servan-Schreiber. 1992. "Context, cortex, and dopamine: a connectionist approach to behavior and biology in schizophrenia." *Psychological Review* 99 (1): 45–77.

Cohn, Neil. 2010a. "Extra! Extra! Semantics in comics!: The conceptual structure of *Chicago Tribune* advertisements." *Journal of Pragmatics* 42 (11): 3138–3146. doi: 10.1016/j.pragma.2010.04.016.

Cohn, Neil. 2010b. "The limits of time and transitions: Challenges to theories of sequential image comprehension." *Studies in Comics* 1 (1): 127–147.

Cohn, Neil. 2011. "A different kind of cultural frame: An analysis of panels in American comics and Japanese manga." *Image [&] Narrative* 12 (1): 120–134.

Cohn, Neil. 2012a. "Explaining "I can't draw": Parallels between the structure and development of language and drawing." *Human Development* 55 (4): 167–192. doi: 10.1159/000341842.

Cohn, Neil. 2012b. "Structure, meaning, and constituency in visual narrative comprehension." Doctoral Dissertation, Psychology, Tufts University.

Cohn, Neil. 2013a. "Navigating comics: An empirical and theoretical approach to strategies of reading comic page layouts." *Frontiers in Psychology—Cognitive Science* 4: 1–15. doi: 10.3389/fpsyg.2013.00186.

Cohn, Neil. 2013b. *The Visual Language of Comics: Introduction to the Structure and Cognition of Sequential Images*. London, UK: Bloomsbury.

Cohn, Neil. 2013c. "Visual narrative structure." *Cognitive Science* 37 (3): 413–452. doi: 10.1111/cogs.12016.

Cohn, Neil. 2014a. "The architecture of visual narrative comprehension: The interaction of narrative structure and page layout in understanding comics." *Frontiers in Psychology* 5: 1–9. doi: 10.3389/fpsyg.2014.00680.

Cohn, Neil. 2014b. "Framing "I can't draw": The influence of cultural frames on the development of drawing." *Culture & Psychology* 20 (1): 102–117. doi: 10.1177/1354067x13515936.

Cohn, Neil. 2014c. "You're a good structure, Charlie Brown: The distribution of narrative categories in comic strips." *Cognitive Science* 38 (7): 1317–1359. doi: 10.1111/cogs.12116.

Cohn, Neil. 2015. "Narrative conjunction's junction function: The interface of narrative grammar and semantics in sequential images." *Journal of Pragmatics* 88: 105–132. doi: 10.1016/j.pragma.2015.09.001.

Cohn, Neil. 2016a. "From Visual Narrative Grammar to Filmic Narrative Grammar: The narrative structure of static and moving images." In *Film Text Analysis: New Perspectives on the Analysis of Filmic Meaning.*, edited by Janina Wildfeuer and John A. Bateman, 94–117. London: Routledge.

Cohn, Neil. 2016b. "A multimodal parallel architecture: A cognitive framework for multimodal interactions." *Cognition* 146: 304–323. doi: 10.1016/j.cognition.2015.10.007.

Cohn, Neil. 2018. "Combinatorial morphology in visual languages." In *The Construction of Words: Advances in Construction Morphology*, edited by Geert Booij, 175–199. London: Springer.

Cohn, Neil. 2019a. "Being explicit about the implicit: Inference generating techniques in visual narrative." *Language and Cognition* 11 (1): 66–97. doi: 10.1017/langcog.2019.6.

Cohn, Neil. 2019b. "Structural complexity in visual narratives: Theory, brains, and cross-cultural diversity." In *Narrative Complexity: Cognition, Embodiment,*

Evolution, edited by Marina Grishakova and Maria Poulaki, 174–199. Lincoln: University of Nebraska Press.

Cohn, Neil. 2019c. "Visual narratives and the mind: Comprehension, cognition, and learning." In *Psychology of Learning and Motivation: Knowledge and Vision*, edited by Kara D. Federmeier and Diane M. Beck, 97–128. London: Academic Press.

Cohn, Neil. 2020a. "Visual narrative comprehension: universal or not?" *Psychonomic Bulletin & Review* 27 (2):266–285. doi: 10.3758/s13423-019-01670-1.

Cohn, Neil. 2020b. "Your brain on comics: A cognitive model of visual narrative comprehension." *Topics in Cognitive Science*. 12 (1): 352-386. doi: 10.1111/tops.12421.

Cohn, Neil. forthcoming. "Making a star out of inference in the neurocognition of visual narratives."

Cohn, Neil, Jessika Axnér, Michaela Diercks, Rebecca Yeh, and Kaitlin Pederson. 2019. "The cultural pages of comics: Cross-cultural variation in page layouts." *Journal of Graphic Novels and Comics* 10 (1): 67–86. doi: 10.1080/21504857.2017.1413667.

Cohn, Neil, and Patrick Bender. 2017. "Drawing the line between constituent structure and coherence relations in visual narratives." *Journal of Experimental Psychology: Learning, Memory, & Cognition* 43 (2): 289–301. doi: 10.1037/xlm0000290.

Cohn, Neil, and Hannah Campbell. 2015. "Navigating comics II: Constraints on the reading order of page layouts." *Applied Cognitive Psychology* 29 (2): 193–199. doi: 10.1002/acp.3086.

Cohn, Neil, and Sean Ehly. 2016. "The vocabulary of manga: Visual morphology in dialects of Japanese Visual Language." *Journal of Pragmatics* 92: 17–29. doi: 10.1016/j.pragma.2015.11.008.

Cohn, Neil, Jan Engelen, and Joost Schilperoord. 2019. "The grammar of emoji? Constraints on communicative pictorial sequencing." *Cognitive Research: Principles and Implications* 4 (1): 33. doi: 10.1186/s41235-019-0177-0.

Cohn, Neil, Ray Jackendoff, Phillip J. Holcomb, and Gina R. Kuperberg. 2014. "The grammar of visual narrative: Neural evidence for constituent structure in sequential image comprehension." *Neuropsychologia* 64: 63–70. doi: 10.1016/j.neuropsychologia.2014.09.018.

Cohn, Neil, and Marta Kutas. 2015. "Getting a cue before getting a clue: Event-related potentials to inference in visual narrative comprehension." *Neuropsychologia* 77: 267–278. doi: 10.1016/j.neuropsychologia.2015.08.026.

Cohn, Neil, and Marta Kutas. 2017. "What's your neural function, visual narrative conjunction? Grammar, meaning, and fluency in sequential image processing." *Cognitive Research: Principles and Implications* 2 (27): 1–13. doi: 10.1186/s41235-017-0064-5.

Cohn, Neil, and Stephen Maher. 2015. "The notion of the motion: The neurocognition of motion lines in visual narratives." *Brain Research* 1601: 73–84. doi: 10.1016/j.brainres.2015.01.018.

Cohn, Neil, Beena Murthy, and Tom Foulsham. 2016. "Meaning above the head: Combinatorial constraints on the visual vocabulary of comics." *Journal of Cognitive Psychology* 28 (5): 559–574. doi: 10.1080/20445911.2016.1179314.

Cohn, Neil, and Martin Paczynski. 2013. "Prediction, events, and the advantage of Agents: The processing of semantic roles in visual narrative." *Cognitive Psychology* 67 (3): 73–97. doi: 10.1016/j.cogpsych.2013.07.002.

Cohn, Neil, Martin Paczynski, Ray Jackendoff, Phillip J. Holcomb, and Gina R. Kuperberg. 2012. "(Pea)nuts and bolts of visual narrative: Structure and meaning in sequential image comprehension." *Cognitive Psychology* 65 (1): 1–38. doi: 10.1016/j.cogpsych.2012.01.003.

Cohn, Neil, Martin Paczynski, and Marta Kutas. 2017. "Not so secret agents: Event-related potentials to semantic roles in visual event comprehension." *Brain and Cognition* 119: 1–9. doi: 10.1016/j.bandc.2017.09.001.

Cohn, Neil, Ryan Taylor, and Kaitlin Pederson. 2017. "A picture is worth more words over time: Multimodality and narrative structure across eight decades of American superhero comics." *Multimodal Communication* 6 (1): 19–37. doi: 10.1515/mc-2017-0003.

Cohn, Neil, Amaro Taylor-Weiner, and Suzanne Grossman. 2012. "Framing Attention in Japanese and American Comics: Cross-cultural Differences in Attentional Structure." *Frontiers in Psychology – Cultural Psychology* 3: 1–12. doi: 10.3389/fpsyg.2012.00349.

Cohn, Neil, and Eva Wittenberg. 2015. "Action starring narratives and events: Structure and inference in visual narrative comprehension." *Journal of Cognitive Psychology* 27 (7): 812–828. doi: 10.1080/20445911.2015.1051535.

Colin, Michel. 1995. "The Grande Syntagmatique revisited." In *The Film Spectator: From Sign to Mind*, edited by Warren Buckland, 45–86. Amsterdam: Amsterdam University Press.

Collins, W. Andrew, Henry Wellman, Allen H. Keniston, and Sally D. Westby. 1978. "Age-Related Aspects of Comprehension and Inference from a Televised Dramatic Narrative." *Child Development* 49 (2): 389–399.

Consortium, Language and Reading Research. 2015. "The Dimensionality of Language Ability in Young Children." *Child Development* 86 (6): 1948–1965. doi:10.1111/cdev.12450.

Cook, Bruce L. 1980. "Picture communication in the Papua New Guinea." *Educational Broadcasting International* 13 (2): 78–83.

Cooper, Tarni Louisa, Yumi Kirino, Silvia Alonso, Johanna Lindahl, and Delia Grace. 2016. "Towards better-informed consent: Research with livestock-keepers and informal traders in East Africa." *Preventive Veterinary Medicine* 128: 135–141. doi: https://doi.org/10.1016/j.prevetmed.2016.04.008.

Cox, Carole. 1999. "Drawing Conclusions: a study in drafting with cartoons." *Changing English* 6 (2): 219–235. doi: 10.1080/1358684990060208.

Cox, Maureen V. 1998. "Drawings of People by Australian Aboriginal Children: the Intermixing of Cultural Styles." *Journal of Art and Design Education (JADE)* 17 (1): 71–80.

Cox, Maureen V., Masuo Koyasu, Hiromasa Hiranuma, and Julian Perara. 2001. "Children's human figure drawings in the UK and Japan: The effects of age, sex, and culture." *British Journal of Developmental Psychology* 19: 275–292.

Crescentini, Cristiano, Alberta Lunardelli, Alessandro Mussoni, Antonietta Zadini, and Tim Shallice. 2008. "A left basal ganglia case of dynamic aphasia or impairment of extra-language cognitive processes?" *Neurocase* 14 (2): 184–203. doi: 10.1080/13554790802108380.

Culicover, Peter W., and Ray Jackendoff. 2005. *Simpler Syntax*. Oxford: Oxford University Press.

Cutting, James E. 2005. "Perceiving scenes in film and in the world." In *Moving Image Theory: Ecological Considerations*, edited by J. D. Anderson and B.F. Anderson, 9–27. Carbondale, IL: Southern Illinois University Press.

Cutting, James E. 2015. "The Framing of Characters in Popular Movies." *Art & Perception* 3 (2): 191–212. doi: 10.1163/22134913-00002031.

Cutting, James E. 2016. "Narrative theory and the dynamics of popular movies." *Psychonomic Bulletin & Review* 23 (6): 1713–1743. doi: 10.3758/s13423-016-1051-4.

Cutting, James E., and Kacie L. Armstrong. 2018. "Cryptic Emotions and the Emergence of a Metatheory of Mind in Popular Filmmaking." *Cognitive Science* 42 (4): 1317–1344. doi: 10.1111/cogs.12586.

Cutting, James E., Jordan E. DeLong, and Christine E. Nothelfer. 2010. "Attention and the Evolution of Hollywood Film." *Psychological Science* 21: 432–439. doi: 10.1177/0956797610361679.

Davidson, Meghan M, and Susan Ellis Weismer. 2018. "A preliminary investigation of parent-reported fiction versus non-fiction book preferences of school-age children with autism spectrum disorder." *Autism & Developmental Language Impairments* 3: 2396941518806109. doi: 10.1177/2396941518806109.

Davis, Megan, Kerstin Dautenhahn, Chrystopher L. Nehaniv, and Stuart D. Powell. 2007. "The narrative construction of our (social) world: steps towards an interactive learning environment for children with autism." *Universal Access in the Information Society* 6 (2): 145–157.

de Beaugrande, Robert. 1982. "The story of grammars and the grammar of stories." *Journal of Pragmatics* 6: 383–422.

de Lange, Rudi W. 2000. "The Effect of Culture on the Efficacy of Pictures in Developing Communities: A Review of Certain Research and Some Guiding Principles." *Journal of Visual Literacy* 20 (1): 59–72.

De Renzi, E., P. Faglioni, M. Savoiardo, and L. A. Vignolo. 1966. "The Influence of Aphasia and of the Hemispheric Side of the Cerebral Lesion on Abstract Thinking." *Cortex* 2 (4): 399–420. doi: http://dx.doi.org/10.1016/S0010-9452(66)80017-5.

Dehejia, Vidya. 1990. "On Modes of Visual Narration in Early Buddhist Art." *The Art Bulletin* 72 (3): 374–392. doi: 10.2307/3045747.

Delong, Katherine A., Thomas P. Urbach, and Marta Kutas. 2005. "Probabilistic word pre-activation during language comprehension inferred from electrical brain activity." *Nature Neuroscience* 8 (8): 1117–1121.

Deregowski, Jan B., and Don Munro. 1974. "An Analysis of "Polyphasic Pictorial Perception"." *Journal of Cross-Cultural Psychology* 5 (3): 329–343. doi: 10.1177/002202217400500306.

Díaz Vera, Javier E. 2013a. "Embodied emotions in Medieval English language and visual arts." In *Sensuous Cognition Explorations into Human Sentience: Imagination, (E)motion and Perception*, edited by Rosario Caballero and Javier E. Díaz Vera, 195–219. Berlin: de Gruyter.

Díaz Vera, Javier E. 2013b. "Woven emotions: Visual representations of emotions in medieval English textiles." *Review of Cognitive Linguistics* 11 (2): 269–284. doi: 10.1075/rcl.11.2.04dia.

Dierick, Mark. 2017. "Visual storytelling in Dutch and Flemish comic books: A corpus analysis across culture and time." Bachelors Thesis, Communication and Information Science, Tilburg University.

Dodich, Alessandra, Chiara Cerami, Nicola Canessa, Chiara Crespi, Sandro Iannaccone, Alessandra Marcone, Sabrina Realmuto, Giada Lettieri, Daniela Perani, and Stefano F. Cappa. 2015. "A novel task assessing intention and emotion attribution: Italian standardization and normative data of the Story-based Empathy Task." *Neurological Sciences* 36 (10): 1907–1912. doi: 10.1007/s10072-015-2281-3.

Donchin, Emanuel, and Michael G. H. Coles. 1988. "Is the P300 component a manifestation of context updating?" *Behavioral and Brain Sciences* 11 (03): 357–374. doi:10.1017/S0140525X00058027.

Duh, Shinchieh, and Su-hua Wang. 2014. "Infants detect changes in everyday scenes: The role of scene gist." *Cognitive Psychology* 72: 142–161. doi: https://doi.org/10.1016/j.cogpsych.2014.03.001.

Duncan, H.F., N. Gourlay, and W. Hudson. 1973. *A Study of Pictorial Perception Among Bantu and White School Children.* Johannesburg: Witwaterstrand University Press.

Durant, L.E. 1981. "The respresentation of time in adolescent drawings." Unpublished Masters Thesis, Boston University.

Eisenbeiss, Sonja, Bill McGregor, and Claudia Maria Schmidt. 1999. "Story book stimulus for the elicitation of external possessor constructions and dative constructions ('the circle of dirt')." In *Manual for the 1999 Field Season,* 140–144. Max Planck Institute for Psycholinguistics.

Farinella, Matteo. 2018. "The potential of comics in science communication." *Journal of Science Communication* 17 (01): Y01–1.

Farran, Emily K., and Christopher Jarrold. 2003. "Visuospatial Cognition in Williams Syndrome: Reviewing and Accounting for the Strengths and Weaknesses in Performance." *Developmental Neuropsychology* 23 (1–2): 173–200. doi: 10.1080/87565641.2003.9651891.

Fedden, Sebastian, and Lera Boroditsky. 2012. "Spatialization of time in Mian." *Frontiers in Psychology* 3. doi: 10.3389/fpsyg.2012.00485.

Fichman, Sveta, Carmit Altman, Anna Voloskovich, Sharon Armon-Lotem, and Joel Walters. 2017. "Story grammar elements and causal relations in the narratives of Russian-Hebrew bilingual children with SLI and typical language development." *Journal of Communication Disorders* 69: 72–93. doi: 10.1016/j.jcomdis.2017.08.001.

Fivush, Robyn, and Jean M. Mandler. 1985. "Developmental Changes in the Understanding of Temporal Sequence." *Child Development* 56 (6): 1437–1446. doi: 10.2307/1130463.

Forceville, Charles. 2005. "Visual representations of the idealized cognitive model of anger in the Asterix album *La Zizanie.*" *Journal of Pragmatics* 37 (1): 69–88.

Forceville, Charles. 2011. "Pictorial runes in *Tintin and the Picaros.*" *Journal of Pragmatics* 43 (3): 875–890.

Forceville, Charles, and Eduardo Urios-Aparisi. 2009. *Multimodal Metaphor.* New York: Mouton De Gruyter.

Forceville, Charles, Tony Veale, and Kurt Feyaerts. 2010. "Balloonics: The Visuals of Balloons in Comics." In *The Rise and Reason of Comics and Graphic Literature: Critical Essays on the Form,* edited by Joyce Goggin and Dan Hassler-Forest, 56–73. Jefferson: McFarland & Company, Inc.

Forsdale, Joan Rosengren, and Louis Forsdale. 1970. "Film Literacy." *AV Communication Review* 18 (3): 263–276.

Foulsham, Tom, and Neil Cohn. forthcoming. "Zooming in on visual narrative comprehension."

Foulsham, Tom, Dean Wybrow, and Neil Cohn. 2016. "Reading without words: Eye movements in the comprehension of comic strips." *Applied Cognitive Psychology* 30: 566–579. doi: 10.1002/acp.3229.

Fresnault-Deruelle, Pierre. 1976. "Du linéaire au tabulaire." *Communications* 24 (1): 7–23.

Friedman, Sarah L., and Marguerite B. Stevenson. 1975. "Developmental Changes in the Understanding of Implied Motion in Two-dimensional Pictures." *Child Development* 46: 773–778.

Friedman, William J. 1990. "Children's Representations of the Pattern of Daily Activities." *Child Development* 61 (5): 1399–1412. doi: 10.1111/j.1467-8624.1990.tb02870.x.

Frith, Chris. 1994. "Theory of mind in Schizophrenia." In *Brain Damage, Behaviour and Cognition Series. The Neuropsychology of Schizophrenia*, edited by J. C. Cutting and A. S. David, 147–161. Hillsdale, NJ: Lawrence Erlbaum Associates, Inc.

Fucetola, Robert, Lisa T. Connor, Michael J. Strube, and Maurizio Corbetta. 2009. "Unravelling nonverbal cognitive performance in acquired aphasia." *Aphasiology* 23 (12): 1418–1426. doi: 10.1080/02687030802514938.

Fuhrman, Orly, and Lera Boroditsky. 2010. "Cross-Cultural Differences in Mental Representations of Time: Evidence From an Implicit Nonlinguistic Task." *Cognitive Science* 34 (8): 1430–1451. doi: 10.1111/j.1551-6709.2010.01105.x.

Fussell, Diana, and Ane Haaland. 1978. "Communicating with Pictures in Nepal: Results of Practical Study Used in Visual Education." *Educational Broadcasting International* 11 (1): 25–31.

Gaby, Alice. 2012. "The Thaayorre think of Time Like They Talk of Space." *Frontiers in Psychology* 3 (300): 1–8. doi: 10.3389/fpsyg.2012.00300.

Gagarina, Natalia, Daleen Klop, Sari Kunnari, Koula Tantele, Taina Välimaa, Ingrida Balčiūnienė, Ute Bohnacker, and Joel Walters. 2012. *MAIN: Multilingual Assessment Instrument for Narratives*: Zentrum für Allgemeine Sprachwissenschaft.

Ganea, Patricia A., Megan Bloom Pickard, and Judy S. DeLoache. 2008. "Transfer between Picture Books and the Real World by Very Young Children." *Journal of Cognition and Development* 9 (1): 46–66. doi: 10.1080/15248370701836592.

Ganis, Giorgio, Marta Kutas, and Martin I. Sereno. 1996. "The search for "common sense": An electrophysiological study of the comprehension of words and pictures in reading." *Journal of Cognitive Neuroscience* 8: 89–106.

Garnham, Alan. 1983. "What's wrong with story grammars?" *Cognition* 15: 145–154.

Gavaler, Chris. 2017. *Superhero Comics*. London: Bloomsbury.

Gavaler, Chris, and Leigh Ann Beavers. 2018. "Clarifying closure." *Journal of Graphic Novels and Comics*: 1–30. doi: 10.1080/21504857.2018.1540441.

Gawne, Lauren. 2016. *A Sketch Grammar of Lamjung Yolmo*. Canberra: Asia-Pacific Linguistics.

Gawne, Lauren, and Gretchen McCulloch. 2019. "Emoji as Digital Gestures." *Language@Internet* 17 (2). doi: urn:nbn:de:0009-7-48882.

Gelman, Rochel, Merry Bullock, and Elizabeth Meck. 1980. "Preschoolers' understanding of simple object transformations." *Child Development* 51 (3): 691–699.

Gernsbacher, Morton Ann. 1990. *Language Comprehension as Structure Building*. Hillsdale, NJ: Lawrence Earlbaum.

Gernsbacher, Morton Ann, and David A. Robertson. 2004. "Watching the Brain Comprehend Discourse." In *Experimental Cognitive Psychology and its Applications*, edited by A. Healy. Washington D.C.: APA Publications.

Gernsbacher, Morton Ann, K. R. Varner, and M Faust. 1990. "Investigating differences in general comprehension skill." *Journal of Experimental Psychology: Learning, Memory, and Cognition* 16: 430–445.

Goldberg, Adele E. 1995. *Constructions: A Construction Grammar Approach to Argument Structure*. Chicago, IL: University of Chicago Press.

Goldberg, Wendy. 2010. "The Manga Phenomenon in America." In *Manga: An Anthology of Global and Cultural Perspectives*, edited by Toni Johnson-Woods, 281–296. New York: Continuum Books.

Goldin-Meadow, Susan. 2003. *The Resiliance of Language: What Gesture Creation in Deaf Children Can Tell Us About How All Children Learn Language*. New York and Hove: Psychology Press.

Goldsmith, Evelyn. 1984. *Research into Illustration: An Approach and a Review*. Cambridge: Cambridge University Press.

Goldstein, Gerald, Sue R. Beers, Don J. Siegel, and Nancy J. Minshew. 2001. "A Comparison of WAIS-R Profiles in Adults With High-Functioning Autism or Differing Subtypes of Learning Disability." *Applied Neuropsychology* 8 (3): 148–154. doi: 10.1207/S15324826AN0803_3.

Gonçalves, Óscar F., Ana P. Pinheiro, Adriana Sampaio, Nuno Sousa, Montse Férnandez, and Margarida Henriques. 2010. "The Narrative Profile in Williams Syndrome: There is more to Storytelling than Just Telling a Story." *The British Journal of Development Disabilities* 56 (111): 89–109. doi: 10.1179/096979510799102943.

Graesser, Arthur C., Keith K. Millis, and Rolf A. Zwaan. 1997. "Discourse Comprehension." *Annual Review of Psychology* 48: 163–189.

Gravett, Paul. 2004. *Manga: Sixty Years of Japanese Comics*. New York, NY: HarperCollins.

Gravoso, RS, and TH Stuart. 2000. "Upland Farmers' Comprehension of Pictorial Messages on Environmental Protection." *Journal of Applied Communications* 84 (3): 1–14.

Green, Jennifer. 2014. *Drawn from the Ground: Sound, Sign and Inscription in Central Australian Sand Stories*. Cambridge, UK: Cambridge University Press.

Green, Michael J., and Kimberly R. Myers. 2010. "Graphic medicine: use of comics in medical education and patient care." *BMJ: British Medical Journal (Online)* 340.

Groensteen, Thierry. 2007. *The System of Comics*. Translated by Bart Beaty and Nick Nguyen. Jackson: University of Mississippi Press.

Gross, Dana, Nelson Soken, Karl S. Rosengren, Anne D. Pick, Bradford H. Pillow, and Patricia Melendez. 1991. "Children's Understanding of Action Lines and the Static Representation of Speed of Locomotion." *Child Development* 62: 1124–1141.

Hagmann, Carl Erick, and Neil Cohn. 2016. "The pieces fit: Constituent structure and global coherence of visual narrative in RSVP." *Acta Psychologica* 164: 157–164. doi: 10.1016/j.actpsy.2016.01.011.

Hagoort, Peter. 2005. "On Broca, brain, and binding: a new framework." *Trends in Cognitive Sciences* 9 (9): 416–423.

Hagoort, Peter. 2016. "MUC (Memory, Unification, Control): A Model on the Neurobiology of Language Beyond Single Word Processing." In *Neurobiology of Language*, edited by Gregory Hickok and Steven L. Small, 339–347. San Diego: Academic Press.

Hagoort, Peter. 2017. "The core and beyond in the language-ready brain." *Neuroscience & Biobehavioral Reviews* 81: 194–204. doi: https://doi.org/10.1016/j.neubiorev.2017.01.048.

Hagoort, Peter, Colin M. Brown, and J. Groothusen. 1993. "The syntactic positive shift (SPS) as an ERP measure of syntactic processing." *Language and Cognitive Processes* 8 (4): 439–483. doi: 10.1080/01690969308407585.

Hamm, Jeff P., Blake W. Johnson, and Ian J. Kirk. 2002. "Comparison of the N300 and N400 ERPs to picture stimuli in congruent and incongruent contexts." *Clinical Neurophysiology* 113 (8): 1339–1350. doi: https://doi.org/10.1016/S1388-2457(02)00161-X.

Happé, Francesca, and Uta Frith. 2006. "The Weak Coherence Account: Detail-focused Cognitive Style in Autism Spectrum Disorders." *Journal of Autism and Developmental Disorders* 36 (1): 5–25. doi: 10.1007/s10803-005-0039-0.

Haspelmath, Martin, Ekkehard König, Wulf Oesterreicher, and Wolfgang Raible. 2001. *Language Typology and Language Universals: An International Handbook*. Vol. 2. Berlin: Walter de Gruyter.

Hayward, Denyse V., and Phyllis Schneider. 2000. "Effectiveness of teaching story grammar knowledge to pre-school children with language impairment. An exploratory study." *Child Language Teaching and Therapy* 16 (3): 255–284. doi: 10.1177/026565900001600303.

Hayward, Denyse V., Phyllis Schneider, and Ronald B. Gillam. 2009. "Age and task-related effects on young children's understanding of a complex picture story." *Alberta Journal of Educational Research* 55 (1): 54–72.

Heaton, Robert K., Lyle E. Baade, and Kathy L. Johnson. 1978. "Neuropsychological test results associated with psychiatric disorders in adults." *Psychological Bulletin* 85 (1): 141–162.

Helland, Turid, and Arve Asbjørnsen. 2003. "Visual-Sequential and Visuo-Spatial Skills in Dyslexia: Variations According to Language Comprehension and Mathematics Skills." *Child Neuropsychology* 9 (3): 208–220. doi: 10.1076/chin.9.3.208.16456.

Helo, Andrea, Sandrien van Ommen, Sebastian Pannasch, Lucile Danteny-Dordoigne, and Pia Rämä. 2017. "Influence of semantic consistency and perceptual features on visual attention during scene viewing in toddlers." *Infant Behavior and Development* 49: 248–266. doi: https://doi.org/10.1016/j.infbeh.2017.09.008.

Hobbs, Renée, Richard Frost, Arthur Davis, and John Stauffer. 1988. "How First-Time Viewers Comprehend Editing Conventions." *Journal of Communication* 38 (4): 50–60. doi:10.1111/j.1460-2466.1988.tb02069.x.

Hochberg, J., and V. Brooks. 1978. "The Perception of Motion Pictures." In *Handbook of Perception*, edited by E. C. Carterette and M. P. Friedman. New York: Academic Press.

Hoeks, John C. J., and Harm Brouwer. 2014. "Electrophysiological Research on Conversation and Discourse." In *The Oxford Handbook of Language and Social Psychology*, edited by Thomas M. Holtgraves, 365–386. Oxford, UK: Oxford University Press.

Holmes, Alan C. 1963. *A Study of Understanding of Visual Symbols in Kenya.* London: Oversea Visual Aids Centre.

Holmes, Alana Maureen. 2001. "Theory of mind and behaviour disorder in children with specific language impairment." Doctoral Dissertation, Clinical Psychology, Lakehead University.

Huang, CT James. 1984. "On the typology of zero anaphora." *Language Research* 20 (2).

Huber, Walter, and Jochen Gleber. 1982. "Linguistic and nonlinguistic processing of narratives in aphasia." *Brain and Language* 16: 1–18.

Huff, Markus, Tino G.K. Meitz, and Frank Papenmeier. 2014. "Changes in situation models modulate processes of event perception in audiovisual narratives." *Journal of Experimental Psychology: Learning, Memory, & Cognition* 40 (5): 1377–1388. doi: 10.1037/0033-2909.133.2.273.

Huff, Markus, Frank Papenmeier, Annika E. Maurer, Tino G. K. Meitz, Bärbel Garsoffky, and Stephan Schwan. 2017. "Fandom Biases Retrospective Judgments Not Perception." *Scientific Reports* 7: 43083. doi: 10.1038/srep43083.

Huntsinger, Carol S., Paul E. Jose, Dana Balsink Krieg, and Zupei Luo. 2011. "Cultural differences in Chinese American and European American children's drawing skills over time." *Early Childhood Research Quarterly* 26 (1): 134–145.

Hutson, John P., Joe Magliano, and Lester C. Loschky. 2018. "Understanding Moment-to-moment Processing of Visual Narratives." *Cognitive Science* 42 (8): 2999–3033. doi: 10.1111/cogs.12699.

Ildirar, Sermin, Daniel T. Levin, Stephan Schwan, and Tim J. Smith. 2018. "Audio Facilitates the Perception of Cinematic Continuity by First-Time Viewers." *Perception* 47 (3): 276–295. doi: 10.1177/0301006617745782.

Ildirar, Sermin, and Stephan Schwan. 2015. "First-time viewers' comprehension of films: Bridging shot transitions." *British Journal of Psychology* 106 (1): 133–151. doi: 10.1111/bjop.12069.

Ingber, Sara, and Sigal Eden. 2011. "Enhancing sequential time perception and storytelling ability of deaf and hard of hearing children." *American Annals of the Deaf* 156 (4): 391–401.

Inui, Toshio, and Kensaku Miyamoto. 1981. "The time needed to judge the order of a meaningful string of pictures." *Journal of Experimental Psychology: Human Learning and Memory* 7 (5): 393–396.

Jackendoff, Ray. 2002. *Foundations of Language: Brain, Meaning, Grammar, Evolution.* Oxford: Oxford University Press.

Jackendoff, Ray. 2007. *Language, Consciousness, Culture: Essays on Mental Structure (Jean Nicod Lectures).* Cambridge, MA: MIT Press.

Jackendoff, Ray, and Jenny Audring. 2018. "Relational morphology in the parallel architecture." In *The Oxford Handbook of Morphological Theory*, edited by Jenny Audring and F. Masini. Oxford: Oxford University Press.

Jackendoff, Ray, and Eva Wittenberg. 2014. "What You Can Say Without Syntax: A Hierarchy of Grammatical Complexity." In *Measuring Linguistic Complexity*, edited by Frederick Newmeyer and L. Preston, 65–82. Oxford: Oxford University Press.

Jackendoff, Ray, and Eva Wittenberg. 2017. "Linear grammar as a possible stepping-stone in the evolution of language." *Psychonomic Bulletin & Review* 24 (1): 219–224. doi: 10.3758/s13423-016-1073-y.

Jain, Eakta, Yaser Sheikh, and Jessica Hodgins. 2016. "Predicting Moves-on-Stills for Comic Art Using Viewer Gaze Data." *IEEE Computer Graphics and Applications* 36 (4): 34–45. doi: 10.1109/MCG.2016.74.

Jajdelska, Elspeth, Miranda Anderson, Christopher Butler, Nigel Fabb, Elizabeth Finnigan, Ian Garwood, Stephen Kelly, Wendy Kirk, Karin Kukkonen, Sinead Mullally, and Stephan Schwan. 2019. "Picture This: A Review of Research Relating to Narrative Processing by Moving Image Versus Language." *Frontiers in Psychology* 10 (1161). doi: 10.3389/fpsyg.2019.01161.

Jenkins, Janet. 1978. "Using Pictures in Non-Formal Education." *Educational Broadcasting International* 11 (1): 32–38.

Jennings, Kimberly Ann, Audrey C Rule, and Sarah M Vander Zanden. 2014. "Fifth graders' enjoyment, interest, and comprehension of graphic novels compared to heavily-illustrated and traditional novels." *International Electronic Journal of Elementary Education* 6 (2): 257–274.

Johnels, Jakob Åsberg, Bibbi Hagberg, Christopher Gillberg, and Carmela Miniscalco. 2013. "Narrative retelling in children with neurodevelopmental disorders: Is there a role for nonverbal temporal-sequencing skills?" *Scandinavian Journal of Psychology* 54 (5): 376–385. doi: 10.1111/sjop.12067.

Johnson, S. P. 2013. "Development of the Visual System." In *Neural Circuit Development and Function in the Brain: Comprehensive Developmental Neuroscience*, edited by John L.R. Rubenstein and Pasko Rakic, 249–269. Elsevier Inc.

Jones, Catherine R. G., Francesca Happé, Hannah Golden, Anita J. S. Marsden, Jenifer Tregay, Emily Simonoff, Andrew Pickles, Gillian Baird, and Tony Charman. 2009. "Reading and arithmetic in adolescents with autism spectrum disorders: Peaks and dips in attainment." *Neuropsychology* 23 (6): 718–728. doi: 10.1037/a0016360.

Juricevic, Igor. 2017. "Analysis of pictorial metaphors in comicbook art: test of the LA-MOAD theory." *Journal of Graphic Novels and Comics*: 1–21. doi: 10.1080/21504857.2017.1313287.

Kaan, Edith. 2007. "Event-Related Potentials and Language Processing: A Brief Overview." *Language and Linguistics Compass* 1 (6): 571–591. doi: 10.1111/j.1749-818X.2007.00037.x.

Kacsuk, Zoltan. 2018. "Re-Examining the "What is Manga" Problematic: The Tension and Interrelationship between the "Style" Versus "Made in Japan" Positions." *Arts* 7 (3): 26.

Kaefer, Tanya, Ashley M. Pinkham, and Susan B. Neuman. 2017. "Seeing and knowing: Attention to illustrations during storybook reading and narrative comprehension in 2-year-olds." *Infant and Child Development* 26 (5): e2018. doi:10.1002/icd.2018.

Karmiloff-Smith, Annette. 1985. "Language and cognitive processes from a developmental perspective." *Language and Cognitive Processes* 1 (1): 61–85. doi: 10.1080/01690968508402071.

Kato, Hiromichi. 2006. "The Formation of Triadic Interpersonal Relationship and Narrative Production: Relationship to the Developmental Process of Meanings." 乳幼児発達臨床センター年報= *Research and Clinical Center for Child Development Annual Report* 28: 89–96.

Kaufman, Alan S., and Elizabeth O. Lichtenberger. 2006. *Assessing Adolescent and Adult Intelligence*. 3rd ed. Hoboken: Wiley.

Kennedy, John M., and A. Ross. 1975. "Outline picture perception by the Songe of Paua." *Perception* 4: 391–406.

Khaleefa, Omar H., and Ikhlas H. Ashria. 1995. "Intelligence testing in an Afro-Arab Islamic culture: The Northern Sudan." *Journal of Islamic Studies* 6 (2): 222–233.

Kim, Minam. 2008. "Korean Children's Self-initiated Learning and Expression through *Manwha*." *Visual Arts Research* 34 (1): 29–42.

Kintsch, Walter, and Teun van Dijk. 1978. "Toward a model of text comprehension and production." *Psychological Review* 85: 363–394.

Kirtley, Clare, Christopher Murray, Phillip B. Vaughan, and Benjamin W. Tatler. 2018. "Reading words and images: Factors influencing eye movements in comic reading." In *Empirical Comics Research: Digital, Multimodal, and Cognitive Methods*, edited by Alexander Dunst, Jochen Laubrock and Janina Wildfeuer, 264–283. New York: Routledge.

Kluender, Robert, and Marta Kutas. 1993. "Bridging the gap: Evidence from ERPs on the processing of unbound dependencies." *Journal of Cognitive Neuroscience* 5 (2): 196–214.

Koelsch, Stefan, Thomas C. Gunter, Matthias Wittfoth, and Daniel Sammler. 2005. "Interaction between syntax processing in language and in music: An ERP study." *Journal of Cognitive Neuroscience* 17 (10): 1565–1577.

Kowalewski, Hubert. 2018. "Heart is for Love: Cognitive Salience and Visual Metonymies in Comics." *The Comics Grid: Journal of Comics Scholarship* 8.

Krafft, H., and Jean Piaget. 1925. "La notion d'ordre des événements et le test des images en desordre chez l'enfant de 6 a 10 ans [The concept of order of events and muddled picture test with 6–10 year olds]." *Archives de Psychologie* 19: 306–349.

Kukkonen, Karin. 2008. "Beyond Language: Metaphor and Metonymy in Comics Storytelling." *English Language Notes* 46 (2): 89–98.

Kunen, Seth, Suzanne A. Chabaud, and Anne L. Dean. 1987. "Figural factors and the development of pictorial inferences." *Journal of Experimental Child Psychology* 44 (2): 157–169. doi: http://dx.doi.org/10.1016/0022-0965(87)90028-2.

Kunzle, David. 1973. *The History of the Comic Strip*. Vol. 1. Berkeley: University of California Press.

Kuperberg, Gina R. 2010. "Language in Schizophrenia Part 1: An Introduction." *Language and Linguistics Compass* 4 (8): 576–589. doi: 10.1111/j.1749-818X.2010.00216.x.

Kuperberg, Gina R. 2013. "The pro-active comprehender: What event-related potentials tell us about the dynamics of reading comprehension." In *Unraveling the Behavioral, Neurobiological, and Genetic Components of Reading Comprehension*, edited by B. Miller, L. Cutting and P McCardle, 176–192. Baltimore: Paul Brookes Publishing.

Kuperberg, Gina R. 2016. "Separate streams or probabilistic inference? What the N400 can tell us about the comprehension of events." *Language, Cognition and Neuroscience* 31 (5): 602–616. doi: 10.1080/23273798.2015.1130233.

Kupersmitt, Judy R., and Sharon Armon-Lotem. 2019. "The linguistic expression of causal relations in picture-based narratives: A comparative study of bilingual and monolingual children with TLD and DLD." *First Language* 39 (3): 319–343. doi: 10.1177/0142723719831927.

Kurby, Christopher A., and Jeffrey M. Zacks. 2012. "Starting from scratch and building brick by brick in comprehension." *Memory & Cognition* 40 (5): 812–826. doi: 10.3758/s13421-011-0179-8.

Kutas, Marta, and Kara D. Federmeier. 2011. "Thirty years and counting: Finding meaning in the N400 component of the Event-Related Brain Potential (ERP)." *Annual Review of Psychology* 62 (1): 621–647.

Kutas, Marta, and Steven A. Hillyard. 1980. "Reading senseless sentences: Brain potential reflect semantic incongruity." *Science* 207: 203–205.

Labitsi, Vasiliki. 2007. "'Climbing to reach the sunset': an inquiry into the representation of narrative structures in Greek children's drawings." *International Journal of Education through Art* 3 (3): 185–193.

Langdon, Robyn, Max Coltheart, Philip B. Ward, and Stanley V. Catts. 2001. "Mentalising, executive planning and disengagement in schizophrenia." *Cognitive Neuropsychiatry* 6 (2): 81–108. doi: 10.1080/13546800042000061.

Langdon, Robyn, Patricia T. Michie, Philip B. Ward, Neil McConaghy, Stanley V. Catts, and Max Coltheart. 1997. "Defective Self and/or Other Mentalising in Schizophrenia: A Cognitive Neuropsychological Approach." *Cognitive Neuropsychiatry* 2 (3): 167–193. doi: 10.1080/135468097396324.

Langdon, Robyn, and Philip Ward. 2008. "Taking the Perspective of the Other Contributes to Awareness of Illness in Schizophrenia." *Schizophrenia Bulletin* 35 (5): 1003–1011. doi: 10.1093/schbul/sbn039.

Laubrock, Jochen, and David Dubray. 2019. "CNN-Based Classification of Illustrator Style in Graphic Novels: Which Features Contribute Most?" In *MultiMedia Modeling. MMM 2019. Lecture Notes in Computer Science*, edited by Ioannis Kompatsiaris, Benoit Huet, Vasileios Mezaris, Cathal Gurrin, Wen-Huang Cheng and Stefanos Vrochidis, 684–695. Cham: Springer International Publishing.

Laubrock, Jochen, Sven Hohenstein, and Matthias Kümmerer. 2018. "Attention to comics: Cognitive processing during the reading of graphic literature." In *Empirical Comics Research: Digital, Multimodal, and Cognitive Methods*, edited by Alexander Dunst, Jochen Laubrock and Janina Wildfeuer, 239–263. New York: Routledge.

Le Guen, Olivier, and Lorena Ildefonsa Pool Balam. 2012. "No metaphorical timeline in gesture and cognition among Yucatec Mayas." *Frontiers in Psychology* 3: 1–15. doi: 10.3389/fpsyg.2012.00271.

Leckey, Michelle, and Kara D. Federmeier. 2019. "The P3b and P600(s): Positive contributions to language comprehension." *Psychophysiology* 0 (0): e13351. doi: 10.1111/psyp.13351.

Lee, James F., and William S. Armour. 2016. "Factors influencing non-native readers' sequencing of Japanese manga panels." In *Manga Vision*, edited by Pasfield-Neofitou and Cathy Sell, 178–193. Clayton, Australia: Monash University Publishing.

Lefèvre, Pascal. 2000a. "The Importance of Being 'Published': A Comparative Study of Different Comics Formats." In *Comics and Culture: Analytical and Theoretical Approaches to Comics*, edited by Anne Magnussen and Hans-Christian Christiansen, 91–105. Copenhagen: Museum Tusculanum Press.

Lefèvre, Pascal. 2000b. "Narration in comics." *Image [&] Narrative* 1 (1).

Lent, John A. 2010. "Manga in East Asia." In *Manga: An Anthology of Global and Cultural Perspectives*, edited by Toni Johnson-Woods, 297–314. New York: Continuum Books.

Leonard, Laurence B. 1998. *Children with Specific Language Impairment*. Cambridge, MA: MIT Press.

Levin, Daniel T., and Lewis J. Baker. 2017. "Bridging views in cinema: a review of the art and science of view integration." *Wiley Interdisciplinary Reviews: Cognitive Science*: e1436–n/a. doi: 10.1002/wcs.1436.

Levin, Daniel T., and Daniel J. Simons. 1997. "Failure to detect changes to attended objects in motion pictures." *Psychonomic Bulletin & Review* 4 (4): 501–506.

Levin, Daniel T., and Daniel J. Simons. 2000. "Perceiving Stability in a Changing World: Combining Shots and Intergrating Views in Motion Pictures and the Real World." *Media Psychology* 2 (4): 357–380.

Levinson, Stephen C., and Asifa Majid. 2013. "The island of time: Yélî Dnye, the language of Rossel Island." *Frontiers in Psychology* 4. doi: 10.3389/fpsyg.2013.00061.

Liddell, Christine. 1996. "Every picture tells a story: South African and British children interpreting pictures." *British Journal of Developmental Psychology* 14 (3): 355–363. doi: 10.1111/j.2044-835X.1996.tb00711.x.

Liddell, Christine. 1997. "Every Picture Tells a Story—Or does it?: Young South African Children Interpreting Pictures." *Journal of Cross-Cultural Psychology* 28 (3): 266–283.

Lipsitz, Joshua D., Robert H. Dworkin, and L. Erlenmeyer-Kimling. 1993. "Wechsler comprehension and picture arrangement subtests and social adjustment." *Psychological Assessment* 5 (4): 430–437.

Loschky, Lester C., John P. Hutson, Maverick E. Smith, Tim J. Smith, and Joseph Magliano. 2018. "Viewing Static Visual Narratives Through the Lens of the Scene Perception and Event Comprehension Theory (SPECT)." In *Empirical Comics Research: Digital, Multimodal, and Cognitive Methods*, edited by Alexander Dunst, Jochen Laubrock and Janina Wildfeuer, 217–238. London: Routledge.

Loschky, Lester C., Joseph Magliano, Adam M. Larson, and Tim J. Smith. 2020. "The Scene Perception & Event Comprehension Theory (SPECT) Applied to Visual Narratives." *Topics in Cognitive Science*. 12 (1): 311–351. doi: 10.1111/tops.12455.

Loucas, Tom, Nick Riches, Gillian Baird, Andrew Pickles, Emily Simonoff, Susie Chandler, and Tony Charman. 2013. "Spoken word recognition in adolescents with autism spectrum disorders and specific language impairment." *Applied Psycholinguistics* 34 (2): 301–322. doi: 10.1017/S0142716411000701.

Lucas, Rebecca, and Courtenay Frazier Norbury. 2018. "The home literacy environment of school-aged children with autism spectrum disorders." *Journal of Research in Reading* 41 (1): 197–219. doi: 10.1111/1467-9817.12119.

Magliano, Joseph P., James A. Clinton, Edward J. O'Brien, and David N. Rapp. 2018. "Detecting differences between adapted narratives." In *Empirical Comics Research: Digital, Multimodal, and Cognitive Methods*, edited by Alexander Dunst, Jochen Laubrock and Janina Wildfeuer, 284–304. New York: Routledge.

Magliano, Joseph P., Katinka Dijkstra, and Rolf A. Zwaan. 1996. "Generating predictive inferences while viewing a movie." *Discourse Processes* 22: 199–224.

Magliano, Joseph P., Karyn Higgs, and James A. Clinton. 2019. "Sources of Complexity in Comprehension Across Modalities of Narrative Experience." In *Narrative Complexity: Cognition, Embodiment, Evolution*, edited by Marina Grishakova and Maria Poulaki, 149–173. Lincoln: University of Nebraska Press.

Magliano, Joseph P., Kristopher Kopp, Karyn Higgs, and David N. Rapp. 2017. "Filling in the Gaps: Memory Implications for Inferring Missing Content in

Graphic Narratives." *Discourse Processes* 54 (8): 569–582. doi: 10.1080/0163853X.2015.1136870.

Magliano, Joseph P., Kristopher Kopp, M. Windy McNerney, Gabriel A. Radvansky, and Jeffrey M. Zacks. 2012. "Aging and perceived event structure as a function of modality." *Aging, Neuropsychology, and Cognition* 19 (1–2): 264–282. doi: 10.1080/13825585.2011.633159.

Magliano, Joseph P., Adam M. Larson, Karyn Higgs, and Lester C. Loschky. 2015. "The relative roles of visuospatial and linguistic working memory systems in generating inferences during visual narrative comprehension." *Memory & Cognition* 44 (2): 207–219. doi: 10.3758/s13421-015-0558-7.

Magliano, Joseph P., Lester C. Loschky, James A. Clinton, and Adam M. Larson. 2013. "Is Reading the Same as Viewing? An Exploration of the Similarities and Differences Between Processing Text- and Visually Based Narratives." In *Unraveling the Behavioral, Neurobiological, and Genetic Components of Reading Comprehension*, edited by B. Miller, L. Cutting and P. McCardle, 78–90. Baltimore, MD: Brookes Publishing Co.

Magliano, Joseph P., and Jeffrey M. Zacks. 2011. "The impact of continuity editing in narrative film on event segmentation." *Cognitive Science* 35 (8): 1489–1517. doi: 10.1111/j.1551-6709.2011.01202.x.

Mandler, Jean M., and Nancy S. Johnson. 1977. "Remembrance of things parsed: Story structure and recall." *Cognitive Psychology* 9: 111–151.

Manfredi, Mirella, Neil Cohn, Mariana De Araújo Andreoli, and Paulo Sergio Boggio. 2018. "Listening beyond seeing: Event-related potentials to audiovisual processing in visual narrative." *Brain and Language* 185: 1–8. doi: https://doi.org/10.1016/j.bandl.2018.06.008.

Manfredi, Mirella, Neil Cohn, and Marta Kutas. 2017. "When a hit sounds like a kiss: an electrophysiological exploration of semantic processing in visual narrative." *Brain and Language* 169: 28–38. doi: 10.1016/j.bandl.2017.02.001.

Manfredi, Mirella, Neil Cohn, Pamella Sanchez Mello, Elizabeth Fernandez, and Paulo Sergio Boggio. 2020. "Visual and verbal narrative comprehension in children and adolescents with autism spectrum disorders: an ERP study." *Journal of Autism and Developmental Disorders*. doi: 10.1007/s10803-020-04374-x.

Manschreck, Theo C., Brendan A. Maher, James J. Milavetz, Donna Ames, C. Cecily Weisstein, and Margaret L. Schneyer. 1988. "Semantic priming in thought disordered schizophrenic patients." *Schizophrenia Research* 1 (1): 61–66. doi: https://doi.org/10.1016/0920-9964(88)90041-2.

Margairaz, E., and Jean Piaget. 1925. "La structure des réits et l'interpretation des images de Dawid chez l'enfant [The structure of children's stories and interpretation of pictures of Dawid]." *Archives de Psychologie* 19: 211–239.

Marini, Andrea, Sergio Carlomagno, Carlo Caltagirone, and Ugo Nocentini. 2005. "The role played by the right hemisphere in the organization of complex textual structures." *Brain and Language* 93 (1): 46–54. doi: https://doi.org/10.1016/j.bandl.2004.08.002.

Marini, Andrea, Sara Martelli, Chiara Gagliardi, Franco Fabbro, and Renato Borgatti. 2010. "Narrative language in Williams Syndrome and its neuropsychological correlates." *Journal of Neurolinguistics* 23 (2): 97–111. doi: https://doi.org/10.1016/j.jneuroling.2009.10.002.

Martín-Arnal, Lorena A., José A. León, Paul van den Broek, and Ricardo Olmos. 2019. "Understanding Comics. A Comparison between Children and Adults through a Coherence/Incoherence Paradigm in an Eye-tracking Study." *Psicología Educativa* 25 (2): 127–137. doi: 10.5093/psed2019a7.

Masuda, Takahiko, and Richard Nisbett. 2001. "Attending Holistically Versus Analytically: Comparing the Context Sensitivity of Japanese and Americans." *Journal of Personality and Social Psychology* 81 (5): 922–934.

Mayberry, Rachel I., Jen-Kai Chen, Pamela Witcher, and Denise Klein. 2011. "Age of acquisition effects on the functional organization of language in the adult brain." *Brain and Language* 119 (1): 16–29. doi: http://dx.doi.org/10.1016/j.bandl.2011.05.007.

Mayer, Richard E. 2009. *Multimedia Learning*. Second ed: Cambridge University Press.

Mazur, Dan, and Alexander Danner. 2014. *Comics: A Global History, 1968 to the Present*. London: Thames & Hudson.

McCloud, Scott. 1993. *Understanding Comics: The Invisible Art*. New York, NY: Harper Collins.

McCloud, Scott. 2006. *Making Comics*. New York, NY: Harper-Collins.

McFie, J., and M.F. Piercy. 1952. "Intellectual impairment with localized cerebral lesions." *Brain: A Journal of Neurology* 75: 292–311.

McFie, J., and J. A. Thompson. 1972. "Picture Arrangement: A Measure of Frontal Lobe Function?" *The British Journal of Psychiatry* 121 (564): 547–552. doi: 10.1192/bjp.121.5.547.

McFie, John. 1961. "The effect of education on African performance on a group of intellectual tests." *British Journal of Educational Psychology* 31 (P3): 232–240. doi:10.1111/j.2044-8279.1961.tb01712.x.

McIntyre, Nancy S., Emily J. Solari, Ryan P. Grimm, Lindsay E. Lerro, Joseph E. Gonzales, and Peter C. Mundy. 2017. "A Comprehensive Examination of Reading Heterogeneity in Students with High Functioning Autism: Distinct Reading Profiles and Their Relation to Autism Symptom Severity." *Journal of Autism and Developmental Disorders* 47 (4): 1086–1101. doi: 10.1007/s10803-017-3029-0.

McKoon, Gail, and Roger Ratcliff. 1986. "Inferences about predictable events." *Journal of Experimental Psychology: Learning, Memory, and Cognition* 12 (1): 82–91.

McNamara, Danielle S, and Joe Magliano. 2009. "Toward a comprehensive model of comprehension." *Psychology of Learning and Motivation* 51: 297–384.

McPherson, W.B., and Phillip J. Holcomb. 1999. "An electrophysiological investigation of semantic priming with pictures of real objects." *Psychophysiology* 36 (1): 53–65.

Mikkonen, Kai, and Ollie Philippe Lautenbacher. 2019. "Global Attention in Reading Comics: Eye movement indications of interplay between narrative content and layout." *ImageTexT* 10 (2).

Milch-Reich, Shoulamit, Susan B. Campbell, Jr. Pelham, William E., Lynda M. Connelly, and Diklah Geva. 1999. "Developmental and Individual Differences in Children's On-Line Representations of Dynamic Social Events." *Child Development* 70 (2): 413–431. doi:10.1111/1467-8624.00030.

Miodrag, Hannah. 2013. *Comics and Language: Reimagining Critical Discourse on the Form*. Jackson: University Press of Mississippi.

Molotiu, Andrei. 2012. "Abstract Form: Sequential dynamism and iconostasis in abstract comics and in Steve Ditko's *Amazing Spider-Man*." In *Critical Approaches to Comics: Theories and Methods*, edited by Matthew J. Smith and Randy Duncan, 84–100. New York: Routledge.

Moore, Stuart. 2003. "In the old days, it woulda been eight pages." In *A Thousand Flowers: Comics, Pop Culture and the World Outside*, edited by Matt Brady.

Mori, Kazuhiko. 1995. "The influence of action lines on pictorial movement perception in pre-school children." *Japanese Psychological Research* 27 (3): 183–187.

Munk, Carmen, Günter Daniel Rey, Anna Katharina Diergarten, Gerhild Nieding, Wolfgang Schneider, and Peter Ohler. 2012. "Cognitive Processing of Film Cuts Among 4- to 8-Year-Old Children." *European Psychologist* 17 (4): 257–265. doi: 10.1027/1016-9040/a000098.

Munn, Nancy D. 1986. *Walbiri Iconography: Graphic Representation and Cultural Symbolism in a Central Australian Society.* Chicago, IL: University of Chicago Press.

Nagai, Masayoshi, Nobutaka Endo, and Kumada Takatsune. 2007. "Measuring Brain Activities Related to Understanding Using Near-Infrared Spectroscopy (NIRS)." In *Human Interface and the Management of Information: Methods, Techniques and Tools in Information Design*, edited by M.J. Smith and Salvendy G., 884–893. Heidelberg: Springer Berlin.

Nakazawa, Jun. 1997. "Development of *manga* reading comprehension: Developmental and experimental differences in adults." *Proceedings of the 8th Annual Conference of Japan Society of Developmental Psychology*, 309.

Nakazawa, Jun. 2002a. "Analysis of manga (comic) reading processes: Manga literacy and eye movement during Manga reading." *Manga Studies* 5: 39–49.

Nakazawa, Jun. 2002b. "Effects of *manga* reading comprehension ability on children's learning by *manga* materials." *Research on Teaching Strategies and Learning Activities* 9: 13–23.

Nakazawa, Jun. 2004. "Manga (comic) literacy skills as determinant factors of manga story comprehension." *Manga Studies* 5: 7–25.

Nakazawa, Jun. 2005. "Development of manga (comic book) literacy in children." In *Applied Developmental Psychology: Theory, Practice, and Research from Japan*, edited by David W. Shwalb, Jun Nakazawa and Barbara J. Shwalb, 23–42. Greenwich, CT: Information Age Publishing.

Nakazawa, Jun. 2016. "Manga literacy and manga comprehension in Japanese children." In *The Visual Narrative Reader*, edited by Neil Cohn, 157–184. London: Bloomsbury.

Nakazawa, Jun, and Sayuri Nakazawa. 1993a. "Development of *manga* reading comprehension: How do children understand *manga*?" In *Manga and Child: How Do Children Understand Manga?*, edited by Y. Akashi, 85–189. Research report of Gendai Jidobunka Kenkyukai.

Nakazawa, Jun, and Sayuri Nakazawa. 1993b. "How do children understand comics?: Analysis of comic reading comprehension." *Annual of Research in Early Childhood* 15: 35–39.

Nakazawa, Jun, and David W. Shwalb. 2012. "Japan and the US comparison of university students' Manga reading literacy." *Proceedings of Annual Conference of 54th Japanese Association of Educational Psychology*, 319.

Nalu, Amber. 2011. "Comics as a cognitive training medium for expert decision making." Doctoral dissertation, Human Factors Psychology, Old Dominion University.

Nalu, Amber, and James P. Bliss. 2011. "Comics as a Cognitive Training Medium for Expert Decision Making." *Proceedings of the Human Factors and Ergonomics Society Annual Meeting* 55 (1): 2123–2127.

Navarrete, Federico. 2000. "The Path from Aztlan to Mexico: On Visual Narration in Mesoamerican Codices." *RES: Anthropology and Aesthetics* (37): 31–48.

Nenadović, Vanja, Miodrag Stokić, Mile Vuković, Sanja Đoković, and Miško Subotić. 2014. "Cognitive and electrophysiological characteristics of children with specific language impairment and subclinical epileptiform electroencephalogram." *Journal of Clinical and Experimental Neuropsychology* 36 (9): 981–991. doi: 10.1080/13803395.2014.958438.

Newton, Douglas P. 1985. "Children's Perception of Pictorial Metaphor." *Educational Psychology* 5 (2): 179–185. doi: 10.1080/0144341850050207.

Nisbett, Richard, and Takahiko Masuda. 2003. "Culture and Point of View." *Proceedings of the National Academy of Sciences* 100 (19): 11163–11170.

Noble, Grant. 1975. *Children in Front of the Small Screen*. London: Constable.

Núñez, Rafael. p.c. "Personal Communication." La Jolla, CA, Jan. 25, 2013.

Núñez, Rafael, and Kensy Cooperrider. 2013. "The tangle of space and time in human cognition." *Trends in Cognitive Sciences* 17 (5): 220–229. doi: http://dx.doi.org/10.1016/j.tics.2013.03.008.

Núñez, Rafael, Kensy Cooperrider, D. Doan, and Jürg Wassmann. 2012. "Contours of time: Topographic construals of past, present, and future in the Yupno valley of Papua New Guinea." *Cognition* 124 (1): 25–35. doi: http://dx.doi.org/10.1016/j.cognition.2012.03.007.

Nurss, Joanne R., and Ruth A. Hough. 1985. "Young Children's Oral Language: Effects of Task." *The Journal of Educational Research* 78 (5): 280–285. doi: 10.1080/00220671.1985.10885616.

Nuske, Heather Joy, and Edith L. Bavin. 2011. "Narrative comprehension in 4–7-year-old children with autism: testing the Weak Central Coherence account." *International Journal of Language & Communication Disorders* 46 (1): 108–119. doi: 10.3109/13682822.2010.484847.

O'Connell, Barbara G., and Anthony B. Gerard. 1985. "Scripts and Scraps: The Development of Sequential Understanding." *Child Development* 56 (3): 671–681. doi: 10.2307/1129757.

Okada, Takeshi, and Kentaro Ishibashi. 2017. "Imitation, Inspiration, and Creation: Cognitive Process of Creative Drawing by Copying Others' Artworks." *Cognitive Science* 41 (7): 1804–1837. doi:10.1111/cogs.12442.

Omori, Takahide, Taku Ishii, and Keiko Kurata. 2004. "Eye catchers in comics: Controlling eye movements in reading pictorial and textual media." (pp. 1–9) *28th International Congress of Psychology*, Beijing, China.

Osaka, Mariko, Ken Yaoi, Takehiro Minamoto, and Naoyuki Osaka. 2014. "Serial changes of humor comprehension for four-frame comic Manga: an fMRI study." *Scientific Reports* 4 (5828): 1–9. doi: 10.1038/srep05828.

Osterhout, Lee, and Phil Holcomb. 1992. "Event-related potentials elicited by syntactic anomaly." *Journal of Memory and Language* 31: 758–806.

Ouellet, Julie, Peter B. Scherzer, Isabelle Rouleau, Philippe Métras, Caroline Bertrand-Gauvin, NadÉRa Djerroud, ÉMilie Boisseau, and Pierre Duquette. 2010. "Assessment of social cognition in patients with multiple sclerosis." *Journal of the International Neuropsychological Society* 16 (2): 287–296. doi: 10.1017/S1355617709991329.

Paczynski, Martin, Ray Jackendoff, and Gina Kuperberg. 2014. "When Events Change Their Nature: The Neurocognitive Mechanisms Underlying Aspectual

Coercion." *Journal of Cognitive Neuroscience* 26 (9): 1905–1917. doi: 10.1162/jocn_a_00638.

Padakannaya, Prakash, M.L. Devi, B. Zaveria, S.K. Chengappa, and Jyotsna Vaid. 2002. *Directional Scanning Effect and Strength of Reading Habit in Picture Naming and Recall.* Amsterdam: Elsevier.

Pallenik, Michael J. 1986. "A Gunman in Town! Children Interpret a Comic Book." *Studies in the Anthropology of Visual Communication* 3 (1): 38–51.

Pantaleo, Sylvia. 2011. "Warning: A Grade 7 Student Disrupts Narrative Boundaries." *Journal of Literacy Research* 43 (1): 39–67. doi: 10.1177/1086296x10397870.

Pantaleo, Sylvia. 2012a. "Exploring the intertextualities in a grade 7 student's graphic narrative." *L1 Educational Studies in Language and Literature* 12, Running Issue (Running Issue): 23–55. doi: 10.17239/l1esll-2012.04.01.

Pantaleo, Sylvia. 2012b. "Middle-school students reading and creating multimodal texts: a case study." *Education 3-13* 40 (3): 295–314. doi: 10.1080/03004279.2010.531037.

Pantaleo, Sylvia. 2013a. "Matters of Design and Visual Literacy: One Middle Years Student's Multimodal Artifact." *Journal of Research in Childhood Education* 27 (3): 351–376. doi: 10.1080/02568543.2013.796334.

Pantaleo, Sylvia. 2013b. "Paneling "Matters" in Elementary Students' Graphic Narratives." *Literacy Research and Instruction* 52 (2): 150–171. doi: 10.1080/19388071.2012.754973.

Pantaleo, Sylvia. 2015. "Exploring the intentionality of design in the graphic narrative of one middle-years student." *Journal of Graphic Novels and Comics* 6 (4): 398–418.

Pantaleo, Sylvia. 2019. "The semantic and syntactic qualities of paneling in students' graphic narratives." *Visual Communication* 18 (1): 55–81. doi: 10.1177/1470357217740393.

Paris, Alison H., and Scott G. Paris. 2001. "Children's Comprehension of Narrative Picture Books." *CIERA Report*: 2–37.

Paris, Alison H., and Scott G. Paris. 2003. "Assessing narrative comprehension in young children." *Reading Research Quarterly* 38 (1): 36–76. doi:10.1598/RRQ.38.1.3.

Parsons, Sarah, and Peter Mitchell. 1999. "What Children with Autism Understand about Thoughts and Thought Bubbles." *Autism* 3 (1): 17–38. doi: 10.1177/1362361399003001003.

Patel, Aniruddh D. 2003. "Language, music, syntax and the brain." *Nature Neuroscience* 6 (7): 674–681. doi: 10.1038/nn1082.

Pederson, Kaitlin, and Neil Cohn. 2016. "The changing pages of comics: Page layouts across eight decades of American superhero comics." *Studies in Comics* 7 (1): 7–28. doi: 10.1386/stic.7.1.7_1.

Peeters, Benoît. 1998 [1991]. *Case, Planche, et Récit: Lire la Bande Dessinée.* Paris: Casterman.

Peirce, Charles Sanders. 1931. "Division of Signs." In *Collected Papers of Charles Sanders Peirce: Vol. 2: Elements of Logic.*, edited by Charles Hartshorne and Paul Weiss, 134–173. Cambridge, MA: Harvard University Press.

Pellicano, Elizabeth, and David Burr. 2012. "When the world becomes 'too real': a Bayesian explanation of autistic perception." *Trends in Cognitive Sciences* 16 (10): 504–510. doi: https://doi.org/10.1016/j.tics.2012.08.009.

Pempek, Tiffany A, Heather L Kirkorian, John E Richards, Daniel R Anderson, Anne F Lund, and Michael Stevens. 2010. "Video comprehensibility and attention in very young children." *Developmental Psychology* 46 (5): 1283.

Petersen, Robert S. 2011. *Comics, Manga, and Graphic Novels: A History of Graphic Narratives.* Santa Barbara, CA: ABC-CLIO.

Pierson, Melinda R., and Barbara C. Glaeser. 2007. "Using Comic Strip Conversations to Increase Social Satisfaction and Decrease Loneliness in Students with Autism Spectrum Disorder." *Education and Training in Developmental Disabilities* 42 (4): 460–466.

Poulsen, Dorothy, Eileen Kintsch, Walter Kintsch, and David Premack. 1979. "Children's comprehension and memory for stories." *Journal of Experimental Child Psychology* 28 (3): 379–403. doi: https://doi.org/10.1016/0022-0965(79)90070-5.

Premack, D., and G. Woodruff. 1978. "Does the chimpanzee have a 'theory of mind'?" *Behavioral and Brain Science* 4: 515–526.

Radvansky, Gabriel A., and Jeffrey Zacks. 2014. *Event Cognition.* Oxford, UK: Oxford University Press.

Ramos, Mary C., and Ann H. Die. 1986. "The Wais-R Picture Arrangement Subtest: What do Scores Indicate?" *The Journal of General Psychology* 113 (3): 251–261. doi: 10.1080/00221309.1986.9711036.

Reilly, Judy, Molly Losh, Ursula Bellugi, and Beverly Wulfeck. 2004. ""Frog, where are you?" Narratives in children with specific language impairment, early focal brain injury, and Williams syndrome." *Brain and Language* 88 (2): 229–247. doi: https://doi.org/10.1016/S0093-934X(03)00101-9.

Richards, John E., and Kim Cronise. 2000. "Extended Visual Fixation in the Early Preschool Years: Look Duration, Heart Rate Changes, and Attentional Inertia." *Child Development* 71 (3): 602–620. doi:10.1111/1467-8624.00170.

Robertson, David A. 2000. "Functional neuroanatomy of narrative comprehension." Doctoral Doctoral dissertation, Psychology, University of Wisconsin, Madison.

Rosset, Delphine B., Cécilie Rondan, David Da Fonseca, Andreia Santos, Brigitte Assouline, and Christine Deruelle. 2008. "Typical Emotion Processing for Cartoon but not for Real Faces in Children with Autistic Spectrum Disorders." *Journal of Autism and Developmental Disorders* 38 (5): 919–925. doi: 10.1007/s10803-007-0465-2.

Rosset, Delphine B., Andreia Santos, David Da Fonseca, François Poinso, Kate O'Connor, and Christine Deruelle. 2010. "Do children perceive features of real and cartoon faces in the same way? Evidence from typical development and autism." *Journal of Clinical and Experimental Neuropsychology* 32 (2): 212–218. doi: 10.1080/13803390902971123.

Roux, Paul, Eric Brunet-Gouet, Christine Passerieux, and Franck Ramus. 2016. "Eye-tracking reveals a slowdown of social context processing during intention attribution in patients with schizophrenia." *Journal of Psychiatry & Neuroscience : JPN* 41 (2): E13–E21. doi: 10.1503/jpn.150045.

Rozema, Robert. 2015. "Manga and the Autistic Mind." *English Journal* 105 (1): 60–68.

Rumelhart, David E. 1975. "Notes on a schema for stories." In *Representation and Understanding*, edited by Daniel Bobrow and Allan Collins, 211–236. New York, NY: Academic Press.

San Roque, Lila, Lauren Gawne, Darja Hoenigman, Julia Colleen Miller, Alan Rumsey, Stef Spronck, Alice Carroll, and Nicholas Evans. 2012. "Getting the story straight: Language fieldwork using a narrative problem-solving task." *Language Documentation and Conservation* 6: 135–174.

Saraceni, Mario. 2001. "Relatedness: Aspects of textual connectivity in comics." In *The Graphic Novel*, edited by Jan Baetens, 167–179. Leuven: Leuven University Press.

Saraceni, Mario. 2003. *The Language of Comics*. New York, NY: Routeledge.

Saraceni, Mario. 2016. "Relatedness: Aspects of textual connectivity in comics." In *The Visual Narrative Reader*, edited by Neil Cohn, 115–129. London: Bloomsbury.

Sarfati, Yves, Marie-Christine Hardy-Baylé, Chrystel Besche, and Daniel Widlöcher. 1997. "Attribution of intentions to others in people with schizophrenia: a non-verbal exploration with comic strips." *Schizophrenia Research* 25 (3): 199–209. doi: https://doi.org/10.1016/S0920-9964(97)00025-X.

Sarfati, Yves, Marie-Christine Hardy-Baylé, Eric Brunet, and Daniel Widlöcher. 1999. "Investigating theory of mind in schizophrenia: influence of verbalization in disorganized and non-disorganized patients." *Schizophrenia Research* 37 (2): 183–190. doi: https://doi.org/10.1016/S0920-9964(98)00154-6.

Sarfati, Yves, Marie-Christine Hardy-Baylé, Jacqueline Nadel, Jean-Francois Chevalier, and Daniel Widlöcher. 1997. "Attribution of Mental States to Others by Schizophrenic Patients." *Cognitive Neuropsychiatry* 2 (1): 1–18. doi: 10.1080/135468097396388.

Sarfati, Yves, Christine Passerieux, and Marie-Christine Hardy-Baylé. 2000. "Can Verbalization Remedy the Theory of Mind Deficit in Schizophrenia?" *Psychopathology* 33 (5): 246–251. doi: 10.1159/000029153.

Schank, R. C., and R. Abelson. 1977. *Scripts, Plans, Goals and Understanding*. Hillsdale, NJ: Lawrence Earlbaum Associates.

Schlaffke, Lara, Silke Lissek, Melanie Lenz, Georg Juckel, Thomas Schultz, Martin Tegenthoff, Tobias Schmidt-Wilcke, and Martin Brüne. 2015. "Shared and nonshared neural networks of cognitive and affective theory-of-mind: A neuroimaging study using cartoon picture stories." *Human Brain Mapping* 36 (1): 29–39. doi: 10.1002/hbm.22610.

Schmidt, Constance R., and Scott G. Paris. 1978. "Operativity and Reversibility in Children's Understanding of Pictorial Sequences." *Child Development* 49 (4): 1219–1222. doi: 10.2307/1128764.

Schmidt, Constance R., Scott G. Paris, and Sheila Stober. 1979. "Inferential distance and children's memory for pictorial sequences." *Developmental Psychology* 15 (4): 395–405.

Schneider, Phyllis. 1996. "Effects of Pictures Versus Orally Presented Stories on Story Retellings by Children With Language Impairment." *American Journal of Speech-Language Pathology* 5 (1): 86–96. doi: 10.1044/1058-0360.0501.86.

Schneider, Phyllis, and Rita Vis Dubé. 2005. "Story Presentation Effects on Children's Retell Content." *American Journal of Speech-Language Pathology* 14 (1): 52–60. doi:10.1044/1058-0360(2005/007).

Schneider, Phyllis, Denyse Hayward, and Rita Vis Dubé. 2006. "Storytelling from pictures using the Edmonton narrative norms instrument." *Journal of Speech-Language Pathology and Audiology* 30 (4): 224–238.

Schodt, Frederik L. 1983. *Manga! Manga! The World of Japanese Comics*. New York: Kodansha America Inc.

Schodt, Frederik L. 1996. *Dreamland Japan: Writings on Modern Manga*. Berkeley: Stonebridge Press.

Schwan, Stephan, and Sermin Ildirar. 2010. "Watching Film for the First Time: How Adult Viewers Interpret Perceptual Discontinuities in Film." *Psychological Science* 21 (7): 970–976. doi: 10.1177/0956797610372632.

Schweitzer, Thomas M., and M. Schnall. 1970. "Sequence Effects in the Abstraction of the Concept of Progressive Change." *Human Development* 13 (3): 201–212.

Shaklee, Harriet. 1976. "Development in Inferences of Ability and Task Difficulty." *Child Development* 47 (4): 1051–1057. doi: 10.2307/1128442.

Shapiro, Lauren R, and Judith A Hudson. 1991. "Tell me a make-believe story: Coherence and cohesion in young children's picture-elicited narratives." *Developmental psychology* 27 (6): 960–974.

Shinohara, Kazuko, and Yoshihiro Matsunaka. 2009. "Pictorial metaphors of emotion in Japanese comics." In *Multimodal Metaphor*, edited by Charles Forceville and Eduardo Urios-Aparisi, 265–293. New York: Mouton De Gruyter.

Short, Jeremy C., Brandon Randolph-Seng, and Aaron F. McKenny. 2013. "Graphic Presentation: An Empirical Examination of the Graphic Novel Approach to Communicate Business Concepts." *Business Communication Quarterly* 76 (3): 273–303. doi: 10.1177/1080569913482574.

Siegel, Don J., Nancy J. Minshew, and Gerald Goldstein. 1996. "Wechsler IQ profiles in diagnosis of high-functioning autism." *Journal of Autism and Developmental Disorders* 26 (4): 389–406. doi: 10.1007/bf02172825.

Silva, Macarena, and Kate Cain. 2019. "The use of questions to scaffold narrative coherence and cohesion." *Journal of Research in Reading.* 42 (1): 1–17. doi:10.1111/1467-9817.12129.

Silva, Macarena, Katherine Strasser, and Kate Cain. 2014. "Early narrative skills in Chilean preschool: Questions scaffold the production of coherent narratives." *Early Childhood Research Quarterly* 29 (2): 205–213. doi: https://doi.org/10.1016/j.ecresq.2014.02.002.

Silver, Lauren Davi. 2000. "Linguistic and pictorial narratives in preschool children: An exploration into the development of symbolic representation." Doctoral Dissertation, Psychology, University of California, Berkeley.

Simcock, Gabrielle, Kara Garrity, and Rachel Barr. 2011. "The Effect of Narrative Cues on Infants' Imitation From Television and Picture Books." *Child Development* 82 (5): 1607–1619. doi:10.1111/j.1467-8624.2011.01636.x.

Simons, Daniel J., and Michael S. Ambinder. 2005. "Change Blindness: Theory and Consequences." *Current Directions in Psychological Science* 14 (1): 44–48. doi: 10.1111/j.0963-7214.2005.00332.x.

Simons, Daniel J., and Daniel T. Levin. 1997. "Change blindness." *Trends in Cognitive Sciences* 1 (7): 261–267. doi: https://doi.org/10.1016/S1364-6613(97)01080-2.

Sinha, Pawan, Margaret M. Kjelgaard, Tapan K. Gandhi, Kleovoulos Tsourides, Annie L. Cardinaux, Dimitrios Pantazis, Sidney P. Diamond, and Richard M. Held. 2014. "Autism as a disorder of prediction." *Proceedings of the National Academy of Sciences* 111 (42): 15220–15225. doi: 10.1073/pnas.1416797111.

Sivaratnam, Carmel S., Kim Cornish, Kylie M. Gray, Patricia Howlin, and Nicole J. Rinehart. 2012. "Brief Report: Assessment of the Social-Emotional Profile in Children with Autism Spectrum Disorders using a Novel Comic Strip Task." *Journal of Autism and Developmental Disorders* 42 (11): 2505–2512. doi: 10.1007/s10803-012-1498-8.

Smith, Nancy R. 1985. "Copying and Artistic Behaviors: Children and Comic Strips." *Studies in Art Education* 26 (3): 147–156.

Smith, Robin, Daniel R. Anderson, and Catherine Fischer. 1985. "Young Children's Comprehension of Montage." *Child Development* 56 (4): 962–971.

Smith, Tim J. 2012. "The attentional theory of cinematic continuity." *Projections* 6 (1): 1–27. doi: http://dx.doi.org/10.3167/proj.2012.060102.

Sousanis, Nick. 2015. *Unflattening*. Cambridge, MA: Harvard University Press.

Spinillo, Carla G, and Mary C Dyson. 2001. "An exploratory study of reading procedural pictorial sequences." *Information Design Journal* 10 (2): 154–168.

Spitzer, Manfred, Ursula Braun, Leo Hermle, and Sabine Maier. 1993. "Associative semantic network dysfunction in thought-disordered schizophrenic patients: Direct evidence from indirect semantic priming." *Biological Psychiatry* 34 (12): 864–877. doi: https://doi.org/10.1016/0006-3223(93)90054-H.

Sprong, Mirjam, Patricia Schothorst, Ellen Vos, Joop Hox, and Herman Van Engeland. 2007. "Theory of mind in schizophrenia: Meta-analysis." *British Journal of Psychiatry* 191 (1): 5–13. doi: 10.1192/bjp.bp.107.035899.

Stainbrook, Eric J. 2016. "A Little Cohesion between Friends; Or, We're Just Exploring Our Textuality: Reconciling Cohesion in Written Language and Visual Language." In *The Visual Narrative Reader*, edited by Neil Cohn, 129–154. London: Bloomsbury.

Stead, Amanda L., Meghan C. Savage, and Hugh W. Buckingham. 2012. "Pictorial and Graphemic Processing in Fluent Aphasia." *Imagination, Cognition and Personality* 31 (4): 279–295. doi: 10.2190/IC.31.4.c.

Stenchly, Kathrin, Tobias Feldt, David Weiss, Jessica N. Andriamparany, and Andreas Buerkert. 2019. "The explanatory power of silent comics: An assessment in the context of knowledge transfer and agricultural extension to rural communities in southwestern Madagascar." *PLOS ONE* 14 (6): e0217843. doi: 10.1371/journal.pone.0217843.

Stoermer, Mary. 2009. "Teaching between the frames: Making comics with seven and eight year old children, a search for craft and pedagogy." Doctoral Dissertation, Curriculum and Instruction of W. W. Wright School do Education, Indiana University.

Stojanovik, Vesna, Mick Perkins, and Sara Howard. 2004. "Williams syndrome and specific language impairment do not support claims for developmental double dissociations and innate modularity." *Journal of Neurolinguistics* 17 (6): 403–424. doi: https://doi.org/10.1016/j.jneuroling.2004.01.002.

Szawerna, Michał. 2017. *Metaphoricity of Conventionalized Diegetic Images in Comics: A Study in Multimodal Cognitive Linguistics, Łódź Studies in Language 54*. Frankfurt am Main: Peter Lang Publishing.

Tager-Flusberg, Helen. 1995. "'Once upon a ribbit': Stories narrated by autistic children." *British Journal of Developmental Psychology* 13 (1): 45–59. doi:10.1111/j.2044-835X.1995.tb00663.x.

Tanaka, Takamasa, Kenji Shoji, Fubito Toyama, and Juichi Miyamichi. 2007. "Layout Analysis of Tree-Structured Scene Frames in Comic Images." International Joint Conference on Artificial Intelligence, Hyderabad, India, January 6–12, 2007.

Tanner, Darren, Maria Goldshtein, and Benjamin Weissman. 2018. "Individual Differences in the Real-Time Neural Dynamics of Language Comprehension." In *Psychology of Learning and Motivation*, edited by Kara D. Federmeier and Duane G. Watson, 299–335. Academic Press.

Tasić, Miloš, and Dušan Stamenković. 2015. "The Interplay of Words and Images in Expressing Multimodal Metaphors in Comics." *Procedia – Social and*

Behavioral Sciences 212: 117–122. doi: http://dx.doi.org/10.1016/j. sbspro.2015.11.308.

Tasić, Miloš, and Dušan Stamenković. 2018. "Exploring pictorial runes in Luca Enoch's comic book series *Gea*." *Facta Universitatis, Series: Linguistics and Literature* 15 (2): 123–141.

Tinaz, Sule, Haline E. Schendan, Karin Schon, and Chantal E. Stern. 2006. "Evidence for the importance of basal ganglia output nuclei in semantic event sequencing: An fMRI study." *Brain Research* 1067 (1): 239–249. doi: http://dx.doi.org/10.1016/j.brainres.2005.10.057.

Tinaz, Sule, Haline E. Schendan, and Chantal E. Stern. 2008. "Fronto-striatal deficit in Parkinson's disease during semantic event sequencing." *Neurobiology of Aging* 29 (3): 397–407. doi: http://dx.doi.org/10.1016/j.neurobiolaging.2006.10.025.

Toku, Masami. 2001a. "Cross-Cultural Analysis of Artistic Development: Drawing by Japanese and U.S. children." *Visual Arts Research* 27: 46–59.

Toku, Masami. 2001b. "What is Manga?: The Influence of Pop Culture in Adolescent Art." *Journal of National Art Education* 54 (2): 11–17.

Trabasso, Tom, and Margret Nickels. 1992. "The development of goal plans of action in the narration of a picture story." *Discourse Processes* 15: 249–275.

Trabasso, Tom, and Nancy L. Stein. 1994. "Using Goal-Plan Knowledge to Merge the Past with the Present and the Future in Narrating Events on Line." In *The Development of Future-Oriented Processes*, edited by Marshall M. Haith, Janette B. Benson, Ralph J. Roberts Jr. and Bruce F. Pennington, 323–349. Chicago: University of Chicago Press.

Trabasso, Tom, and Nancy L. Stein. 1997. "Narrating, representing, and remembering event sequences." In *Developmental Spans in Event Comprehension and Representation: Bridging Fictional and Actual Events*, edited by Paul van den Broek, Patricia J. Baur and Tammy Bourg. New York: Lawrence Erlbaum Associates.

Tseng, Chiao-I, and John A Bateman. 2018. "Cohesion in Comics and Graphic Novels: An Empirical Comparative Approach to Transmedia Adaptation in City of Glass." *Adaptation* 11 (2): 122–143. doi: 10.1093/adaptation/apx027.

Tsimpli, Ianthi Maria, Eleni Peristeri, and Maria Andreou. 2016. "Narrative production in monolingual and bilingual children with specific language impairment." *Applied Psycholinguistics* 37 (1): 195–216. doi: 10.1017/S0142716415000478.

Tulsky, David S, and Larry R Price. 2003. "The joint WAIS-III and WMS-III factor structure: development and cross-validation of a six-factor model of cognitive functioning." *Psychological Assessment* 15 (2): 149–162.

Tversky, Barbara, Sol Kugelmass, and Atalia Winter. 1991. "Cross-cultural and developmental trends in graphic productions." *Cognitive Psychology* 23 (4): 515–557.

Ukrainetz, Teresa A., and Ronald B. Gillam. 2009. "The Expressive Elaboration of Imaginative Narratives by Children With Specific Language Impairment." *Journal of Speech, Language, and Hearing Research* 52 (4): 883–898. doi:10.1044/1092-4388(2009/07-0133).

Ullman, Michael T., and Elizabeth I. Pierpont. 2005. "Specific Language Impairment is not Specific to Language: the Procedural Deficit Hypothesis." *Cortex* 41 (3): 399–433. doi: https://doi.org/10.1016/S0010-9452(08)70276-4.

van Berkum, Jos J. A. 2009. "The neuropragmatics of "simple" utterance comprehension: An ERP review." In *Semantics and Pragmatics: From*

Experiment to Theory, edited by Uli Sauerland and Kazuko Yatsushiro, 276–316. Basingstoke: Palgrave.

van Berkum, Jos J. A., Colin Brown, Pienie Zwitserlood, Valesca Kooijman, and Peter Hagoort. 2005. "Anticipating upcoming words in discourse: Evidence from ERPs and reading times." *Journal of Experimental Psychology: Learning, Memory, and Cognition* 31 (3): 443–467.

van Berkum, Jos J. A., Arnout W. Koornneef, Marte Otten, and Mante S. Nieuwland. 2007. "Establishing reference in language comprehension: An electrophysiological perspective." *Brain Research* 1146 (0): 158–171. doi: http://dx.doi.org/10.1016/j.brainres.2006.06.091.

van Daal, John, Ludo Verhoeven, and Hans van Balkom. 2004. "Subtypes of Severe Speech and Language Impairments: Psychometric Evidence From 4-Year-Old Children in the Netherlands." *Journal of Speech, Language, and Hearing Research* 47 (6): 1411–1423. doi: 10.1044/1092-4388(2004/105).

van Daal, John, Ludo Verhoeven, and Hans van Balkom. 2007. "Behaviour problems in children with language impairment." *Journal of Child Psychology and Psychiatry* 48 (11): 1139–1147. doi: 10.1111/j.1469-7610.2007.01790.x.

van Daal, John, Ludo Verhoeven, Jan van Leeuwe, and Hans van Balkom. 2008. "Working memory limitations in children with severe language impairment." *Journal of Communication Disorders* 41 (2): 85–107. doi: https://doi.org/10.1016/j.jcomdis.2007.03.010.

van Dijk, Teun, and Walter Kintsch. 1983. *Strategies of Discourse Comprehension*. New York: Academic Press.

van Middelaar, Lincy. 2017. "It ain't much, if it ain't Dutch: Visual morphology across eight decades of Dutch and Flemish comics." Bachelors Thesis, Communication and Information Science, Tilburg University.

Van Petten, Cyma, and Marta Kutas. 1991. "Influences of semantic and syntactic context on open- and closed-class words." *Memory and Cognition* 19: 95–112.

Van Petten, Cyma, and Barbara J. Luka. 2012. "Prediction during language comprehension: Benefits, costs, and ERP components." *International Journal of Psychophysiology* 83 (2): 176–190. doi: http://dx.doi.org/10.1016/j.ijpsycho.2011.09.015.

Verano, Frank. 2006. "Spectacular consumption: Visuality, production, and the consumption of the comics page." *International Journal of Comic Art* 8 (1): 378–387.

Verhoeven, Ludo, and Anne Vermeer. 2006. "Sociocultural variation in literacy achievement." *British Journal of Educational Studies* 54 (2): 189–211. doi: 10.1111/j.1467-8527.2006.00341.x.

Veroff, Amy E. 1978. "A structural determinant of hemispheric processing of pictorial material." *Brain and Language* 5 (2): 139–148. doi: https://doi.org/10.1016/0093-934X(78)90014-7.

Wallesch, Claus W., Hans H. Kornhuber, Christian Köllner, H. Christian Haas, and J. Michael Hufnagl. 1983. "Language and cognitive deficits resulting from medial and dorsolateral frontal lobe lesions." *Archiv für Psychiatrie und Nervenkrankheiten* 233 (4): 279–296. doi: 10.1007/bf00345798.

Wang, Zezhong, Shunming Wang, Matteo Farinella, Dave Murray-Rust, Nathalie Henry Riche, and Benjamin Bach. 2019. "Comparing Effectiveness and Engagement of Data Comics and Infographics." *CHI 2019*, Glasgow, Scotland UK, May 4–9, 2019.

Watkins, Kate E., N. F. Dronkers, and F. Vargha-Khadem. 2002. "Behavioural analysis of an inherited speech and language disorder: comparison with acquired aphasia." *Brain* 125 (3): 452–464. doi: 10.1093/brain/awf058.

Wechsler, David. 1981. *WAIS-R Manual: Wechsler Adult Intelligence Scale-Revised*: Psychological Corporation.

Weissman, Benjamin, and Darren Tanner. 2018. "A strong wink between verbal and emoji-based irony: how the brain processes ironic emojis during language comprehension." *PLoS ONE* 13 (8): e0201727.

Weist, Richard M. 2009. "Children think and talk about time and space." In *Language, Science, and Culture*, edited by P. Łobacz, P. Nowak and W. Zabrocki. Poznań: Wydawnictwo Naukowe UAM.

Weist, Richard M., Marja Atanassova, Hanna Wysocka, and Aleksandra Pawlak. 1999. "Spatial and temporal systems in child language and thought: a cross-linguistic study." *First Language* 19 (57): 267–308. doi: 10.1177/014272379901905701.

Weist, Richard M., Paula Lyytinen, Jolanta Wysocka, and Marja Atanassova. 1997. "The interaction of language and thought in children's language acquisition: a crosslinguistic study." *Journal of Child Language* 24 (01): 81–121.

Wellman, Henry M., Simon Baron-Cohen, Robert Caswell, Juan Carlos Gomez, John Swettenham, Eleanor Toye, and Kristin Lagattuta. 2002. "Thought-bubbles help children with autism acquire an alternative to a theory of mind." *Autism* 6 (4): 343–363.

Wellman, Henry M., David Cross, and Julanne Watson. 2001. "Meta-Analysis of Theory-of-Mind Development: The Truth about False Belief." *Child Development* 72 (3): 655–684.

Wellman, Henry M., Michelle Hollander, and Carolyn A. Schult. 1996. "Young children's understanding of thought bubbles and thoughts." *Child Development* 67: 768–788.

West, W. Caroline, and Phil Holcomb. 2002. "Event-related potentials during discourse-level semantic integration of complex pictures." *Cognitive Brain Research* 13: 363–375.

Wichmann, Søren, and Jesper Nielsen. 2016. "Sequential Text-Image Pairing among the Classic Maya." In *The Visual Narrative Reader*, edited by Neil Cohn, 282–313. London: Bloomsbury.

Wildfeuer, Janina. 2013. *Film Discourse Interpretation: Towards a New Paradigm for Multimodal Film Analysis*. New York: Routledge.

Wilkins, David P. 1997/2016. "Alternative Representations of Space: Arrernte Narratives in Sand." In *The Visual Narrative Reader*, edited by Neil Cohn, 252–281. London: Bloomsbury. Original edition, 1997. Proceedings of the CLS Opening Academic Year '97 '98, edited by M. Biemans and J. van de Weijer, 133–164. Nijmegen: Nijmegen/Tilburg Center for Language Studies.

Willats, John. 1997. *Art and Representation: New Principles in the Analysis of Pictures*. Princeton: Princeton University Press.

Willats, John. 2005. *Making Sense of Children's Drawings*. Mahwah, NJ: Lawrence Erlbaum.

Wilson, Brent. 1974. "The Superheroes of J.C. Holz: Plus an Outline of a Theory of Child Art." *Art Education* 27 (8): 2–9.

Wilson, Brent. 1988. "The Artistic Tower of Babel: Inextricable Links Between Culture and Graphic Development." In *Discerning Art: Concepts and Issues*, edited by George W. Hardiman and Theodore Zernich, 488–506. Champaign, IL: Stipes Publishing Company.

Wilson, Brent. 1999. "Becoming Japanese: Manga, Children's Drawings, and the Construction of National Character." *Visual Arts Research* 25 (2): 48–60.

Wilson, Brent. 2016. "What happened and what happened next: Kids' visual narratives across cultures." In *The Visual Narrative Reader*, edited by Neil Cohn, 185–227. London: Bloomsbury.

Wilson, Brent, and Marjorie Wilson. 1977. "An Iconoclastic View of the Imagery Sources in the Drawings of Young People." *Art Education* 30 (1): 4–12.

Wilson, Brent, and Marjorie Wilson. 1979a. "Children's Story Drawings: Reinventing Worlds." *School Arts* 78 (8): 6–11.

Wilson, Brent, and Marjorie Wilson. 1979b. "Figure Structure, Figure Action, and Framing in Drawings by American and Egyptian Children." *Studies in Art Education* 21 (1): 36–43.

Wilson, Brent, and Marjorie Wilson. 1982. *Teaching Children to Draw*. Englewood Cliffs, NJ: Prentice-Hall.

Wilson, Brent, and Marjorie Wilson. 1984. "The themes of children's story drawings: A tale of four cultures." In *Art in Education: An International Perspective*, edited by R. Ott and A. Hurwitz, 31–38. University Park, PA: The Pennsylvania State University Press.

Wilson, Brent, and Marjorie Wilson. 1987. "Pictorial Composition and Narrative Structure: Themes and Creation of Meaning in the Drawings of Egyptian and Japanese Children." *Visual Arts Research* 13 (2): 10–21.

Wilson, Brent, and Marjorie Wilson. 2010. *Teaching Children to Draw*. Second ed. Englewood Cliffs, NJ: Prentice-Hall.

Winter, W. 1963. "The perception of safety posters by Bantu industrial workers." *Psychological Africana* 10 (2): 127–135.

Wittenberg, Eva, Martin Paczynski, Heike Wiese, Ray Jackendoff, and Gina Kuperberg. 2014. "The difference between "giving a rose" and "giving a kiss": Sustained neural activity to the light verb construction." *Journal of Memory and Language* 73: 31–42. doi: http://dx.doi.org/10.1016/j.jml.2014.02.002.

Wong, Simpson W. L., Hoyee Miao, Rebecca Wing-yi Cheng, and Michael Chi Wing Yip. 2017. "Graphic Novel Comprehension Among Learners with Differential Cognitive Styles and Reading Abilities." *Reading & Writing Quarterly* 33 (5): 412–427. doi: 10.1080/10573569.2016.1216343.

Worth, Sol, and John Adair. 1972. *Through Navajo Eyes: An Exploration in Film Communication and Anthropology*. Bloomington: Indiana University Press.

Yano, Masataka. 2018. "Predictive processing of syntactic information: evidence from event-related brain potentials." *Language, Cognition and Neuroscience* 33 (8): 1017–1031. doi: 10.1080/23273798.2018.1444185.

Zacks, Jeffrey M. 2014. *Flicker: Your Brain on Movies*. Oxford, UK: Oxford University Press.

Zacks, Jeffrey M., Todd S. Braver, Margaret A. Sheridan, David I. Donaldson, Abraham Z. Snyder, John M. Ollinger, Randy L. Buckner, and Marcus E. Raichle. 2001. "Human brain activity time-locked to perceptual event boundaries." *Nature Neuroscience* 4 (6): 651–655.

Zacks, Jeffrey M., and Joseph P. Magliano. 2011. "Film, narrative, and cognitive neuroscience." In *Art and the Senses*, edited by D.P. Melcher and F. Bacci, 435–454. New York: Oxford University Press.

Zalla, Tiziana, Nathalie Bouchilloux, Nelly Labruyere, Nicolas Georgieff, Thierry Bougerol, and Nicolas Franck. 2006. "Impairment in event sequencing in disorganised and non-disorganised patients with schizophrenia." *Brain Research Bulletin* 68 (4): 195–202. doi: http://dx.doi.org/10.1016/j. brainresbull.2005.04.020.

Zampini, Laura, Chiara Suttora, Laura D'Odorico, and Paola Zanchi. 2013. "Sequential reasoning and listening text comprehension in preschool children." *European Journal of Developmental Psychology* 10 (5): 563–579. doi: 10.1080/17405629.2013.766130.

Zampini, Laura, Paola Zanchi, Chiara Suttora, Maria Spinelli, Mirco Fasolo, and Nicoletta Salerni. 2017. "Assessing sequential reasoning skills in typically developing children." *BPA-Applied Psychology Bulletin (Bollettino di Psicologia Applicata)* 65 (279): 44–50.

Zhang-Kennedy, Leah, Khadija Baig, and Sonia Chiasson. 2017. "Engaging children about online privacy through storytelling in an interactive comic." In *Proceedings of the 31st British Computer Society Human Computer Interaction Conference*, 1–11. Sunderland, UK: BCS Learning & Development Ltd.

Zhao, Fang, and Nina Mahrt. 2018. "Influences of Comics Expertise and Comics Types in Comics Reading." *International Journal of Innovation and Research in Educational Sciences* 5 (2): 218–224.

Zwaan, Rolf A., and Gabriel A. Radvansky. 1998. "Situation models in language comprehension and memory." *Psychological Bulletin* 123 (2): 162–185.

INDEX